Poetic Voices Without Borders 2

edited by
Robert L. Giron

Arlington, Virginia

Copyright © 2009 by Gival Press, LLC.

Introduction © 2009 by Robert L. Giron.

All rights reserved under International and Pan-American Copyright Conventions. Printed in the United States of America.

With the exception of brief quotations in the body of critical articles or reviews, no part of this book may be reproduced or transmitted in any form or by any means, graphic, electronic, or mechanical, including photocopying, recording, taping, or by any information storage or retrieval system, without the permission in writing from the publisher.

After publication, all rights revert to the individual poets.

Published by Gival Press, an imprint of Gival Press, LLC.

For information please write:
Gival Press, LLC, P.O. Box 3812, Arlington, VA 22203.

Website: www.givalpress.com
Email: givalpress@yahoo.com

First edition ISBN 13: 978-1-928589-43-3
Library of Congress Control Number: 2008907132

Bookcover artwork *Intuiting the Everpresent Tide*
Copyright © 2008 by JETIII (www.JETgallery.com).

Format and design by Ken Schellenberg.
Set in 10.5/11.5 Monotype Octavian and Franklin Gothic

Contents

Poems in English

After the Flood	Arthur Rimbaud	1
Afterwards	John Amen	2
All Men Kill the Thing They Love	Arthur Ginsberg	3
All Saints' Day	Carolyn Kreiter-Foronda	3
Amulet from the Andes	Ye Chun	5
Angels of the Tsunami	Ernie Wormwood	6
Anne Frank in '45	Walter R. Holland	6
Anti-Father	Rita Dove	7
An Apple in Hand	Gary Lehmann	8
The Apple Orchard	Dana Gioia	9
Architects of the Imaginary (A fragment)	Marta López-Luaces	9
At the Pentecostal Baths	Pablo Miguel Martínez	11
August Eve	Anika Paris	12
Autumn Inaugural	Dana Gioia	12
The Balkan Bridge	Vladimir Levchev	14
The Baltimore Sun	Donald Berger	14
Being Happy	Dana Gioia	15
Betrayers	Gary Beck	16
Big Ship	Sydney March	17
Black Book	Michael Montlack	17
Blue Dusk	Donna J. Gelagotis Lee	18
Blue Jay Passion of Flight	Benito Pastoriza Iyodo	19
Body in need	JoseMarGuerr	20
The Border	Martha Collins	21
Border Line	Anika Paris	22
Bread Boy	Dante Micheaux	24
The Candidate	John Gilgun	24
Carpooling with a Stranger	Benjamin S. Grossberg	24

Carry Me Away	Mario Meléndez	26
Cascade of Faces	Alfred Corn	27
Castile I-II-III	Andrés S. Fisher	28
Casualties of War	Gloria Vando	29
Cat Scrabble Ode	Ron Singer	30
Chancellorsville	Jeff Mann	31
Chemistry Lessons	Nina Corwin	33
Children of the Stones	J. Glenn Evans	33
Chrysanthemum is Prettiest in the Ninth Moon	Ye Chun	34
Cicada	Vladimir Levchev	35
City	Arthur Rimbaud	36
Clearance Questionnaire	Richard Peabody	36
The Climb	Randy Koch	38
Closure	Greg Baysans	41
Confession	Don Cellini	42
Confession	Kim Jensen	43
The Courtship of the Morticians	Peter Klappert	44
The Cricket:	Benito del Pliego	45
La Cucaracha	Grace Cavalieri	45
Damaged Goods	Jill Williams	46
Dawn	Arthur Rimbaud	46
[Deaf is the night...]	Raymond Queneau	47
Death	Alta Ifland	48
Delft	Rita Dove	48
A Deluge of Script	Yvette Neisser Moreno	49
The Disappeared	Colette Inez	50
The Dog:	Benito del Pliego	50
[don't paint yourself invisible]	Claire Joysmith	51
The Door	Bernadette Geyer	52
During the War	Philip Levine	52
Eastern Village with Factory	Daniele Pantano	53
Ecstasy	J. E. Robinson	54
Edge	Karren LaLonde Alenier	54
Elena Mesa	Carolyn Kreiter-Foronda	55
Every Name Has a Face*	E. Ethelbert Miller	56
Every Throat	Naomi Ayala	57
The Explanation of Metaphors	Raymond Queneau	57
Fairy Tales for Writers: Little Red Riding Hood	Lawrence Schimel	59
Faith	Edward Falco	60
A Fantastic Sapphic	Karren LaLonde Alenier	61
Farewell Kiss	Ron Singer	61
[Fifi, the dangerous fag dog]	John Del Peschio	62
Final Approach	Lucille Gang Shulklapper	62
First Breath Last Breath	Antler	63
The Floor Is Sticky	Kim Roberts	64
The Fly:	Benito del Pliego	65

Forgive Us Our Sins	Katharina Yakovina	65
Fortune	Katherine Soniat	66
[from the desert]	Raymond Queneau	66
The Ghosts of the Confederacy	Richard Peabody	67
Givenchy Lavender	Paula Goldman	68
Global Notes	M. A. Schaffner	68
The Gods Just Appeared	Jason Tandon	69
The Good Fight	Miles David Moore	69
Green-Eyed Mexican Boy: Little Brother #1	Alicia Gaspar de Alba	70
Hardcovers	Anita Vélez-Mitchell	72
The Heart of the Matter	Dana Gioia	73
Heile Welt	Walter R. Holland	74
Hero, Posthumous	J.D. Smith	74
Hieros #14	Marie Lecrivain	75
Hometown	Gerard Wozek	75
Honeys	Jeff Mann	77
The Horse:	Benito del Pliego	78
How to Make a Human	Lawrence Schimel	78
[i recall a day in cordoba]	Jesús Encinar	79
If I Get This Far	Kay Murphy	80
Imagine The Shock	Joseph Ross	81
Immigrant Story	Jason Tandon	82
Immigration Interview	Gunilla Theander Kester	82
Improvised Poetic Device (IPD)	Rodrigo Toscano	83
In Adams Morgan, Two Years of Neighborhood-wide Reconstruction Comes to a Halt for the Night	Naomi Ayala	86
In Lower East Side, Looking at an Apartment	Raymond Luczak	86
In the Attic of My Grief	Grace Cavalieri	87
In the Valley of the Kings	Yvette Neisser Moreno	88
Instructions to Be Followed at the Time of My Death: The Service is Optional.	Ron Singer	89
Introduction to Economics	J. D. Smith	90
Iranian Boys Hanged for Sodomy, July 2005*	Stephen S. Mills	90
It's Seven	Luis Cremades	91
Jazz Funeral	Bruce Lader	92
Judas Kiss	Shannon Gilreath	93
Jumper	Jeff Walt	93
Kismet	Christopher Soden	94
Kristallnacht	Lawrence Schimel	94
Labor	Barbara Louise Ungar	97
Last Night in London	Jonathan Tilley	98
The Last World of Fire and Trash	Joy Harjo	99
Late in the Day	Patricia Gray	100
Laughter	Isaac Goldemberg	101
The Law	Isaac Goldemberg	102
Legacy	Sydney March	102

Les Places Numérotées	Peter Klappert	103
Like the Children of Bororo	Kathryn Kirkpatrick	104
Listen	Don Cellini	105
Litany of Waves	Don Cellini	106
La Llorona Considers the State of Tortillas	Norma Elía Cantú	106
A Long Marriage	Mary Kay Rummel	107
Lost Voice	Mark Saba	108
Love Affairs	Naomi Shihab Nye	109
Lucky	Jody Bolz	110
[magnetic karma]	Arnold Melleby	111
Man High*	C. M. Mayo	112
The Manifestation of Sisíism	Robert L. Giron	114
March 20, 2003	Edward Falco	116
The Marvelous Child	Alta Ifland	116
Memories of the Future	Mario Meléndez	117
[Metaphor has died.]	Mercedes Roffé	117
Michelangelo's Last Pietà	Paula Goldman	118
Miles and the Shofar	Mel Belin	118
The Milky Way	Anita Vélez-Mitchell	119
Morning Star Children	Suzan Shown Harjo	120
My Language	Alta Ifland	122
Naiveté	Anika Paris	122
Nameless	Lucille Gang Shulklapper	123
Native Land	Marcelle Kasprowicz	123
Navigating the Warning	Joy Harjo	125
Neologism	David Bergman	125
The Night Last Night	Luis Martínez de Merlo	126
Nights at Maya's	Teri Ellen Cross	127
No-Man's Land	Randy Koch	128
Not This	Emily Lupita Plum	130
Ö	Rita Dove	131
An Obsidian Path	Claire Joysmith	132
Okie Monarchs	John Domini	132
An Old Uncle Held Them	Patricia Gray	133
On U.S. 11 (Bear Station, Tennessee, 1968)	Anthony W. Reevy	134
The Outskirts	Raymond Queneau	135
The Ox:	Benito del Pliego	135
Patrimonial Recipe	Daniele Pantano	136
The Pavlovian Crux	G. Tod Slone	136
Persimmons	George Klawitter	137
The Philosophy Lesson	Isaac Goldemberg	138
The Pilgrimage	Robert L. Giron	139
Pirateology	Barbara Louise Ungar	140
Plastic Hen	Miles David Moore	140
Poema como TRANSLENGUAJE A Trans-L=A=N=G=U=A=G=E Poem	Marta López-Luaces	141

Poetry Offender	Thaddeus Rutkowski	143
[Poets are bad for the economy.]	Mark Saba	144
The Pond Does Not Ripple	Shome Dasgupta	144
Prove To Me	Antler	145
Prozac	Chris Tusa	146
Radiolaria	Kim Roberts	146
Raptors	Katherine Soniat	148
Reality Show	Joy Harjo	148
Redemption	Gerard Wozek	149
Red, White and Blue	Josh Gilman	150
Reformation of the Arsonist	Jeff Mann	151
The Religion Lesson	Isaac Goldemberg	152
A Retired Voodoo Priestess Dreams of Revenge from The Psych Ward in Charity Hospital	Chris Tusa	153
Rip Tide	Julie Marie Wade	154
The Road	Dana Gioia	154
Robinson	Raymond Queneau	155
[St. Anthony's Church]	Clifton Snider	155
Saved	Naomi Ayala	156
Secrets	Daniel W. K. Lee	157
Seigneurial Rights	Marcelle Kasprowicz	157
Sexing the Dancers	Edmund Miller	158
Sexual Paradox	Jill Williams	159
Short Cuts	Steve Fellner	159
A Short History of the Corset	Kristy Bowen	161
The Slave's Critique of Practical Reason	Rita Dove	162
Smokers on Break	Jeff Walt	163
Social Intercourse	Edmund Miller	164
Song for Fernand Léger	Colette Inez	165
The Sound of Grass	Paula Goldman	166
The Speech of Cretans	Thaddeus Rutkowski	166
Sperm	Clifford Browder	167
Spires and Tunnels	Gunilla Theander Kester	168
Starkweather: Numbered for the Bottom	Christopher Conlon	169
Staying Home on Mother's Day	Janet I. Buck	169
Suburban Blues	Piotr Gwiazda	170
[The suicide bomber is tightening the Laces of his boots.]	Jody Bolz	171
Taking Our Measure	Patricia Garfinkel	172
Telling Time	Nina Corwin	172
Testament	Luis Alberto Ambroggio	173
[They saw Christ ...]	Mercedes Roffé	175
This Precise Morning, February	Sean Ross	175
[Tighter and tighter...]	Mercedes Roffé	176
To Your Shadow Beast: In Memoriam	Alicia Gaspar de Alba	176
Translation as Memory La traducción como recuerdo	Marta López-Luaces	178

Traveling Southeast Asia	Josh Gilman	179
Truce	Allison Whittenberg	179
Trying to Sleep, Chicago-Paris, Economy	John Domini	180
Turning 60	Arthur Ginsberg	181
The Twinkle	Antler	181
Valentines for a Friend Who Caught Fire	Kay Murphy	182
Virginia Woolf's Pockets, Full of Stones	Thomas March	183
Virtual Freedom	Bruce Lader	184
Voices	Mary Kay Rummel	184
Waking In a Borrowed Place, West 85th	Judith McCombs	185
Wall	Isaac Goldemberg	186
The Wall	Donald Berger	186
Weather Warning	Jason Tandon	186
Wedding (after the feast)	Alta Ifland	187
What Are You Dreaming?	Gregg Shapiro	187
When You Ask About Your Native Country	Beverly Burch	188
[When you crossed the line]	Karren LaLonde Alenier	189
The Whole Man Blooms	Blake Robinson	190
Wind Chill Factor	Gloria Vando	190
The Winding Path	Marcelle Kasprowicz	191
Wing by Wing	Emily Lupita Plum	192
The Women	Donna J. Gelagotis Lee	193
Work	Greg Baysans	194
[You're back from Provincetown]	John Del Peschio	194
You're Looking at the Love Interest	Denise Duhamel	195
[You've become clear]	Luis Cremades	197

Poems in French

Aquarelle	Hedy Habra	199
Le café turc	Hedy Habra	200
Chute libre	Hedy Habra	200
Délire	Hedy Habra	201
Droit de Seigneur	Marcelle Kasprowicz	201
L'enfant merveilleuse	Alta Ifland	202
L'Ettersberg	Marcelle Kasprowicz	203
Filles du feu	Hedy Habra	203
Ma langue	Alta Ifland	204
Mort	Alta Ifland	205
Niagara	Hedy Habra	205
Les Noces (après la fête)	Alta Ifland	206
Le Sentier Sinueux	Marcelle Kasprowicz	206

Terre Natale	Marcelle Kasprowicz	207
La vieille femme	Hedy Habra	208
Vouloir qu'on veuille	Alfred Corn	209

Poems in Spanish

Adagio por una viola d'amore olvidada	Hedy Habra	211
Alfa amor	Fanny Carrión de Fierro	213
Blue jay paixao de vôo	Benito Pastoriza Iyodo	214
El buey:	Benito del Pliego	215
Cabalgadura del siglo actual	Efraín E. Garza	216
El caballo:	Benito del Pliego	216
Cartografía sin inventariar	Efraín E. Garza	217
Castilla I-II-III	Andrés S. Fisher	217
Confesión	Don Cellini	218
Contrapunto	Hedy Habra	219
Cuero fresco	Rodrigo Toscano	221
[descubrir noches pintadas por poetas]	Benito Pastoriza Iyodo	223
[Dicen los del pueblo]	Rose Mary Salum	223
Donde nació la luz	Fanny Carrión de Fierro	224
Escucha	Don Cellini	225
Espacio abierto	Leonel Bernal	226
Geografía del corazón	Fanny Carrión de Fierro	227
El grillo:	Benito del Pliego	228
[el impulso sexual vestido de fiera]	Benito Pastoriza Iyodo	228
Lección de filosofía	Isaac Goldemberg	229
Lección de religión	Isaac Goldemberg	229
Letanía de las olas	Don Cellini	230
La ley	Isaac Goldemberg	230
Llévame	Mario Meléndez	231
Luchar	María-Elvira Luna-Escudero-Alie	232
Mapas	Hedy Habra	232
Mis manos	Leonel Bernal	233
La mosca:	Benito del Pliego	234
Mujer	Desirée Marín	234
Muro	Isaac Goldemberg	235
Necesidad de cuerpo	JoseMarGuerr	236
La noche de anoche	Luis Martínez de Merlo	236
Nonos de la estrella de la aurora	Suzan Shown Harjo	237
Paisajes de USA	Luis Alberto Ambroggio	239
Pasajero de la memoria	Benito Pastoriza Iyodo	240
El perro:	Benito del Pliego	242

Quince Pangas	Desirée Marín	242
Recuerdos del futuro	Mario Meléndez	243
[recuerdo que un día en córdoba]	Jesús Encinar	243
Risas	Isaac Goldemberg	244
[El sol también tiene su lado oscuro]	Hedy Habra	245
Soneto a la indiferencia	Leonel Bernal	246
Son las siete	Luis Cremades	247
Sodoma	Juan M. Godoy	248
Sueños hechos añicos	Efraín E. Garza	249
"Te beso"	Rose Mary Salum	249
Te has vuelto claro	Luis Cremades	250
Testamento	Luis Alberto Ambroggio	251

Author Biographies — 253

Acknowledgments — 275

Index of Authors — 281

**for the Source
that provides Energy**

Introduction

In trying to make this a short introduction, let me begin by extending a sincere thank you to everyone who helped make this anthology possible for without their patience I don't believe it would have been possible, given that I survived two major back surgeries in the process of getting this book into form.

As you leaf through the book, you will find that its format is not customary in that the works of the poets are arranged intentionally by title and are not grouped by the poets' last name. In keeping with the desire to cross borders, perhaps even break them down, the desire is that you will take to the content like a fish to water and be surprised by who wrote the poem. Some of the poems in French and Spanish have English translations but some do not; we hope you welcome the inclusion of these two major languages of North America.

The voices found within these pages are passionate and enlightening while echoing a desire in their own way to transform, to change, to transcend borders, be they personal, cultural or national, in a poetic manner as if to say that within literature there isn't a border for the human spirit, for it is that energy that keeps us going.

I would like to thank the following individuals: Rita Dove, Dana Gioia, Joy Harjo, David Garrett Izzo, Peter Klappert, Philip Levine, and Naomi Shihab Nye for their gracious support; Fran Jordan for her proofing and patience for detail; Ken Schellenberg for his patience and design; Joel E. Traylor, III for his art; Dr. Andrew Siekanowicz, Dr. Joshua Ammerman, Dr. Richard Wells, and the late Dr. Bruce Ammerman for their healing powers and commitment to making people well; Lawrence Lapidus and Jonathan Beiser for their help during my trying times; Francine Jamin, Sharon Mandel, Marcia Bronstein, Margaret Kirkland, Rowena D'Souza, Paula D. Matuskey, Carolyn Terry, Amy Gumaer, Haoua Welsh, Carolyn Waddy, and Julie Wakeman-Linn for their support; Richard Peabody, John Domini, Donna J. Gelagotis Lee, Paula Goldman. Barbara Louise Ungar, Patricia Garfinkel, Gunilla Theander Kester, C. M. Mayo, Kim Roberts, Gregg Shapiro, Judith McCombs, Rose Mary Salum, and Gloria Vando for their encouragement and support; to all the contributors of *Poetic Voices Without Borders 2* who helped make this project possible; The New York Center for Independent Publishing; the Arlington Arts Center; Busboys and Poets Café and Bookstore; Marianne Moerman, Anne Smith, Helen Hong, and Jimmy Dill for their support; Tante Germaine, Anne-Marie Chaix née Giron, and Pierre Mangin for their inspiration and support; my cousins Stephen and Lenny for their support; and finally my parents, sisters Jeannie and Judy, brother Joey, and my family in spirit for their countless prayers and support.

ə❦ RLG

Poems in English

After the Flood

As soon as the idea of the flood went stale,

    A hare paused in the clover and the swaying flower bells, and said a prayer through the spider's web that went straight through to the rainbow.

    The cherished stones were un-revealed and the flowers opened.

    The butchers' blocks rose up everywhere on the filthy street and boats were launched on the sea, stacked high as in pictures.

    Blood flowed in Bluebeard's house, in the slaughter houses, at the circuses, where God's seal paled the windows. Blood and milk poured everywhere.

    Beavers went about their work. Coffee steamed in the taverns. In the huge house with the windows all wet, sorrowful children looked upon lively pictures.

    A door slammed shut. On the square, a child has moved his arms all around and was comprehended by the weather vanes and the steeple cocks, against the pelting rain.

    Madame X…placed a piano in the Alps. Mass and first communions were celebrated at one hundred thousand alters in the Cathedral.

    The caravans went away. And the Hotel Splendid was constructed within the chaos of ice and polar night.

    Since then, the Moon has listened to jackals howling in the thyme deserts and pastoral dialogs in the wooden shoes growl in the garden. In the blooming violet grove, Eucharis whispered to me that Spring was here.

—Erupting waters of the pond.

Foam, flowing over the bridge and through the forest. Black veils and organs, lightening and thunder, arise, and cover everything. Water and Sorrows rise up and return the floods.

Since they've departed—oh! Precious stones buried and the open flowers,—we are bored. The Queen, the witch, igniting her coal in the clay pot, will never tell us what she knows and what we will never be allowed to know.

                       ❧ Arthur Rimbaud
                       ❧ New translation by Louis E. Bourgeois

Afterwards
(for Dan and Alix)

And so
in a spell of song and autumnal glow,
I put down my glorious hammer.

My unfinished castles
loomed on the other side of the river.

I forgot them, something began.
Ripe fruit hung from an empty sky.

Sometimes what falls still stands forever.

After thirty years of arguing with ash,
I've finally befriended failure.

Now I will give
the seat of honor to something I find repulsive.

Finally, dear comrades, this leads nowhere.

                     ❧ John Amen

All Men Kill the Thing They Love

         At the bottom of a hill,
my brakes fail,
    the pedal under my foot
squeezing slowly through the floorboard
    like a spatula through honey,
striped black and yellow concrete,
    a gathering tidal wave.
I peel into reverse, ram
    into the car behind me,
crush the hood,
    rip the engine from its mounts.
Woman flung to asphalt,
    spurting red from face and lung.

O' Jesus Christ! What have I done?

        You arrive to solace me
with your arms and eyes,
    as I kneel by the body
I have broken, as if
    I did not know who she was,
until, through the cataract of my dream,
    your face sharpens into focus,
there, in the dark,
    as I listen for your breathing
on the far side of the bed.

         ❧ Arthur Ginsberg

All Saints' Day
 I want to sleep a while, . . . a minute,
 a century; but let everyone know that I am
 not dead.
 —Federico García Lorca

When I was eight, no one believed there were ghosts
in our house, except a close friend who heard them

turn on the upstairs faucet once, the air chilled
when we arrived in time to catch them disappearing

through the hallway's blanched walls. Truth is
they were there all along. I heard their heels

tapping the floorboards. At night they slithered
beneath my bed, terrified me until Mother cradled

my head so I could doze off, phantoms, demons,
ghouls, wickedness vanishing in her presence.

*

At sixteen I nearly became a ghost,
illness squeezing the will and drive out of me.

That night I floated above myself into a lucid sky,
the fear of dying gone so that over the years

I have come to respect ghosts, their unexpected
appearance, the need to suspend belief

in order to feel their presence. I suppose
you might say I'm good at it after all this time.

*

Recently in Bolivia on All Saints' Day, my basket
overflowed with sacks of flour, candy, fruit

and drink for the spirits of the dead. My husband
and I had just returned from market, our deceased

relatives about to visit. We prepared beans in hot
sauce, egg biscuits, chicha morada, a rich corn drink.

Legend says the dead protect us if we take care
of them. To highland Indians, this means strong rains

for crops. We lined a table with bread-baked llamas,
sheep and birds to carry souls back from far-off lands.

At noon, church bells rang the arrival of the souls.
My husband and I ate enough for two, knowing

that whatever we consumed would, by faith, satisfy
the dead. The next day we set a small feast

on cemetery graves. Resiris, supplicants, prayed
for the dead while we bid farewell to our relatives.

*

Back home, I mull over Lorca's words, mull over

how not to die, how to leave something behind:

a sculpture, a well-taught child. Mull over
if the highland Indians have it right: that after we die

our souls climb out of the prayers of descendants,
bowed over our graves, so they can release us

from death once a year to wander earth and revere it
the way we should have when we were alive.

                       ❧ Carolyn Kreiter-Foronda

Amulet from the Andes

A shell without ocean

An animal all bone

A secret that can't be shared
hardened into a stone bag

Can you say: I'll give you
dimness and riches
treasures of a soiled palace

Can you say: Because of you
those invisible wings

in the sky those invisible beds

those parasols and straw-shoes

You say: Curl your body in me
I'll wrap you with un-uttering

I say: Clouds rumble along my house
Bird-calls nail my ceiling

                       ❧ Ye Chun

Angels of the Tsunami

In the night they emerge
from the same surge
that took them.
The moon comes round to shine
illuminating them all in a line
at the edge
of the Indian Ocean.
So many beloved, from so many lands
holding hands
wearing their red heart-wings,
humming their worldless, wordless
song that sings.

                         ❧ Ernie Wormwood

Anne Frank in '45

She looks across the fence
hopeful for the bare package to be tossed—
ice and snow of Bergen-Belsen –
sister and sister
were bunked near each other—
the bed at the front
by the door that never seemed
to close—
lice and the early signs of typhus
just two months to liberation—
Anne's insight that none
of her family would be left—
and so the two bodies
were added to the pile
and when the British arrived—
the guards were made to clean the mess
dig shallow trenches—
but the words are left behind on the page
and live in a lonely thinness all their own—
so I could equate her fate with AIDS
and how I took
from the ashes of my time a survivor's guilt—

Primo Levi knew of it,
the full effect
of stories that could not be told—
history had ended—
the writer cannot dispel
the naked swell of words
their stacked weight and stiffened
composures like Anne
stares back from passport photos never sent—
a universe of dark eyes,
serial repetitions of smiling poses—
joined with others taken on some beach—
there at the edge of falling waves—
not the listener in the attic
while the soldiers searched below—
or the girl sealed in the train—
seventy, eighty to a boxcar, one chamber pot, a hole
for air, the flicker of forests and fields outside—night's strangeness—
but she who in the schoolroom sits
with coal-dark eyes
like a doe's
caught by surprise
at something hurtling
toward
her.

                          ❧ Walter R. Holland

Anti-Father

Contrary to
tales you told us

Summer nights when
the air conditioner

broke—the stars
are not far

apart. Rather
they draw

closer together

with years.

And houses
shrivel, un-lost,

and porches sag;
neighbors phone

to report cracks
in the cellar floor,

roots of the willow
coming up. Stars

speak to a child.
The past

is silent. . . .
Just between

me and you,
woman to man,

outer space is
inconceivably

intimate.

                           ❧ Rita Dove

An Apple in Hand

It's like turning an apple
in your hand
in the bright sunshine.

All apples are red at first blush,
but as slowly rotated,
you see nascent green,
some hints of age,
like orange,
and even brown.

In the bright light of day,

the apple
has no single color
but partakes of its present
and its afterlife
all at once.

                         ❧ Gary Lehmann

The Apple Orchard

You won't remember it—the apple orchard
We wandered through one April afternoon,
Climbing the hill behind the empty farm.

A city boy, I'd never seen a grove
Burst in full flower or breathed the bittersweet
Perfume of blossoms mingled with the dust.

A quarter mile of trees in fragrant rows
Arching above us. We walked the aisle,
Alone in spring's ephemeral cathedral.

We had the luck, if you can call it that,
Of having been in love but never lovers—
The bright flame burning, fed by pure desire.

Nothing consumed, such secrets brought to light!
There was a moment when I stood behind you,
Reached out to spin you toward me . . . but I stopped.

What more could I have wanted from that day?
Everything, of course. Perhaps that was the point—
To learn that what we will not grasp is lost.

                         ❧ Dana Gioia

Architects of the Imaginary (A fragment)

[For Frost's echoes.] *I have been one acquainted with the night*[1] and los motives of *Let us go then, you and I, when the evening spread against the sky Like a patient etherized upon a table; Let us go*,² through the paths less traveled by the gardener of dreams until we reach Pound's prison where he looks to the south of Lope de Vega and the east of the haiku, *The Cantos of Pisa*, poligraphy that exorcises the west from its modernity.

For the never of Cernuda like a pattern for the ceremony of life, the *always* is never, don't ask for particulars, never apologize, never is the intermittent pause, never is the other breath that one never finds in the foliage, never is to breathe in the interstices of ritual, never is the Argonaut who travels through the signs and will never reach far ports. Without the viaticum of the father nor the bastion of a mother the old riverbanks return him home.

for the lullaby of Hart Crane to Aunt Emily *you fed your hunger like an endless task*,³ who breastfeeds from her pristine breasts, overflowing with darkness, so much purity stained with puritan hunger and thirst without being satiated in the ocean of a black angel in whose lap…Are you resting?

for the sky without taste of childhood, sky without the touch of far countries, sky without the memory of death that involves the soul's entire voyage, sky without a drawing by Breton nor by Michaux, sky without a perfectly open line that recalls el *estado de mi cuerpo*⁴, sky that echoes in the presence of Gide's sky of invocations—ruddy face of the brimming vortex of modernity—with shooting stars over their heads. Where will my angel be?

for the orphanage that pursues evil like a profession, the orphanage, the craziness of a language, the orphanage that pursues the hysteria of a language, the orphanage that pursues the universe that unites life and poetry, the orphanage that pursues (raven perched on the shoulder of life) following the fury of Ibarborou's grin, the fury of Girondo's white horse, the fury of the witches's sabbath's frenetic dance, HD *el secreto de los dioses se encuentra en el idioma de los hombres*,⁵ persisting in the flight of an owl made of ashes so that it rains libations with a melancholy smell over Storni's expatriots, but where will my angel be? Prophets make mistakes. Tú has (lo que no se debe hacer..)⁶. Said Abimalac to Abraham), pursue the visionary poet without answer, without articulation, who does not act, does not reject, does not accept, does not include, Leviatan, ENDIAGO of a sign, without dew, without breeze, without spring; sickness of the metaphor, without casting a spell. Celan, why when the sparrows kept replacing souls for our response, you went *gentle, gentle into that good night?*

for the holocaust of the universe inside of Celan to an apparition that becomes a representation, a representation that becomes an incarnation, an incarnation that becomes a body, a body that becomes a text that becomes a reading, a reading that becomes an apparition for the interior universe of Celan. *¿Con cuántos comprenden, y luego a quién?*⁷

                      ❧ Marta López-Luaces
                      ❧ Translation by Alexandra Van de Kamp

1 The quotations are, for the most part, by the poets mentioned in the poem. When the poet is not mentioned, the reference can be found in a footnote. Frost, "Acquainted with the Night" (Me he familiarizado con la noche).
2 From T. S. Eliot's "The Love Song Of J. Alfred Prufrock".
3 *alimentaste tu hambre como una tarea interminable.* Versos de Hart Crane a su madre poética Emily Dickinson.
4 *the state of my body*
5 The secret of the gods is found in the language of man.
6 *You have done with me what you should not have done.*
7 *How much do they understand and later for whom César Vallejo*

At the Pentecostal Baths

Tactile, yes. In total darkness, yes.
As if eclipsed. As on his lips.
As if in secret retreat,
finding his way, eagerly. Yes.

A room filled with men, yes.
Lightness years away.
He waits for the coming
of the Paraclete,

a proper businessman, yes,
on his knees, imploring,
waits for ecstasy, yes.
Glory revealed in silver-

dollar holes. Halos, yes.
Come with thy grace
and heavenly aid,
he begs.

There are no tongues
of flame. Is this
how it ends? This is
how it ends, yes.

                 ❧ Pablo Miguel Martínez

August Eve

The scent of gardenias and smoky cigars
have come to visit me again,
seeping through my window
on this August eve.

I hear the crickets pause,
feel a lukewarm breeze tap my shoulder
and wake to palm leaves catching raindrops
while the curtains part the way
preparing my room for song.

And I, sprawled on my back
between my rough-and-tumble sheets,
smile.

I asked her not to scare me
when she crosses over
but still give me a sign,
and she, with witted humor
visits me in mixed metaphors.

                      ❧ Anika Paris

Autumn Inaugural

I.

There will always be those who reject ceremony,
Who claim that resolution requires no fanfare,
Those who demand the spirit stay fixed
Like a desert saint, fed only on faith,
To worship in no temple but the weather.

There will always be the austere ones
Who mount denial's shaky ladder
To drape the statues or whitewash the frescoed wall,
As if the still star of painted plaster
Praised creation less then the evening's original.

And they are right. Symbols betray us.
They are always more or less than what

Is really meant. But shall there be no
Processions by torchlight because we are weak?
What native speech do we share but imperfection?

II.

Look at the trees that surround our ceremony—
These skinny saplings barely kept upright
By wooden poles and braided wire.

They constitute no stately grove of academe,
They give the merest inklings of an avenue. And yet
The skittering whisper of their leaves suggest

A promise rooted local to the soil—
To care and cultivate these slender silhouettes
Until they shade the games of children yet unborn.

III.

Praise to the rituals that celebrate change,
Old robes worn for new beginnings,
Solemn protocol where the mutable soul,
Surrounded by ancient experience, grows
Young in the imagination's white dress.

Because it is not the rituals we honor
But our trust in what they signify, these rites
That honor us as witnesses—whether to watch
Lovers swear loyalty in a careless world
Or a newborn washed with water and oil.

So praise to innocence—impulsive and evergreen—
And let the old be touched by youth's
Wayward astonishment at learning something new,
And dream of a future so fitting and so just
That our desire will bring it into being.

                            ❧ Dana Gioia

The Balkan Bridge
(for Ismail Kadare)

For millennia we have quarreled,
for millennia we have built and demolished
the Balkan bridge
(over the Drina, over the Danube,
over Ujana e Keqe
in Albania).

For millennia we have asked ourselves:
Where is the Golden City—East
or West?
Where is the true Prophet?
And what will be our profit
from that bridge
between sunrise and sunset?

With knives in our teeth,
we have asked our neighbors:
Is it true that living people,
our people,
have been immured here
to make the bridge stronger?

For millennia we have quarreled, and fought,
died and killed, built and demolished.

Meanwhile
they invented the airline.
Today no traveler can even see
that ancient bridge.

                   ❧ Vladimir Levchev
                   ❧ Translation with Alicia Suskin Ostriker

The Baltimore Sun

With the proper tools she shows me how
The bullet ricocheted
Off the refrigerator—I fought for
This image, fall, autumn, me.

Why I don't know.
How often
Why I do the things I do,
Trying to write about it. A
Masterpiece? That's probably
Why you were fascinated, it
Was just like this book I'm
Reading for my English class,
More appealing to me than
Whether some law gets passed.
One of my editors died, like that.
You don't know, you don't care,
At all. Maybe, maybe to me,
I guess, famous but not necessarily
For writing. What's that burning?
Do you think that's a fair way to
Answer it? To see
Your poems in anthologies, sitting
At the computer, it just comes.
I don't ask for that. I ask
For contentment, like wine-tasters,
Standards to make things great.
Why don't you know, a professional
Poet. I don't know something
More active. She wasn't
Moving at all. She was just there.

                 ❧ Donald Berger

Being Happy

Of course it was doomed. I know that now,
but it ended so quickly, and I was young.
I hardly remember that summer in Seattle—
except for her. The city seems just a rainy backdrop.
From the moment I first saw her at the office
I was hooked. I started visiting her floor.

I couldn't work unless I caught a glimpse of her.
Once we exchanged glances, but we never spoke.
Then at a party we found ourselves alone.
We started kissing and ended up in bed.

We talked all night. She claimed she had liked me
secretly for months. I wonder now if that was true.

Two weeks later her father had a heart attack.
While she was in Chicago, they shut down our division.
I was never one for writing letters.
On the phone we had less to say each time.
And that was it—just those two breathless weeks,
then years of mild regret and intermittent speculation.

Being happy is mostly like that. You don't see it up close.
You recognize it later from the ache of memory.
And you can't recapture it. You only get to choose
whether to remember or forget, whether to feel remorse
or nothing at all. Maybe it wasn't really love.
But who can tell when nothing deeper ever came along?

                   ❧ Dana Gioia

Betrayers

Old men dream wars,
fondling remembered weapons
as they watch the skies for omens,
then sleep invasions.
They are America's betrayers,
the men of World War II,
who went in millions,
bearing the burden of democracy
to distant, underprivileged shores.
They came home with grosser appetites,
hungry for their share of pleasures
and their nation's endless treasures.
They became the makers of power,
the abusers of tomorrow,
the slayers of the sandman.

                   ❧ Gary Beck

Big Ship

As a child
I daydreamed
you brought me
bananas
breadfruit
mangoes
and Robinson Crusoe.

You were
all possibilities
inventing continents
inventing seas
and destruction.
You brought Colon
and Cortez,
horses and muskets,
Raleigh, seeking El Dorado,
settling for tobacco.

You came with sugarcane.
From barracoons
you bought flesh
at forty glass necklaces
and two pistols per head
and whips
to set aflame
sweating
African backs.

≈ Sydney March

Black Book

At the end of the '80s,
he threw away his phone book;
everyone in it was dead.

Now strolling Christopher Street
to brunch and therapy,
he gazes into familiar doorwells,

remembering leaning figures, handlebar mustaches
curling, like fingers through denim belt loops:
those five o'clock shadows in the shadows.

He's 66, paunchy and gray
but they still wink at him from the grave:
cool invitations
to the piers, the truckyard,
back to their place.

Crossing the cobblestones,
he's still too stunned to be amazed
by all those faded one-nighters
lined up and waiting
for him to come.

                     ᓫ Michael Montlack

Blue Dusk
(Lésvos, Greece)

Blue is its eggshell demeanor
in its stillness and its blur of division,

forcing the land grey on its way to sea then
sky spreading over like a nightcap.

This is the hour the women meet,
the last light hovering on the head of a needle,

words threaded through the afternoon's dismissal to this point
like a yawn of inhale. The men have all left

for coffee, cigarettes, and local politics. They'll return
to lie down with the blue of night, which the women

know, though only some will speak it. The women nod
in recognition—dusk a large eye of a needle.

Watch them pull it through and before you look
again, the space will be empty of them, like

a dusty field, with a few olive trees turning
silver with moonlight, wearing jewelry that clacks

when a breeze picks up a blue note on the wind.
O Aeolus, let open your door. Free them

before the sea and the blue mountains of dusk
unsettling us before time, upsetting

the men who seek the women's womb in sleep,
who take the coastal road like a birthright,

an umbilical cord they dangle from in denial,
their fists welled up in a moment of panic.

And then silence will stay like a blue night.
And they will sleep, and their children

in some far-off land, where I, too, touch the dusk.
Toward me, I pull it, blue as can be.

It's slipped through my photograph.
And yet it keeps me company with its lack of charity.

                         ❧ Donna J. Gelagotis Lee

Blue Jay Passion of Flight
(for Estela Porter Seale)

the drop falls immaculate
into the perennials of red
blue bird jay of the night
yes at least I shall say yes
the drop falls immaculate
at the curve of your passionate waist
made transparent by light
and there it is deposited
deprived of the need for dreams
that remind it
that pure sweat
a pure labor of love
an epidermis that in you burns
like a chant of flowering flames
to remember the force the strength
of your hands
of your muscles

the purity of your fingers
that hammer with the fury
of a young carpenter
of the carpenter who constructs
the fence that divides the yards
the properties the divisions
and there the blue bird jay of the night
establishes itself in its flight of passion
observing your manly labor
of a human who knows himself well
the lines the separations
the borders of Robert Frost
good fences good neighbors
and the bird overwhelmed in its flight
hops from fence to fence
until arriving at your side
man who constructs
fences properties
and looks you in the face
directly in the face
spreading its wings
blue and black
and you smile like an accomplice
of a single word
of a single phrase
that you know well
man who constructs
fences and properties

                         ❧ Benito Pastoriza Iyodo
                         ❧ Translation by Bradley Warren Davis

Body in need

Come play my guitar
and write me a song
or a poem, or a ballad

Remind me of my son
mention the good times
make the tune a smile

Perhaps, a reveille
to wake my senses
of belonging

Come play my guitar
and write me a song
or a poem, or a ballad

About the father I never knew
about the grandmother I did
and the influence of both

The melody can be Irish
but not German or Dutch
Spanish but not French

Either one I'll understand
since the soul of both
is in the same embrace

Come play my guitar
and write me a song
or a poem, or a ballad

                             ❧ JoseMarGuerr

The Border

Hasta luego and over you go and it's not
serapes, the big sombreros, not even coyotes,
rivers and hills, though that's more like it, towers
with guards, stop! or we shoot and they do but you don't
need a border for that, a fence will do, a black
boy stuck to its wire like a leaf, a happy gun
in the thick pink hand that wags from the sleeve, even
a street, the other side, a door, a skin, give
me a hand, and she gives him a hand, she gives him both
her hands, the bones of her back are cracking, the string
has snapped, she's falling, she's pleated paper, paper
is spreading and there you are again, over
the edge, you open your hands and what have you got
but confetti and what can you do with confetti, our
side won, a celebration, shaken hands, it matters

now, whatever it is, but how close
you are, your street, the fence behind your house
is the zero border where minus begins, roots
turn branches, cellar is house, you close your busy
mouth to speak, an anti-lamp darkens
the day, and you love that street, its crazy traffic,
you climb that fence, you wave across, there's a rock
in your hand but it's not your fault, you like to travel,
the colorful people, but what if you fell, your house,
your children, the work that gets you up in the morning,
the language gone, the grammar, the rules, the family
talent, those searching eyes, but think of the absence
of eye, a higher tower, a little more wire—
Border? You crossed the border hours ago.

                                       ꙮ Martha Collins

Border Line

Puerto Nuevo or New Port in English
is 40 miles from the border of Mexico.
It's Saturday and there's a slight
overcast on our venture

¿Quieren comida? they say courting us
with brown sugar smiles and honey-glazed eyes,
men like paparazzi perched outside their restaurants
begging to cook us a meal
pleading to serve us anything
as we glitter their muddy streets.

The salty air hangs heavy
on my conscience,
on the roof of this restaurant,
on the rim of my margarita,
bittersweetly blended in chartreuse.

We sit over looking the village
and sing out to the mariachi band below
"La cucaracha, La cucaracha, ya no puede caminar"
till all twelve trot up the stairs playing
guitars, horns, drums and violins

busting at the seams of indigo blue
wearing tiny red vests, shiny sombreros
and a little bit of boredom on
their belts by their cell phones.
I trace the sound with the tips of my fingers
And lose myself for a moment.

Still, I can't help noticing across the street
a woman on the roof of a tenement that's
burnt to a seaweed crisp
its coffee-stained sheets unable to hide
the naked rooms inside
this building sagging slightly to the left
barely held together with wire hangers
pouts over the junked cars
climbing the doorway like spiders

And amidst all this American novelty
and façade of celebration
she washes her family's clothes
scrubs each shirt, each pair of pants
each mud-stained sock
unable to rinse out their future

"Se sirve el almuerzo,
langosta deliciosa para todas
las señoritas hermosas," the owner says
as he unfolds a blanket of food,
his wife and children catering to us like royalty
filling our cups till they overflow
basting our plates with homemade salsa, tortillas
guacamole, beans, rice,
and succulent lobster in melted butter.

The mariachi band's still playing
my friends are laughing and clapping in rhythm
dancing on the rooftop
even the sun decides to finally visit.

But I can't eat.

                     ❧ Anika Paris

Bread Boy
(for Ruzdo Gasi)

The weight of the loaves isn't heavy enough
to break the sway of his hips
through the narrow alleys of Venice.

He is a local delivery boy
on his way to leave bread on the window sills
of the vecchiettas that run pensions for tourists.

The look over his shoulder and smile
tells me that, like the bread, he wants to be
kneaded, baked, dipped in oil, and eaten.

                   ❧ Dante Micheaux

The Candidate

If he wins...
It will be a bad dream. I will not wake
up from it. My queer heart will crack, then break.
No expatriation to Mozambique. I'm condemned to remain and take
it: the loss of my civil rights, the ache
in knowing that I'm again unspeak-
able—non-being, pervert, faggot, freak.
If he wins,
my computer screen goes dark
as all the hounds of hatred look up and bark.

                   ❧ John Gilgun

Carpooling with a Stranger

A fork. That might have been
my favorite detail. And coke: how you opened

with coke. How your life might have been

if not for coke: right there

in Miami, 1981, those two men doing lines
on a beach-front bar, and the big one—

like a marine, you said—offered you the straw.
How your life might have been

if you'd refused. The tines of a fork
turning as if wrapping spaghetti. The quick

disappearance of powder, disappearing
up a vacuum. On a beach, the rush

inside you. The fork. I loved it. I looked
out the window at West Virginia, shook my head

and waited. The basement. Set up
for it, you said. Dungeon, you said. Did you?

At first it was okay, what you wanted, too.
Then it was hours; they wouldn't

stop; and somehow you didn't quite
realize what they were doing to you.

And when you tried to get up, one of them
hit you, side of the head with

something. Who knows what?
A wrench. Did you say wrench? A fork.

I'm sure you said fork. And coke. And
your life which you then understood

to be in danger. But yet didn't understand
what they were actually doing

inside you, opening you: your body
dilating like an iris in the dark.

The details a haze, a halo over top
of your story: a fork, a wrench, no

commercial break now, not now, the gentle
churning of white powder inside a snow globe

in which you lie on a long table, a basement,
bare cinderblock walls, chains, did you

say that? In the endless poverty
of West Virginia. Bare walls, dirt floor.

Did you? And the two of them, one
like a marine, you said, and how your life

might have been different, and
the emergency room, how you bled

for months after, and the doctor, his face
when you brought up your hand

covered in blood. Wait, you didn't say that—
I'm sure you didn't—

in West Virginia, endlessly rural
West Virginia. Better than

a movie. Dripping. And the glint of metal
behind you, and the snow globe, and then

you finished talking, and we were silent
the four-hour ride back home.

                         ❧ Benjamin S. Grossberg

Carry Me Away

Carry me away to the south
of your hips
where the humidity
envelops the trees
that issue from your body.
Carry me away to the deep earth
that looms between your legs
to that small north of your breast.
Carry me away to the cold desert
that menaces your mouth
to the exiled oasis of your navel.
Carry me away to the west of those feet
that were mine,
of those hands that encircled
the sea and the mountains.

Carry me away to other villages
with the first kiss,
to the interminable region
of language and flowers,
to that genital route
to that river of ash that overflows.
Carry me away to all points, love,
and to all places drive my fingers
as if you were the homeland
and me, your only inhabitant.

                   ❧ Mario Meléndez
                   ❧ Translation by Ron Hudson

Cascade of Faces

Five seconds of fame drag them down
the screen, ranks, names, faces, ages:
Staff Sergeant Hannah Nagel, 24.
Private Tom Abeel, 19.
Major Luís Moreno, 33.
Lance Corporal Rafiq Ibrahim, 20.
Captain Roger Kean, 31.
Candid American faces, unblinking,
unafraid, unvenal, snapped
a year, two years ago, not yet reviled
or revered, the newscast's evening crop.

Images swallowed up, transfigured,
launched into an unlived future.

            *

On the Oval Office desk,
dead center, one hot white spot
lights the briefing's final page.
A chief executive is working late,
behind him, tall windows onto
a sky petroleum black,
strewn with trembling sparks.

            *

In another hemisphere, noon towers over

a desert city where his signature ignited
hair, skin, and eyes of the unknown civilian.
One by one, for how many terrorized
hundred-thousands the precedent was set,
roofs, walls, thundering down on their screams.

*

He reaches to snap out the lamp, ambles
to a door that closes on his steps.
Official darkness. Clockwise stellar bodies,
in their long-term impartiality, continue
rinsing the blackboard,
rinsing the blackboard—
which in a decade, or a century,
will free itself from any obligation
to save a chalked-up tally of the cost.

            ප් Alfred Corn

Castile I

            i.
The wheat already covered the knolls before there was someone to write about it.

            ii.
The wheat and the sunflowers forming geometries beneath the skies of Castile:

            iii.
the stubbles and bundles of wheat endowing the plain with its own calligraphy.

Castile II

            i.
The power lines opening other paths into the plains of Castile.

            ii.
Extending its elliptical geometry to the knolls covered of wheat.

iii.
The steel and concrete towers until eternity over the fields of Castile.

Castile III
(for Antonio Machado)

i.
A stone crucifix atop the knolls of wheat.

ii.
Trees barely grow on the plains.

iii.
Cars on the local roads that cross the fields of Castile.

                     ❧ Andrés S. Fisher

Casualties of War
(February 14th)

On this day I think of the widows
who awoke before dawn and planned
a morning of strenuous exercise,
five times around the mall
until the stores open, then new
linens for the bed, a down pillow
or two, scented paper for
the closet empty in the hall.
An afternoon of cleaning windows
and attics, discarding clothes
snug to the point of pain.

On this day I think of the widows
who busy themselves in kitchens,
clanging pots and pans like tocsins
warding off despair, who dedicate
an hour before tea to scouring

grease off burners on the stove,
who fall to their knees, as in prayer,
and wax each linoleum square
until it glows and they can see
reflected in its speckled grey their
own neglected faces.

On this day I think of the widows,
my friends, who fall asleep exhausted
at day's end, the television hawking
its relentless, heartless lie.

                         ❧ Gloria Vando

Cat Scrabble Ode

While you were out tonight
the cats played Scrabble.
Of course that's not to say
they played it the way
you and I would play.
But that's a cavil:
the cats played Scrabble.

Once they'd knocked it to the floor,
of course they ignored the board.
Playing as a team, together no slouch,
if you assume intention from proximity
and count the "L" half under the couch
as an "I," their best word was "GTIER"
(by chance), though neither spotted "TIGER,"
which would have been obvious to you or me
(as obvious as that little irony).
But humans are mammals of a different stripe,
and each mammal plays according to type.

Asleep, myself, on the self-same couch,
from a hard day's work and a beer, I avouch,
catatonic, completely zonked,
contemptuous of concerns ergonomical,
while the cats spelled "MIA" and "AWOL,"
I dreamt of old ladies in the Bronx.

At a big green table on a summer's day,
having tired of manifold hands of cards,
to gossip continuo, a buzz-saw of words,
they slapped away at a game of mah jong
while a small red radio sang them a song.

My dream was triggered by batted tiles,
the cats cavorting all the while.
In scribble-scrabble, mix and match,
they skidded, scampered, in and out of turn.
Little Albert takes a pipe while at play.
Claude the Orange likes to scratch,
to pill and pull at cloth and fern.
In chaos and fury their play is war,
though no one dies or even keeps score.

Well, dear, how's life at the old PTA?
I'm glad you're home, it gets lonely here,
my only company two cats and a beer.
If we could but find some twenty-odd tiles,
might we ourselves try a bit of play
(admittedly not in feline style)
to wile the rest of the night away?

                       ❧ Ron Singer

Chancellorsville
> "Let us cross over the river, and rest under the shade of the trees."
> —Stonewall Jackson's last words

Late April, the sarvisberry blossoms
fall like frayed lace. Where that fool
bullet shattered you, petals scatter
the brittle-leaf forest floor.

Today, a tourist at Chancellorsville,
I stroll the battlefield, lag by relic cases,
staring at photographs, buttons
and uniforms, the threadbare Stars and Bars

I would have fought for,

born a century sooner.
You too were a mountaineer,
from the wild hills west of here,

slopes snowy in spring with sarvis,
resurrection's first proof,
sparkling with redbud,
or the creamy dogwood bearing

Christ's rusty wounds.
Sometimes, a soldier
shrapneled with family deaths,
failed ambitions, lost lovers,

I add a slice of lemon to iced tea
and think of you, chewing lemons
even inside battle, inuring
yourself to the acids that war requires.

Here, off Route 3's roar,
I stand by the stone
that marks where you fell,
shot by your own mistaken men.

On the surgeon's table
your left arm was lost, buried
before you in a grave of its own.
If not courage, perhaps pride

would have armed me, would have
lined me up behind you.
Perhaps I might have seized as relic
some drained lemon you tossed away,

hoping that war's chances
would allow me such courage,
such a comrade, who rests now
on the river's far bank, in the shade of the trees.

                         ᛞ Jeff Mann

Chemistry Lessons

1. Chemistry reduces the mysteries of life to their lowest common denominator.

2. Opposite ions are magnetically drawn to one another.

3. When oxygen and friction collide in sufficient supply spontaneous combustion will occur.

4. The body employs anti-oxidizing agents to neutralize those free radicals that threaten to upset the status quo.

5. Life is simply a matter of molecules that can be reproduced in test tubes and petrie dishes.

6. Love, like any other toxic substance, has its half-life, and in due time will be flushed out.

7. Sooner or later, every thought or passion will be traceable to the firing of a detectable neuron pathway.

8. A laboratory animal has generally exhausted its useful scientific life after a single experiment and will then be put to sleep.

9. There are no monsters. There is only Man. This is the truth.

                    ಲ Nina Corwin

Children of the Stones
—With an acknowledgment to the Syrian poet Nizar Qabbani, (1923-1998)

You throw stones against steel.
You throw stones. The others shoot bullets.
Your mothers shed golden tears in sunlight.
Your fathers shed silver tears in moonlight.

Your parents helpless and weakened.
Your homes bulldozed. Their olive trees swept away.
You return at night to mounds of broken bricks

and concrete. The roads are only for the others.

Those soldiers not much older than you.
You mock the authority of their steel.
They are secure in their tanks and towers.
You of the stones have a different destiny.

O Children of Ramallah!
O Children of Rafah!
You who mock the authority of steel
lost in the rubble of your homes.

O Children of Jerusalem!
O Children of Jenin!
You who mock the authority of steel,
You who rebel against your fathers.

O Children of the Stones!
You who mock the authority of steel,
You who rebel against your fathers,
Who will grieve for you?

                 ❧ J. Glenn Evans

Chrysanthemum is Prettiest in the Ninth Moon

The window has moved.
My grey-haired elders are still there,
counting chrysanthemum petals in the sun,
each petal a sad shoe.

                 ❧ Ye Chun

Cicada

My name is Lazarus.
I came from the grave.
seventeen years I waited, waited
perched on a damp root
on the opposite side of life.
There the sky is dark and firm.

My name is Lazarus.
I came from the grave.
I woke up one morning
in Paradise
together with millions
of awakened kindred souls:
We flew up into a green tree—
a fleet of old-fashioned
brown motorcycles
with two red headlights.

Our song is
the song of time:
it says good morning,
and it says goodbye
with one high pitched note—
a growing song
under the sun.

My name is Lazarus.
I came from the grave.
seventeen years of life in death,
seventeen years in a sky of stone,
seventeen years of silence
don't exist anymore. . . .
What is time?

I will die in a month.
(A month in Paradise!)
But what is time, what is time?

My name is Lazarus.
I came from the grave.
I came to tell you
good morning and goodbye.

          ॐ Vladimir Levchev
          ॐ Translation with Alicia Suskin Ostriker

City

I'm fleeting; I'm a quite dissatisfied citizen of a modern metropolis, where all known decency has been left out of the architecture and out of the general design of the city itself. Here you will find absolutely no totems of any superstitions whatsoever. In brief, morality and conversation are reduced to their most vulgar expressions of normalcy. These millions and millions of people do not know each other and conduct their business, education, and even their old age in accordance with some insane statistics. At my window, I see new ghosts drifting through the coal smoke—our shadows in the forest becoming more shadow, our summer night! Death without tears, desperate loves, and a beautiful crime screams out from the mud in the street.

                               ❧ Arthur Rimbaud
                               ❧ New translation by Louis E. Bourgeois

Clearance Questionnaire

To your knowledge has the subject ever voted for a Democrat?

Have they ever run for political office?

Does the subject have anything in their demeanor that could be used against them? Did they do drugs? Are they alcoholic? Do they pay for sex?
      Wear the opposite sex's underwear? Use a dildo?

Does the subject, to the best of your knowledge, pick their nose? Masturbate? Commit adultery? Attend a church?

Has the subject ever attended a Broadway musical?

Have they ever lived in a Blue state or city? Visited a Blue state or city in the past year? Do they have friends or family in a Blue state or city?

Do they possess a passport?

Do they speak a foreign language?

Do they like any of the following:
      Michael Jackson? Liberace? Elton John? k.d. lang? Ellen Degeneres? Rufus Wainwright? Morrissey? Ru Paul? Will and Grace?

Do they listen to Rap music, wear flashy clothes, or show too much jewelry?

Do they have an American flag in their yard or visible in any window?

Have they ever been heard to utter—[Expletive] Bush, or anything else demeaning or threatening to our President?

Do they fish? Own firearms?

Do you know their ethnic persuasion?

Pureblooded American
Southern Baptist
Non-White
Foreigner

Do they have long hair? A beard? Or wear funny or odd-looking clothes?

We're almost done. I realize all of these questions don't pertain to your [wife/husband; friend; family member], but please bear with me.

To your knowledge does the subject ever say anything anti-American?

Have they ever traveled to

a. Cuba

b. Russia

c. North Korea

d. Iran

e. France

Could they be vegetarians?

Do they look or behave like a terrorist?

Do they read books? And/or subscribe to magazines like:

f. *The Nation*

g. *The Progressive*

h. *Mother Jones*

i. *kanky Possum*

Do they have friends named:

j. Omar

k. Mustapha

l. Francois

m. Clinton

Do they teach anywhere? Perhaps in a liberal university setting?

Have they ever worked in Hollywood for the biased liberal media? In publishing?

Are they or have they ever been:

n. Jewish

o. Islamic

p. Huguenot

Thank you for your time.

Your friends at the RNC.

                     ❧ Richard Peabody

The Climb

Juan de Lara, probably from Cordoba, Spain, was captured by the Mexica at the battle of Xochimilco. He and several other Spaniards, among them Alonso Hernández, were sacrificed, their arms and legs scattered to nearby towns to show that the Mexica were winning the war with the Europeans.

One hundred and thirteen steps led to the top of the Great Temple of Tenochtitlán where sacrifices were held. A priest cut the heart from a living victim; then, the victim's limbs and head were cut off and the torso thrown down the steep steps of the Temple just as Coyolxauhqui, the Mexica deity associated with the moon, was beheaded and thrown down the mountain by her brother, Huitzilopochtli, the war god associated with the sun.

29 April 1521: the Great Temple of Tenochtitlán

his fist grips my hair
my scalp shifts across the bone
I lift my own feet
my thighs, my hips, my chest—
white as hen's feathers
the stone spotted brown
as if from rust
as if they knew iron
the scar on my shin
like a long pale worm
I'm cold—my hands sweat
I feel the drums inside my chest
behind my eyes between my wrists
and I climb
they say that we will sit
on the sun that we will be
the eagle's companions
for four years and sing
war songs and fight again
old battles and sit on
the sun that we are precious
water and that each
morning we will carry
their god to the middle
of the sky and in four years
return as hummingbirds
men die quickly
I have seen them
struck down their arms
there their legs in the jaws
of dogs their heads
rolling on the ground
and stopping against
a wall and the light
has gone from their eyes
even before they stop
and the echoes of their
screams swarm around
their bodies like flies
I climb after my scalp
the shadow of his arm
like a bridge to my head
the stone steps like waves
and our shadows rise and
fall across them and I

feel like I'm coming
apart that my feet move
without me that my legs
follow that my shoulders
fall in that my chin
drops that the cries of men
form a wall around my heart
I can feel the sky and
a warm breeze from the
south and the eyes of the
stone frogs on either side
and the earth has fallen
away I don't remember who
I am or when I was a child
my bare feet in the narrow
streets filled with sunlight
the white walls and counting
the sixteen arches of the
bridge near the castle and
picking olives in the grove
I can smell it the steps
are wet here they're red like
granite my god my feet it's
on my feet already I can't
go I can feel it on my feet
it's still warm and it's
on my feet my god that's me
and the knife and it's warm
and it's on my feet and his
feet and it runs down and
we take it back up and then
me coming down christ I
feel the knife already
hail mary mother of god
protect me and guide me
hail mary holy virgin
give me strength and
victory over their idols
hail mary mother of god
in whom I place my trust
who has guided us and
delivered us many times
from the hands of these
savages help me
and give me the strength

to face this hour
beyond the priest I see the sky
it's blue and his hair is black
it's blue and his ears are torn
it's blue and his face is smeared
with blood it's blue and his face
and arms are black it's blue and
he's neither young nor old it's blue
and his shirt is black and damp
with blood it's blue now as if
the sky shows through him and my
shadow stretches past his feet
and beneath the stone slab blood
puddles and I can't move my eyes
or my feet no don't but they lift me
and drag me through the blood hail
mary christ Alonso's head stuck on
the rack four black priests stand one at
each mother of god corner of the slab
and they lift me and lay me in the
blood hold me one at each shoulder
one at each ankle hail mary the knife
mother and now his hand and my heart

                         ❧ Randy Koch

Closure

Broken eggs, the mess albumin, cumin
everywhere, a rolling barn dance, never a chance
mention of adventure nor sensational

cereal accusations commonplace sunlight
answers, echo streams in e-mail for cement snow
weather changes, those eggs again, a Halloween

mask broken spell that, and that fits too, lies
lonesome in some angel glory found
and lost at the grace gloss halftime

score known days before dinosaurs could
have tramped there, trampled there, trampled

their progeny littering atheist orange groves

humanely harvested of clues amid morning dews
and free to pay to choose your poison pen letter
to be read on stage by (insert your name here).

                   ❧ Greg Baysans

Confession

Weeding and watering,
I come upon a chartreuse
caterpillar so bright
I watch until it moves
to see if it is real.

Suddenly I remember
a similar caterpillar,
two young boys
and an empty coffee can
filled with torn newspaper

wondering what would happen
if we lit a match —
a haunting image
lost for some
fifty years until now.
Nearby, the orange
daylilies face the sun,
yesterday's blossoms
withered and forgotten,
no need for absolution.

I finish the gardening
with a stone in my shoe.

                   ❧ Don Cellini

Confession

I gave birth to a child
and placed her inside
a plastic bottle

then buried her
beneath a foot
of sand.

I understand
this may seem
a savage thing to do.

But I assure you—
you've done it too.
And at midnight

when you turn off the TV
and climb beneath quilted covers
when your children are snug in bed

dreaming the orgies of lies
an endless feverish dance of selfish pleasures.
Sometimes

it occurs to you
to remember.
And you wonder

whether she will live or die.
As it happens, friend.
Last night I did some digging

And I can say this:
I have no answer
to your question.

                       ❧ Kim Jensen

The Courtship of the Morticians

1

Nothing human or inhuman revulses them.
After the formaldehyde, the Lano-Flo and powder,
after roses and chrysanthemums and gladioluses,
after a cozy soprano in the dolorous chapel or
folding chairs and accordion under elms and weeping cherries,
after tea and cakes and marmalade and little cookies
brought in upon a platter, after laying a few long greens
tenderly across the sexton's pink calluses, leaving Forest Lawn
and heading back to the glassy mortuary, they park
for almost an hour at the end of a dirt road
in an untamed part of the cemetery. Their eyes
reflect a minor entanglement of convolvuluses,
reflect bindweed and dodder and railroad vine
and the small red morning glories, which are closed now
because it is later afternoon. They sit close together
on the silver-gray banquette; they do not force
the moment to a crisis, but they sit close together
on the rayon-velvet banquette, in the front row,
as it were, and hold each other's pulses.

2

The courtship of the morticians
was not notably different,
was not better or worse, more
or less passionate, histrionic,
disingenuous, manipulative, tough
or tender than other courtships,
except in this one small regard only:
after wine and candlelight, after
cocktails and inflected chatter,
after the play, concert, or drive-in movie,
after wine and candlelight and violins,
after beer and kielbasa and accordions, they parked
in the cemetery with the other compulsives,
and held each other's pulses.

                     ❧ Peter Klappert

The Cricket:
(for Alejandra Jaramillo)

"The one who, disturbed by the noise of the insect that entered through a crack, crushes it underfoot, will afterwards hear in greater clarity the mysterious awe of darkness and the vast emptiness of the land.

What is hard to hear is, more often than not, what we hear more often, and more disturbingly."

                 ॐ Benito del Pliego
                 ॐ Translation by Robin Ouzman Hislop

La Cucaracha

I usually liked to put on a turban
at age ten and
become Carmen Miranda
with a tablecloth skirt
ruffled at the bottom and pinned
at the waist with a big red flower.
I can't say what got over me
the night Uncle Phil was to be shipped out.
He sat all sad in his brown uniform downstairs
waiting for the music to start,
but I was frozen beside my plaster statue
of the Virgin Mary.
My mother came up and begged me,
"Just this once. Dance for your Uncle Phil
who's going away to war and might get killed."
Finally the day slipped away taking my
uncle with it, leaving me with a
turban filled with fruit on the bed,
big hooped earrings, and an old record,
although I could not sing, even if
life and death were at stake.
Maybe that's why the little girl held out.
Maybe that's why one day Uncle Phil took grief
for a bride and died of cancer.
Maybe that's why we should
always dance when asked, especially
if we made the costume ourselves.
                 ॐ Grace Cavalieri

Damaged Goods

She hates herself for being so turned off,
For begging Fate to cut that final tie.
His voice is thick, a smoker's hacking cough.
And when he breathes, her soul begins to cry.

She loved him true and fair, far more than well.
His boyish eyes, his tawny summer tan.
But when his head cracked open like a shell,
He lost his chance to grow into a man.

He isn't mean, just maddeningly slow,
Devoid of any charm or social grace.
She winces when he drools and croaks "hullo."
For she was raised with forks and knives in place.

Her shame is great for praying he be gone,
For pleading with her God to get it done.
" Don't let him wake this day to see the dawn."
How could a mother wish this on her son?

                       ❧ Jill Williams

Dawn

I embraced the summer dawn.

Nothing stirred in front of the palaces. The water was dead. The shadows lodged on the woodland road. I walked, awakening tepid breaths; and precious stones watched, and wings rose without sound.

The first danger was on a path filled with incipient dim flashes, and a flower told me her name.

I laughed at the waterfall that rumpled through the fir trees: on the silver mountain top I saw the goddess. Then, one after another I raised her veils. On the road, I waved my arms. Across the glade I condemned her to the cock. She fled to the city among the steeples, running like a rogue on the marble wharves, and I chased her.

Far up the road near the laurel wood, I wrapped her in veils and felt just a hint of her boundless form. Dawn and the child sank down at the edge of the wood.

Waking, it was noon.

                 ❧ Arthur Rimbaud
                 ❧ New translation by Louis E. Bourgeois

[Deaf is the night...]

Deaf is the night the shadow the fog
Deaf is the tree deaf the pebble
Deaf is the hammer on the anvil
Deaf is the sea deaf the owl

Blind the night and the stone
Blind the grass and the grain
Blind is the mole under the ground
Blind the kernel inside the fruit

Mute the night and misery
Mute are the days and the plain
Mute is the air's clarity
Mute the forest the lake the cry

Crippled is all of nature
Crippled are rocks and creatures
Crippled is the caricature
Crippled the idiot healed

But who sees? Who hears? Who speaks?

                 ❧ Raymond Queneau
                 ❧ New translation by Daniela Hurezanu and
                    Stephen Kessler

Death

An Arab friend once told me: "I find so reassuring the thought that one day I will be no longer."

This is a very natural way of seeing things; but who among us Westerners could say this? We fight against death and we fight against life.

There is somewhere a company that transforms the body of your dearly departed into a diamond. You can take it everywhere with you, even when he is gone. "Nothing is lost in nature, everything is transformed," we have been taught in school.

Even death is no longer final.

                 ❧ Alta Ifland

Delft

Flat, with variations. Not
the table but the cloth.
As if a continent
raging westward, staggered
at the sight of
so much water, sky
on curdling sky.

Wherever I walk
the earth's soft
mouth suckles.
These clumps of beeches,
glazed trunks
green with age.
Each brick house the original
oven, fired to stay
incipient mold,

while in the hour
of least resolve
the starched sheets
scratch the insomniac wife
to bravado. *At least,*
she whispers,

we dine in style.
And our sceneries
please. We may be standing
on a porch
open to the world
but the house behind us
is sinking.

        ❧ Rita Dove

A Deluge of Script

The junk man's song floated over Cairo
like driftwood—every morning I listened
to its rise and fall and didn't understand
as its three flat notes tumbled along with me
past the empty bench outside my building,
past a turbaned man in a white *galabayya*
rolling a wagon of green figs, their smooth skin
pocked by thorns—past the mangos in mesh bags
above the juicer's stall, past the hint
of open doorways, the scent of frying chick peas
and oil sizzling in metal vats,
past boys on bicycles
balancing trays piled with bread,
past the hunched back of one man,
spine curved like a perfect horseshoe,
head below his shoulders.

I was submerged in a sea of Arabic, a deluge of script.
By the time my eyes tuned in,
my feet had already moved on,
so I was still absorbing the *ta* from the last sign
as the next *alif* rolled into vision.
On every building, every billboard,
letters looped together right to left, saying something
I desperately wanted to grasp.

        ❧ Yvette Neisser Moreno

The Disappeared

Dear Sister Paul's keyhole at which I kneeled
like a supplicant asking for answers
from her vanished hair,
the uncertain gender beneath her robe,

rooms where compass points spun, chalk wiped clean,
hypotenuse erased, and x standing for what sorrow
caused them to hand me over to others.
A shudder before the last rite.

My father has joined the order of dust.
I was the truth of my mother's secrets.
When I fingered her name incised into stone,
a defiant snail, bareback, traveled the arc

of what was not said by the mourners.
Dear wind, brace these sleepers in their passage,
buttress these bodies of dreams.

                 ஐ Colette Inez

The Dog:

"Fidelity burns with a dimming flame. What fidelity adds to happiness is prodigious, and immense its capacity to rot.

Whoever paints a dog on a gravestone knows that waiting is a loss —awaiting a pleasure arising out of thin air.

He who loves the bread the hand feeds, will defy any threat to that feeding hand: the mouth would defy itself were its jaws is a threat."

             ஐ Benito del Pliego
             ஐ Translation by Robin Ouzman Hislop

[don't paint yourself invisible]

don't paint yourself invisible
the geography of your being
is where it was
meant to be—

daughter of the sun
and the milky moon
you don't need obsidian hair
to know you have found
the soil you call home

you wear long trenzas and, yes,
they shine in the sun
but you, la güerita,
want to cut them off
dye every strand black
shy away from
lo descolorida
even though you were given
mother-milk in this
beloved tawny-colored land

on the sacred mountain
huichol bird-whispers
guided your eyes into the
night: you saw at the ceremonial
site ancient webs of light

then you knew

tierra que parió mi alma en altar de piedra
al son de mil y un tambores
los dioses de tez morena lloran sangre—
con arcilla y canto se engendrará nueva luz

                         ❧ Claire Joysmith

The Door

The door is immeasurable.

The door opens or closes; it is all the same to her. The door is still a door.

The door prevents her from hearing the pissy trickle of the water fountain in the courtyard. Tossing coins is forbidden.

The door moves, gives slightly beneath her slick, desperate palms, it jiggles in its frame, loose as a body beneath its clothes.

He is on the other side of the door.

The door is just a door. Only when she wakes and washes the night from her skin can she understand this.

The door is painted yellow, the color of abandonment, to match the ribbons in her front yard (in the branches of her hair, binding her limbs, her torso).

Perhaps he will always be on the other side of the door.

How to sum up the nature of a door: if one passes through it often enough it
       becomes irrelevant.

                                  ஐ Bernadette Geyer

During the War

When my brother came home from war
he carried his left arm in a black sling
but assured us most of it was still there.
Spring was late, the trees forgot to leaf out.

I stood in a long line waiting for bread.
The woman behind me said it was shameless,
someone as strong as I still home, still intact
while her Michael was burning to death.

Yes, she could feel the fire, could smell
his pain all the way from Tarawa—
or was it Midway?—and he so young,
younger than I who was only fourteen,

taller, more handsome in his white uniform

turning slowly gray the way unprimed wood
grays slowly in the grate when the flames
sputter and die. *I think I'm going mad,*

she said when I turned to face her. She placed
both hands on my shoulders, kissed each eyelid,
hugged me to her breasts and whispered wetly
in my bad ear words I'd never heard before.

When I got home my brother ate the bread
carefully one slice at a time until nothing
was left but a blank plate. *Did you see her,*
he asked, *the woman in hell, Michael's wife?*

That afternoon I walked the crowded streets
looking for something I couldn't name,
something familiar, a face or a voice or less,
but not these shards of ash that fell from heaven.

                       ❧ Philip Levine

Eastern Village with Factory

Dogs bark in untended fields. Outside, artificial light
pools the road nobody's died on with men sauntering
the graveyard shift, unafraid to sing alone. I stretch out
and find I married a woman who doesn't care that they
have picked up the ambrosial bouquet of sex—neatly
wrapped in tissue paper—at the foot of our bed. She
welcomes the rabid charge. Anything that reminds her
she belongs to the faint hinterland. She keeps the doors
unlocked. I say nothing. Men or dogs. There will be no
other end.

                       ❧ Daniele Pantano

Ecstasy

The heat makes us go.
Stifling, like a starched shirt,
it bids us to disrobe and
stand naked in the window,
dripping.

A cube of ice passes over
our lips and cools them. It feels
electric, like the moment
we called each other and eloped
to where no one knew us, let alone
cared who we were,

or what we were doing
with each other. Bathe me now
in your sweat again. Let it pool
on my chest once more, and trace a cross
on my forehead, and let me go out

among the world as clean as
a virgin's smock, clothed in your
blessing.

                          ❧ J. E. Robinson

Edge

If I could live
in her world, penetrate
her culture, speak

her language, ululate
with her sisters—Jews
and Arabs, aren't we sparked

and spanked from the same,
the same daddy, Oh! Abraham,
lying with Sarah, lying

with Hagar—the desert
sand sifts into my bed.

No, maybe it's her

grain, those mountains
of barley, wheat, oats,
her shining black

eyes and hair, her
laughter in the market
wilder than a hyena

alerting her clan.
Come quick I'll guard
the feast for the family—

that could be me running
toward her, tight in the hungry
herd. Me without limp

to retard my progress.
I know the tasty morsel
could be me: her gobbling

my flesh, bones, nails, hair,
leaving my parts in pellets
far from her cave. If I could live

in her world, reach that edge,
my own darkness, the abyss
would liberate me from fear.

                      ❧ Karren LaLonde Alenier

Elena Mesa
In 1931, shortly after 22-year-old Elena Mesa died of tuberculosis, her doctor exhumed her body and lived with the mummified remains in a hideaway in Key West, Florida.

Señor von Cosel, you were never my lover,
though you forced me to lie with you,
breathed air into my hardened lungs, covered
my bones with spun silk, pursued
me. May Holy Mary undo your sin.

The night you took me from the tomb
I saw myself in the stars, skin
pocked and hollowed, my hair's bloom
gone, my voice echoing, but no one there.
Did you, sick with love, think you could bring life
back with netting and wax, repair
my hands and feet, make me your wife?
Unholy man, I'm stunned by your disgrace.
Erase these years. Give me back my resting place.

                 ❧ Carolyn Kreiter-Foronda

Every Name Has a Face*
No man knows
How empty a woman feels
When she gets blue.
—Norman Jordan

Every name has a mother
Every name has a face

Words are bridges
Linking the past to the future

Tears falling to earth
Can be heard in the heart

Life is sometimes a sip of water
Too short to quench one's thirst

Death speaks to everyone
Sometimes it whispers—sometimes it shouts

Mothers weeping against cold walls
Our hands must always touch.

                 ❧ E. Ethelbert Miller

* This poem was written for the Afghan Memorial Project for Child Victims of Murder—Wrapped In Love

Every Throat

A coquí choir grades
the song of hedgegrass.
Dark water lapping at the bank.
This way,
where tabaqueras once
carried lanterns
to fields of spent hands,
cancered mouths and throats.
The way of the river
is clear eyes and fishing poles.
The old man, abuelo,
draws bait from a bucket.
I claw the ground for earthworms.
A black, slick water
slitherer, our first catch.
The dark sky seals my mouth.
The bent back man
does not fear Satan.
The word of God
breathes in every throat.
You can eat it, he says,
like butterfish we have for breakfast
with day-old
bread and ripe plantain,
bitter coffee to remember
how we wear this skin that hurts.

ଌ Naomi Ayala

The Explanation of Metaphors

Outside of time and space, a man is lost
Thin as a hair, wide as the light of dawn,
Foam in his nostrils, eyes bulging aghast,
And hands reaching out in search of the scene

--Unreal in fact. So, one will likely ask,
What is the meaning of this metaphor:
"Thin as a hair, wide as the light of dawn"
And why these less than three-dimensional nostrils?

If I should speak of time, it hasn't happened,
If I should speak of a place, it's disappeared,
If I should speak of a man, he'll soon be dead,
If I should speak of time, it's come and gone.

If I should speak of space, a god's destroyed it,
If I should speak of years, it's to erase them,
If I hear silence, a god comes roaring through it,
And his repeated cries give me great grief.

Because these gods are demons; they crawl through space,
Thin as a hair, wide as the light of dawn,
Foam in their nostrils, slobber on their face,
And hands reaching out in search of the scene

--Unreal in fact. So, one will likely ask,
What is the meaning of this metaphor:
"Thin as a hair, wide as the light of dawn"
And why this less than three-dimensional face?

If I should speak of gods, they span the sea,
With their infinite weight, their perpetual flight,
If I should speak of gods, they haunt the air,
If I should speak of gods, they never die,

If I should speak of gods, they're underground,
Breathing their vital breath into the soil
If I should speak of gods, they nurture iron,
They gather carbon and distill cinnabar.

So, are they gods or demons? They fill time
Thin as a hair, wide as the light of dawn,
Foam in their nostrils, hollow enamel eyes,
And hands reaching out in search of the scene

--Unreal in fact. So, one will likely ask,
What is the meaning of this metaphor:
"Thin as a hair, wide as the light of dawn"
And why these less than three-dimensional hands?

Yes, they are demons. One goes down, one up.
A day for every night, a valley for every hill,
A night for every day, a shadow for every tree,
A No for every being, an evil for every good,

Yes, they're reflections, negative images,
Moving about like immobility,

Hurling their many selves into the void
And creating a double for every truth.

But neither god nor demon, man is lost,
Thin as a hair, wide as the light of dawn,
Foam in his nostrils, eyes bulging aghast,
And hands reaching out in search of the scene

--Unreal in fact. For he is truly lost;
He isn't thin enough, nor wide enough
Too many muscles flexed, saliva swallowed.
Calm will return when he sees the Temple's
Form ensuring his own eternity.

> 🕊 Raymond Queneau
> 🕊 New translation by Daniela Hurezanu and
>   Stephen Kessler

Fairy Tales for Writers: Little Red Riding Hood

Sometimes a young girl goes out into the world
unprepared for who or what she'll find out there.
It's not that she hasn't been forewarned, but
sometimes she just doesn't recognize the wolf
in his disguises, or that she should be wary of him.
When he points out the flowery language of the contract
she is entranced: it's all so complicated, this seems to be
the real thing. How exciting it is to be published!
And she's won a prize, the best of the volume!
She readily agrees to buy copies
of the book that her poem is in.
She gives one to her grandmother.

Her grandmother, too, falls prey to the wolf's flattery;
she has her own dreams—and poems,
set aside for all these years.
The grandmother, too, wins a prize!
Good writing must run in the family, they tell one another,
and celebrate with a picnic feast
in a wood they have both written about.

Along comes a well-meaning fellow,
who's been around the block a time or two.

He's a professor at the local community college
where the girl has enrolled in school, and in his day
he's published a book or few. He informs them
of the scam, the wool that's been pulled over their eyes
by this wolf in sheep's clothing.

Who is he to ruin their happiness? they wonder.
They look at the small literary journals
where his recent poems have been published,
 compare those to the handsome hardbound anthology
where their own work appears. He is jealous, they decide.

And even though, in their disillusionment,
they deride him and give him no thanks
for his disturbing their sleep in the belly of the wolf,
he cannot regret what he's done.

                         ❧ Lawrence Schimel

Faith

In the dark in the no-light at the field's center. Cows. Two cows. This is about what I believe. There are two cows in the center of a field that I can not see. Two cows in the dark. I attribute my belief to a small part of the soul where knowledge resides and informs faith. That in the field there are two cows I can not see. Not-cows which I can not see. I know the cows are there because I know the owner of the field. He lives in town. He sold off the herd, he said, except two cows. These two cows. I know the cows are here because I can hear them. I hear them here making cow sounds which are mostly munching and chomping sounds. Moo. Moo. That's me. I say Moo, Moo. I don't know why. Sometimes I talk to myself. I tell myself to have faith. Here in the center of this dark field where I can't see a blessed thing, this seems like a good time. How did I get here? I don't know. I don't have the faintest idea. I wouldn't even swear that I'm here, it's so dark, except I hear the cows munching and I started out to cross the field. I was bored. That was before I got scared. Now I'm not bored. I'm scared because I can't see. I'm completely in the dark. It's exciting. I'm lost. Here I go. I'm walking toward what I'm sure are two cows. Moo, I say. So they know I'm coming.

                         ❧ Edward Falco

A Fantastic Sapphic

Gertrude, Alice, mime Marcel Marceau meet
beach side, U.S. Virgin Islands, one hot dusk.
"Welcome," G.S. says as perfect host but
    swatting noseeums.

Waving first, the great clown smirks, then scratches
right leg, left leg, both knobbed elbows together.
Rearranging her skirt, Miss Toklas asks,
    "Are there mosquitoes?"

"Wind, without wind, trade winds blowing strongly,
people like us become targets, the bull's-eye."
Writer Stein concludes this discourse, fingers
    cocked like a trigger.

Hands held high but knees sinking in the sand,
Bip, the martyr, surrenders, prone to the pests.
"Bored Marceau dead, huh, Pussy?" Alice nods—
    silence unbroken.

                           ❧ Karren LaLonde Alenier

Farewell Kiss

The Navajo way to say "kiss" is
"Two round objects meet."
When we kissed it was more like
two pairs of parallel lines
meeting at various points.
Of course, the geometry was complicated
by the fact that arms were also wrapped
around bodies which pressed each other,
all of these parts, too,
being somewhat straight
as well as somewhat round.

Now since this was a farewell kiss,
the straight round objects were parting
as well as meeting.
Yet by meeting as we parted

—and I believe some of the objects
also parted as they met
we—and they—were perhaps agreeing
or even asking
to meet again.

                 ❧ Ron Singer

[Fifi, the dangerous fag dog]

Fifi, the dangerous fag dog,
makes guys nervous,
gay or straight.
She's so femme!
Pink ribboned,
she knows
drag queens' stones
were Stonewall's first stones.
She knows mincing gaits got there.
Fifi, strut,
you feisty bitch,
strut your dangerous rhinestones.

                 ❧ John Del Peschio

Final Approach

Survivors don't want to live
and live and ask themselves (?), if

human beings: who wonder (?) why chance:
appears to be no obvious

reason to be selected so randomly: they
crash on final approach, and never

understand survival, no matter the
asking: remember only one flight

meeting a mountain and hear the plane echo
the thunder of a summer storm, passengers

losing the sky: please hear their terror:
 they must suffer, for disaster jangles

sleeping nerves, frequently underneath:
those stirring fear so when the living

continue on, a father tells his
daughter crusted with blood: you must

repay for your life as long as
you live, and the young woman

bolting (exploding wreckage): that could
be death: or worse: returns for a passenger;

it might have meant her surviving
as a human being: leaving others

to determine the cause of the shaking jet,
survivors don't know: except they lie awake

and drench themselves in asking (?) crashing is together and
together crashing: live and pay for your own ticket.

                       ❧ Lucille Gang Shulklapper

First Breath Last Breath

When a baby boy is born
and the midwife
holds him up
as he takes
his first breath,
place him over
the Mother's face
so when the baby exhales
his first breath on Earth
the Mother breathes it.

And when the Mother dies,
her middle-aged son

the baby grew up to be—
by her side,
his head next to her head—
follows her breathing with his breath
as it becomes shorter,
and as the dying Mother
exhales her last breath,
her son inhales it.

                 ॐ Antler

The Floor Is Sticky

Robert is on a mission:
he wants to learn how to say the floor
is sticky in every language,
or rather, every language in which its countrymen
(its women) drink beer in bars.
He thinks it's a good ice-breaker.
He's just learned it in Dutch, and now
I can't get it out of my head:
de vloer plakt, de vloer plakt.

I love the way other languages feel
in the back of my throat, the parts of the mouth
that English doesn't use.
When I was a kid, I used to speak
a gibberish that I thought sounded
convincingly foreign.
I would bicycle to the beach where I could speak it
into the wind loudly without embarrassment.
I thought if I could only live somewhere else

I could leave the me of me behind,
take only the shell of my body
and fill it with someone new.
That's how desperate I was.
I only know a few phrases in French:
I can say I am tired,
You are my little cabbage,

Do you want to go to bed with me tonight?
There's been a terrible accident.
                         ઢ Kim Roberts

The Fly:

"Perseverance is virtue and doom. 'Insist on your ruin and find your salvation,' a poet once said.

One can endure hunger and cold; dissatisfaction is a knife we thrust in ourselves.

Desire turns a world, so narrow and mean, into a honeycomb: inciting, satiating, imprisoning."

                         ઢ Benito del Pliego
                         ઢ Translation by Robin Ouzman Hislop

Forgive Us Our Sins

The Earth has much beauty yet.
Because many people have an admiration with
Her
Calm snow
Strong rivers
Soft rains
Heavy green grass
White clouds
. . .

The Earth reflects the feeling of love to people.
Her
Soft rains play the music of dreams.
Calm snow covers the troubles of people.
The sky paints beautiful pictures with white clouds.

The Earth has much beauty yet.
As a beloved woman who can forgive the pain.

                         ઢ Katharina Yakovina

Fortune

I

In the mine, a man's eyes belong to the panther. Wariness
in a circle of black.

Something with teeth marks him as feline,
designed to tunnel for life. An energy with talons
straps a lamp to the man's head,

then drives him down on an empty belly.

An old surgery, these men who try to cut veins and
breathe air inside a mountain.

II

Rag-heap of flies sits up in the hut, rubs its eyes. It's a boy.
One day his dreams may catch fire and brighten, until he thinks
he sees more than the family pig in the door, garbage-slide
down to the highway.

Rainbow flags blow from the market stalls stacked with sacks
of coca leaves. Not a ceremonious tea but enough to dull
stomachs of the hungry. Leaves at the bottom
of a cup tell of children who flicker and go out
on the slopes while the miners go under.

                               ❧ Katherine Soniat

[from the desert]

from the desert
from the ungrowing flowers
where the light's sign slips by
between salty herbs
and swimming skeletons

from the desert
reaching for the horizons
thirty thousand horizons
thirty thousand watering holes

from the desert
the caravan moves slowly
to the right to the left
everything comes at once
nothing behind the dunes

from the desert the transforming fire
variousness of the last oasis
thirty thousand palms
thirty thousand watering holes

from the desert
we take its road
from various oases
toward the oneness of thirty thousand horizons
toward the transforming fire
sky
earth

           ❧ Raymond Queneau
           ❧ New translation by Daniela Hurezanu and
             Stephen Kessler

The Ghosts of the Confederacy

Stir along the ridge tops and sunken lanes
like dreams remembered upon waking.
They pitch shadowy tents in southern pines
amid twilight campfires and darting fireflies.
Southern children grow up believing the ghosts are family.
Part of the tapestry that knits their DNA together.
They are schooled daily in bittersweet nostalgia—
uniforms and lost causes. As grounded in the now
as Gone with the Wind and Elvis Presley.
Southern children are thus rarely surprised by love or loss
or gray ghosts that climb down from monuments on red moon nights
to chase tattered flags across endless fields of wildflowers.
Generations of Southern children have learned to accept
these battles that fade like watercolors left out in the rain.

           ❧ Richard Peabody

Givenchy Lavender
Body my house . . .
—May Swenson

mother not buried
in my lavender silk
dress but ten pieces
of white shroud
prescribed by our faith
my younger brother kept
secret over a year
a mistake he said
not knowing what
to do with the dress
or satin shoes I'd laid out
for her to go proud
to hide her nakedness
from the crowd
she'd let herself go
all to hell yelling
she'd go to the poorhouse
on my account
mark my words
then a slap across the mouth

                             ❧ Paula Goldman

Global Notes

But pigs do fly in Japanese Great Chess,
and blue moons do arrive. Our days erode
at irregular intervals, pausing
for particular sunsets and bottles.
The work of the world continues beneath
self-satirizing offices: termites,
and sewer inspectors, linesmen and cops.
Some create commercial entertainments
when no one has the energy for truth.
Last night I looked up; the local city
lit up the clouds with its own fragile stars.
A preference for the unseen abounds

in sentimental literature. Change
comes naturally to those holding remotes.
For me, wonder flew with the airplane lights,
the thoughts of the pilots and controllers,
the travelers spanning time zones; mechanics;
the clerks marking inventories of parts

                       ❧ M. A. Schaffner

The Gods Just Appeared

I built my Aztec temple without stairs
And Mrs. Glover flunked me.
I thought the gods just appeared
Bursting from jags of light,
Head of a hawk, body of a man writhing snakes.

But the priests, she said,
Who perform human sacrifice,
How will they get up there?
I went home and cut a trap door
So these men could emerge and beg for rain.
I did not pass this unit of history.

Mrs. Glover must have wondered, too,
How at noon precisely
Thirty books hit the floor with a thunderous clap,
How the tacks on her chair
Punctured that heavy dress.

                       ❧ Jason Tandon

The Good Fight
(for my mother)

The English Channel surged below you,
its waves licking American bones.
It was D-Day Plus Fifty, Utah Beach,

and all five-foot-three of you
with a thousand other nurses, helmeted,
full-field-packed, clambered down
the rope ladders swaying against the ship.
The transports were children's toys
bobbing below. Don't look down,
don't slip, your commanders told you.
Your pack will drag you straight to the bottom.
The Norman fields boomed in the distance
as the waves moaned their hunger.
Sixty summers distant from France,
the explosion was in your brain.
You take lessons on how to lace a shoe,
how to walk with a cane.
Your voice, musical as always,
lilts over the nursing center's phone:
Honey, I'm going home today.
Can you call my mom and dad
and tell them to come get me?
Mother, you ascend a ladder now.
The sky is hazy above you,
a fog of dreams and memories.
The decades are your backpack now.
Please don't look down. Please don't slip.
You fight the good fight, now as then.

                       ❧ Miles David Moore

Green-Eyed Mexican Boy: Little Brother #1

From the back that man bending over his breakfast tacos in the San Antonio airport could be my brother. Same brown spiky hair, thick neck, heavy jowls bouncing as he chews.

I remember my brother as a fifth-grader, yellow-haired, green-eyed Mexican boy jumping over the back fence, escaping the big boys he'd just ripped off at marbles or Hot Wheels, me coming after them with a stick or a brick, talking big sister talk: "What you want with my little brother?"

Slice-of-midnight-black mad dog eyes and a Catholic girls' school uniform. Later he'd go, "you saved my life, Sis." And I'd knuckle his towheaded cowlicks.

They were afraid of me, those boys, even the one who wanted to kiss me underwater, write my name on the inside of his arm. He was the worst of the bullies and I swung my stick at him, warning him to keep his gringo ass away from my brother or else risk losing my favors in the deep end of his father's pool.

Summers in the old house, in the orchard of peach, plum, and apricot trees that Pa' Carlos had planted in the backyard, we'd have swinging contests, see who could swing higher and let go—bungee jump from the swing and land without spraining an ankle or smashing into Mima's rosebushes. We'd play astronauts on the thick branches of mulberries that shaded the patio. When we landed on the moon, we'd find pomegranates that looked just like the ones we stole from the neighbor's bush.

We never talked about the other bully, the one married to our mom, who used to beat him hard enough to break his skull open or push him up against a wall-heater and scald his butt, buckle marks running up and own the scrawny length of his arms and legs.

He was the one I really wanted to hurt. And when my brother would show up at my grandparents' house, skinny and spiky-haired and battered, carrying two paper bags filled with toys and clothes to spend the summer with us, or part of the school year, however long it took to heal from the beatings, I wanted to pummel someone else. Our mom for marrying that man. Our dad for loving his girlfriends more than us.

Years later, both of us in high school, me living in my mom's turf for the summer—the house in Juárez where my mom was raising the two children she'd had with that man we never deigned to call "stepfather"—my brother and I made a plan. Parked our new ten-speeds (bought with the money we made at our summer sweat shop job) on the side of the house, and plotted our attack.

The next time that man came after my brother with his fists or his belt or whatever else he felt the right to use against the son of the man he hated for being my mother's first husband and way more good-looking than his red-eyed, squat-bodied, big-headed Yucatecan ass, we'd kill him. Choke him. Kick him in the balls or the head. Punch him in the belly. Do whatever it took to erase him out of our lives. And we'd jump on our ten-speeds and hot-pedal it across the border.

Back to El Paso and the safety of Mima's house on the East side, where the Yucatecan's henchmen couldn't catch us and we could sit in front of the television watching "Leave it to Beaver" and "The Partridge Family." Just a fantasy.

One morning, still too early to get up for school, I woke up in the bed I shared with my little half-sister, and there he was, that man standing over me in his short bathrobe. Our mom was in the hospital, high blood pressure after too many years of suppressing rage and fear, and this man thought I'd be the next piece of meat on his platter.

"You touch me and I'll tell my mother," I said, "and my grandmother and my uncles that you tried to rape me." I could see it in his red-rimmed eyes, the urge to strike this uppity big-mouth of a sixteen-year-old girl. Cabrón left the room in a hurry.

This man who would have flayed my brother's hide just for being another man's son, who burned to a rightful crisp in a Sinaloa jail more than thirty years ago, taught me the meaning of hatred.

This is what I'm thinking about today at the San Antonio airport watching a man who looks like the hungry heavy-set man my brother has become, who heals his wounds in the over-protective love he feeds his own two children.

               ❧ Alicia Gaspar de Alba

Hardcovers

Stroll the sidewalks of New York
and you'll find Manhattan
enlightened with hardcovers.
Like old beggars in distress
they line the busy sidewalks,
beckoning to one's book-wormy
conscience, begging to be read.
I stop to open one at random,
lowering my eyes to the text—

Arise and drink your bliss,
writes Blake, for everything is holy.
A book's half-erased spine by Tolstoy
sighs, open me: "The recognition of
the sacredness of everyman's life is first and only...."
I linger, long admiring the gilt edges,
touching their moldy jackets, knowing
they compress realms of wisdom.

Phrases underlined like authors' eyes
after a night of vigil waiting for the Muse
to sing or sigh, link me to the anonymous lover
of belles-lettres who once held

these creative renderings in her hands.

I, too, tenderline the touching passages
and highlight the quotable stuff.
I, too, scribble in margins,
quarreling with the author's vanity,
comparing the earthly with the gods.

I walk home embracing
these affordable life-works that once
tutored my esprit and savoir-faire.
I read from them in intimate prayer,
forging my future from the past.

I put up a hard bargain for
Colette, Shakespeare, Edna St. Vincent Millay,
Cervantes, Mistral, Octavio Paz,
stack the six immortals I've rescued
from the gutter, like steps leading to an altar.
How can anyone throw such faithful friends away?
Friends come in handy when one
is lonely; especially those that thrive and
must be expert in street-smarts—
like these urchins who refuse to die.

                       ❧ Anita Vélez-Mitchell

The Heart of the Matter

The heart of the matter, the ghost of a chance,
A tremor, a fever, an ache in the chest.
The moth and the candle beginning their dance,
A cool white sheet on which nothing will rest.

Come sit beside me. I've waited alone.
What you need to confess I already know.
The scent of your shame is a heavy cologne
That lingers for hours after you go.

The dregs of the bottle, the end of the line,
The laggard, the loser, the last one to know.
The unfinished book, the dead-end sign,
And last summer's garden buried in snow.

You stand by the window and follow the cars
As their headlights climb the hill's black dome,
The lives that they carry are distant as stars,
And none will return to carry us home.

                     ❧ Dana Gioia

Heile Welt

Seated in the middle of the young men that chat
we drink our cold martinis, as all around they gossip
with smiling faces, just come from work.
Nollendorfplatz is a block away where Isherwood and Auden
stayed in the Twenties to cavort with the street toughs—
working class youths thirsty for a beer, who, for a few marks were easily steered
under the S-Bahn tracks. In the districts of "degenerate love," David Bowie
lived for a time; here where "die Schwulen"
were exterminated, shipped off to Sachsenhausen's pits—
now we sit, sipping martinis and watching a boy lie
flat on the couch, his head cradled lovingly in his boyfriend's lap.

                     ❧ Walter R. Holland

Hero, Posthumous

The safety off. One false move would mean death.
He would not move for nothing. He'd seen death.

Though perfect and rare was the bloody ballet,
The blatant full-stop of on-screen death,

More likely were long months on life support,
Dialysis for years, a machine death,

If not memory's decay, a heart lined with plaque,
Or cancer's forced march. An obscene death.

Only an instant to reach for the gun
And shout God is gracious! A clean death!

                     ❧ J.D. Smith

Hieros #14

sesa's ruminations
on a sunny afternoon
in 21st century los angeles

how ancient is the urge
to paint a sigil on a wall,
sketch a rune into flesh,
carve mystical numbers
onto a park bench or
into a tree?

how far back will
collective memory reach
for sun gods,
genocide, or vestigial
aquatic cells awakened
by a still body
of cool water?

how many times
are the life-lines
of a hand
overwritten,
over-traveled, or
ignored altogether?

what is the difference
between
life and existence,
love and reliability,
habit and karma?

                       ❧ Marie Lecrivain

Hometown

My two feet planted
on this hostile terrain,
in something that resembles
my hometown. The earth

still pliant, despite mining,
poisonous landfills,
repeated experimental
bombings that birth
resilient debris. My assembled
particles bombarded with data,
and tagged by invisible cameras,
pivot on this uncertain plateau,
this soft earthbed,
this overtilled soil,
this trampled Gaia.
They call it a hamlet,
a suburban refuge.
Subdivide it with names like
Monarch's Landing or Fieldcrest.
They put blueprints over it,
despite the insecticide fog.
The drive-bys and the fickle posses.
Bad feng shui here.
No matter, I stand
over the spirits of plants,
soil erosions, decay. Heat
still flecking off my hand.
Irradiation for lunch.
I consider the viral load
of the meat at supper.
The ozone sunburn
on my neck and shoulders.
I am still breathing
in something they call
a village. A dot placed
on a geographical timezone,
infrared spacemap, a blur
in a photo from a spaceship
I can't see. My breath
goes out into the finite
universe, seeking communion,
craving alliance, affirmation:
I am alive and well
in something they call
a little town in America.

                   ❧ Gerard Wozek

Honeys

I don't know what to call it.
Not that insanity I've felt for others—lesser men,
your predecessors—
madness I admittedly miss. I've never learned how
to speak well
and passionately about something other than
rapture and sorrow,
those romantic specialties. Each attachment's
a different chemical
amalgam, a different honey hived in the wax cells
of heart and brain.
One season, clover's predominant; another season,
wildflower, sourwood,
basswood, heather, or the mountain laurel, hallucinogenic.
I don't know
how to make art from comfort, how to love
what's kind, accessible,
when there's no point to my fangs,
scars and rage.
We spend the evening cooking for one another,
then settle
onto the couch, listen to music,
sip Sambuca,
while freezing rain coats car hoods, somewhere
someone else
curses, catches sleet on his lips, sleeps alone,
yearns.
All night I will dream beside you, boat drifting
on the dark
sea-swell of breath, wake to stroke your honey
blond goatee
in winter-morning light. For a time, it is my time
to be moderate,
to rejoice in learning something new.

                                        Jeff Mann

The Horse:
(for Agusto Monterroso)

"They lie who tell you they are free because nobody handles them.

I am told there were horses without masters, but I think about their riders.

The one who nails your hooves and saddles you —he, too, is spurred by a boot and also spurs the flank."

                         ☙ Benito del Pliego
                         ☙ Translation by Robin Ouzman Hislop

How to Make a Human

Take the cat out of the sphinx
and what is left? Riddle me that.

Take the horse from the centaur
and you take away the sleek grace,
the strength of harnessed power.
What is left can still run across fields,
after a fashion, but is easily winded;
what is left will therefore erect buildings
to divide the open plains, so he no longer
must face the wide expanse where once
his equine legs raced the winds
and, sometimes, won.

Take the bull from the minotaur
but what is left will still assemble
a herd for the sake of ruling over it.
What is left will kill for sport,
in an arena thronged with spectators
shouting "Olé!" at each deadly thrust.

Take the fish from the merman:
What is left can still swim,
if only with lots of splashing; gone
is the smooth sliding through waves,
alert to the subtle changes in the current.
What is left will build ships

so he can cross the oceans without
getting his feet wet; what is left won't care
if his boats pollute the seas he can no
longer breathe, so long as their passage
can keep him from sinking.

Take the goat from the satyr
but what is left will dance out of reach
before you have a chance
to get that Dionysian streak of mischief,
the love of music and wine, the rutting parts
that like to party all the day through.
What is left will be stubborn and refuse
to give way; what is left will lock horns
and butt heads with anyone who challenges him.

Take the bird from the harpy
but the memory of flying, a constant yearning ache
for the skies so tantalizingly distant,
will still remain, as will the established pecking orders,
the bitter squabblings over food and territory,
and the magpie eye that lusts for shiny objects.
What is left will cut down the whole forest
to feather their sprawling urban nests.

At the end of these operations,
tell me: what is left? The answer: Man,
a creature divorced from nature,
who's forgotten where he came from.

                         ❧ Lawrence Schimel

[i recall a day in cordoba]

i recall a day in cordoba
at the exit of the mosque
a gypsy read my palm:
i see a journey in your life, a woman and two children.
i knew she lied
because in the cards of my life
only men appear.
even so i paid

and continued down the street

i would like to tell you this story
right now
to see you laugh
but you're sleeping.
and if i wake you?

                 ❧ Jesús Encinar
                 ❧ Translation by Lawrence Schimel

If I Get This Far

How long it takes loneliness
to figure me out. The length of shadow
the fir makes falling over the house,
your house. A lattice across the front window,
behind it, silence; the warbling sky
I lie under, my back in the snow
while the neighbor spills sunseeds
into her balcony feeder for cardinals.
When I rise here I am again
standing before your door.
Have I knocked yet?
A nest of gutter birds scatters
from the rotting eaves
spilling brown notes
with edges like pine cones,
clusters in the brittle sky.
My wrist is empty of time
but the tick tick goes on, needles
on the glass. The door you're behind
has always opened for me.
Only a handful of heroes
steps back through, to this—
not about thresholds but you to hold me.
Don't look back I tell myself.
How long it takes
for my rapping to reach you

for you to put down your book of puzzles
heave weariness from your lap
cross the country to where touch
changes everything.

                   ❧ Kay Murphy

Imagine The Shock

Imagine the shock
at seeing my name
anger-scratched
on a bathroom wall,
two words small
but deep
slicing steep
carving a canyon
of raw.

They are cut into
green paint
by a furious blade,
a knife-wielding tirade
of pressing, cutting,
crushing, shutting
us down, way down.

It's a simple message really,
these two words
fired bent
as a head hits cement,
followed by the
slow awareness
of spreading pain.
They are mouthed so calmly
from a gun
loaded with only two-words:
"die faggot."

                   ❧ Joseph Ross

Immigrant Story

I've failed to donate bags of old clothes
Now moldy and moth-bitten.
My closet smells like my grandfather's apartment
I used to search as a kid, thinking I'd find a gun.

He had fought in the Second World War
And there was a hole behind his ear
Where my older brother said
A bullet was still lodged.

On Grandparents' Day in school
We recited the Pledge of Allegiance.
Everyone removed his hat, except my grandfather
Who didn't rise or try to mouth the words.

He came over for dinner many nights
With stitches in his face and a black eye,
Having been mugged walking home
From his weekly game of skat.

                                 ❧ Jason Tandon

Immigration Interview

Early morning in late summer rain I drive downtown
big drops hit the car as if to break the glass.
While I review dates, names, wars, the Constitution,
they drown out the noise of traffic;
they try to reach me, soak me.

The morning of my immigration interview,
I leave two daughters sleeping behind curtains.
They look safe. They make me happy even when they sleep.
I check again for my green card, my foreign passport.
I look at my books, think, stay, be here for me when I come back.

Some books are native, most are translated.
Today I translate myself from foreign student
to immigrant, to citizen. So much rain. So many books.
So many roles. The children and the books accept them.
My oldest daughter says, Mom, you're so weird.

A badge of honor from a fifteen-year-old
who looks at me and sees different faces even when she
wants one, sees fissures, scars, seams where she
craves smoothness, a healing gesture, like I do
as I peer through the rain seeking a parking space.

                         ઢ Gunilla Theander Kester

Improvised Poetic Device (IPD)

The ribcage wrapped
—as per usual—
in muscle, skin

The head mounted
—as per usual—
on the trunk

The eyes tautly tied
—as per usual—
to the skull

The little ones prance
gazelles
are the way they are

Dates in the heat
—as per usual—
are sweet, pungent

Days at their end
(such days are welcomed)
bring on the night

The long night
—as per usual—
can be terrifying

You could
patch in
very punchy, very gnarly
appropriately
first-world-wealthy

stuff
anywhere
you
damn
well
please

The thighs
are elegantly and complexly tied
to the hips

The hips
—as per usual—
buttress the spine

The hips at times
expand
to twice their width

Old men
given time, given space
play chess

Mud bricks, well-made
—as per usual—
absorb the hot sun

The spines of middle-aged women
leopards
are the way they are

You could
Cut out
very savvy, very quippy
appropriately
first-world-snarky
stuff
anytime
you
damn
well
please

The ears
—as per usual—
come in twos

The nose
sits at the top of the mouth
co-coordinative

The mind is
—as per usual—
in dispute

The ass
is like hands
dependant & rebellious

You could
sync in
very sexy, very tarty
appropriately
first-world-prickly
stuff
anyhow
you
damn
well
please

The ubiquitous cotton plaid shirt
—as per usual—
is sewn by young girls

Cialis, Viagra, Propecia
are smuggled goods
for the porker class (there)

The porker class (here)
is about to reward you
—as per usual—

The ubiquitous singular ass
with a beef
is what's for dinner

Here's an IPD for you
Here's an IPD for you
Here's an IPD for you

                           ❧ Rodrigo Toscano

In Adams Morgan, Two Years of Neighborhood-wide Reconstruction Comes to a Halt for the Night

And now, where the moon
rose behind here,
three stories loom—
inexplicable to the eye.
Flood lights lift
the puddles in the alley
to sad perfection.
No other brightness
to make beautiful
the edges of the dark.
Progress comes—
mocking visitor, a snoop—
to awed spaces
where we hold up
our pots and pans,
brush sweat
from the brow, wipe hands
on threadbare dishrags,
scold and kiss our children.
We should be glad—
some people tell us—
life is precious, move on.
Others say poverty
is redemption, go,
and, waiting to wake,
we stir all night. We pray.
Our father, god
of the cupboard and the ladle,
redeem us.

                        ❧ Naomi Ayala

In Lower East Side, Looking at an Apartment

His building made me wonder which windows were his,
the ones he had looked out for six years. Oh, would he catch me,
my eyes scanning the windows on each floor for some sign of him?

Was this really where he once paid $331 a month?
The squalor from those Riis photographs could not match
my own vacant warehouse padlocked with empty aches.

I felt more condemned, a harking back to the noise of tired tenements,
from where patent-leather shoes sidestepped puddles and horse dung
toward the synagogue. The thunder of the Torah seemed sweeter

than back home, while the streets boiled from breathsweat.
Funny-voiced families took turns flushing the soon-to-be-clogged
toilet,
a stomached stench from paying the rent.

I went up in that blue building of his, curious
though not wild about the idea of having the same address as him.
In the plaster-cracked dimness, I felt ghosts of all sizes seeping

beneath the many coats of paint in the not-very-large two rooms.
I saw a trail of table legs dragged through the thick dust,
but there were no footprints. Did this place really belong to
specters,

or to him whom I knew enough not to seek or haunt?
Below one window, a poultry truck bounced over a pothole.
I thought of eggs cracking, a far cry from home.

                            ❧ Raymond Luczak

In the Attic of My Grief
(for Hilary Tham)

I am writing here. Hilary is correcting my poem. (I liked it
the way it was, vivid with reds and yellow.) "Too bright,"
she says, retreating back into the shadows.
I begin again. This time I describe the plain pine box
they buried her in.
She sweeps a blue scarf over my eyes,
the color of bluebirds on Chinese New Year.
I scratch out the line about the plain coffin.
Hilary wants only the truth from this poem, and I—so lost—
cannot find it. She shows me
brown chocolates from Florence,
a gray silk shawl from Rome,

a well in Lucca where a young girl drowned in despair.
She holds image after image, reaching out to me.
I am crying while I write.
She smiles. "Find the truth. Your breath is like snow on the page."
Now I go to the orange trees transplanted
across the river Huai, the river of death
where it is said the same fruit thrives on both sides.
Hilary comes closer. I can tell she likes this one. "Go on" she says.
I talk about my husband, the sketchbook she gave him
when he could no longer sculpt,
my daughters she put in her poems,
She smiles. We are getting closer.
I come up with just one line from the Bible:
"How beautiful upon the mountains are the feet of the messenger
announcing the green of memory."
She thinks I'm ready to begin.

                               ❧ Grace Cavalieri

In the Valley of the Kings

I liked to imagine the artists there on ladders,
paintbrushes dipped in azurite, covering the ceiling
of the tilted entranceway with the blue

of a night sky, patched with yellow stars.
Their pigments filled every inch
of those walls leading to the tomb.

A language of pictures—beetle, horned viper,
a jagged line, an arm bent at the elbow,
hieroglyphs cutting slices of story

into the sequence of friezes
pushing forward across the walls,
one scene leading into another

in the manner of life or memory:
boys yoking a bull to sacrifice,
men fishing the Nile, a woman kneeling,

pounding bread on a flat stone. An offering
of incense scrolls into a procession

of chariots rolling toward some unseen destination

and so on down to the wall's cracked edge,
down to the burial chamber. The journey
of the sun beneath the earth ends there

on the ceiling above the tomb, in a deep blue,
the color of the sea leading to death,
within the golden torsos of two goddesses—

Day and Night facing each other,
volleying the sun along
the length of their bodies.

This is how I picture the passage
to eternity: an endless circling
into deeper and deeper shades of blue.

                       ❧ Yvette Neisser Moreno

Instructions to Be Followed at the Time of My Death: The Service is Optional.

Cremate me,
that would be best.
Have a party
in the living room,
but, for god's sake,
no matter how cold the day,
don't make a fire!
Not only would that be
in dubious taste,
but our faulty chimney
would smoke out the guests.

                    ❧ Ron Singer

Introduction to Economics

Assume a world of many lenses,
each focused on its own set of facts.
Assume another lens encompasses the rest
and concentrates their powers
as, on a sunny day,
a boy's magnifying glass
is trained upon an ant.

Unless you are holding up that lens,
assume you are the ant.

                         J. D. Smith

Iranian Boys Hanged for Sodomy, July 2005

We have their last photograph,*
a magazine cutout of the blind-
folded boys, with nooses round
their necks and masked men
behind. Men with thick hands,
hands that keep everything
in order, everyone blind.

We let the picture drift around
the apartment like an omen
that will one day make perfect
sense. Some mornings I stick it
on the bathroom mirror before
you shave, the next you have it
on the fridge or tucked inside
my O'Hara Collected. Some nights
I slip it in a shoebox marked
"private" and forget we ever cut it

out, but by the following evening
it's under our mattress as we make
love. Each time I thrust into you,
I'm thrusting into them, creasing
their boyish bodies, one only 16.
On Sunday morning I ask you

if you think the Iranian boys
loved each other like I love you

here in America where true love
must be complicated. You're sure
they did, believe being hanged together
reeks of romance, of epic novels,
and Hollywood love stories, but
I fear it's just a case of being
in the wrong place at the wrong time.

All I can see are two terrified boys,
hands bound, about to be hanged
for public view. And I need to know
if it was quick. If the rope did what
ropes are meant to do or if the boys
found freedom in the dark
of their twitching eyelids?

                         ❧ Stephen S. Mills

* The poem refers to the event that occurred on July 19, 2005 when two young men (one rumored to be 16) were publically hanged in Iran for the crime of sodomy. They were held in prison for 14 months where they were beaten until they confessed to having gay sex. An estimated 4,000 lesbians and gay men have been put to death in Iran since 1979 when the ayatollahs took power. The incident was reported in The Advocate, July 2005.

It's Seven

It's seven and I walk
the city, the morning,
I don't know how, my steps
confused, two sentences
of comfort and few enough
concerns except
the time, wandering.

I dream, with uncertain light
on the bay, hours
that find no owners.
Without remembering I walk
the morning of trenches,
the work of the convent.

A young woman smiled:
"He was lost there," she says,
"my lover without memory."
I look at her and I don't remember,
from so much not remembering
I get a feeling:
I am a child who looks
and forgets, as if
he were looking anew.

The city at seven,
I walk and it dissolves.

                       ❧ Luis Cremades
                       ❧ Translation by Lawrence Schimel

Jazz Funeral

The crowd crescendos in Congo Square, turns up St. Peter Street,
         handkerchiefs waving at
a ghost in a horse-drawn open carriage, the soul cut loose
         from earthly limits
flying away free, a gleaming angel sung up to a river valley
         accompanied by Kid Ory's
Creole ensemble, it rambles beyond any tempestuous
         scenario of weather
to a realm where disaster and war never can be imagined.
         Satchmo blowing like Gabriel
with the raggedy oddfellows moan tubas, pass Preservation Hall,
         St. Louis Cathedral,
the procession of blues-wailing trombones lament a phantom
         steamboat that ploughs
Basin Street to the cemetery of swamps where scattered
         shells decorate gravestones,
African emblems of the bleached and watery world of the dead.

Then two Neptunian trumpet blasts herald the refugees'
         return from the diaspora
to their parishes, snare drums roll spirited rhythmic flavors,
         the second line lengthens
a parade of deliverance that rivers the French Quarter
         with dancing Storyville

hustlers and good-time Charlies pirouetting brassy umbrellas
        the colors of sunset,
celebrating jamboree the way tambourines jingle and splash
        dazzling green dolphins,
marimbas and banjos dialog with jubilant clarinets and saxes,
        zydeco swings in the bayous.

                      Bruce Lader

Judas Kiss

Your kisses, previously like burning embers on my tongue,
        now drop as cold stones from my lips.
I twist up my face and my courage to embrace you,
        but moments of truth come too few.

I am simply not in love with you anymore.

                      Shannon Gilreath

Jumper

The roof held his sad weight.
Curtains reached from open windows as he plummeted.
The fire hydrant, dry mouthed, just sat there,
stoic, stone-faced: Third one this year.
The dog watched the soul
rise—odd, he thought, how
it resembled steam
after a long piss on the snow.
A mosquito buzzed away in disgust—
all that wasted blood.
The shadows ironed their dark suits.
Flies washed up for dinner.
The sidewalk wanted to catch him, but in the end
could only lie there, knowing
the gutter—just a few feet away—
was waiting, like always, mouth open wide.

                      Jeff Walt

Kismet

What can you do when he slakes
your taste for poison? When
the privilege of his smile transfigures
you? Naked glory of the radiant
and dissolute. What can you do
when suddenly you recognize
a stranger, who might be, but isn't
a friend? What can you do when
your best strategy is shutting down?
When you are determined to do
what's right by him, by you,
and might as well hoist a bridge
to the moon. What can you do
when he recalls your dad, when
every path ends in catastrophe?
When regret climbs into bed, brushing
crumbs of mildew and clay?
What can you do when his voice
mocks breath of wind: your sole
companion in somber dark?
What can you do when God
hands you a key of glass,
but close your eyes
and swallow?

                                          ❧ Christopher Soden

Kristallnacht

She wore glass spectacles
for her vision was clouded,
as if that night her family's home
was burned to the ground in a pogrom
the smoke had gotten into her eyes
and never left them.

They named her Cinderella
when they pulled her from the ashes,
their hearts going soft because
she was only three years old.

Years later, her stepsisters teased
that she was named Cinderella
because she was dark as soot.
They pinched her bold nose
and pulled her black hair
and powdered their pale faces
to go to parties with the Viennese elite.

Cinderella, of course, was never invited
to attend these lavish social functions;
her foster family happily left her at home,
working while they danced, dreaming
of the day she was asked to accompany them.
She was always certain it would not be long,
and therefore worked unfailingly, hoping
for approval.

While her stepsisters primped and prepped
to waltz among princes, Cinderella walked
to the market, stepping over sewage in the gutters,
dodging the nimble rats that boldly crossed
the streets in search of food. A kindly frau
who sat beside a cart of squash—yellow gourds
and fat pumpkins like lumpy little suns—stopped her.
She took Cinderella's hands into her own.
"You look so sad, dear. I will help you."
The woman drew Cinderella into the shadows
of the alleyway, and pulled papers from her pocket.
"Take these," she said. "They are mine,
but I am old. Go to America instead of me.
Find a new life. Send for your family,
if any are still alive. I am too old to begin again.
But for you, there is still hope for you."

Cinderella stared at this woman. "I am
no Jew," she said, handing back the papers.
She walked away, but the frau's words—
the insinuations, the generosity—
haunted her. She walked faster,
trying to outrun the echoes in her mind.

Passing a shop window, Cinderella saw
a pair of slippers made of glass.
If she had been invited to the ball,
she thought, she would love to wear
those slippers. She stared at them,

longing, and her reflection stared back:
swart, square. Semitic.

She bought the slippers with the grocery money
and hurried back to the now-empty house.
Cinderella powdered her face
with the stepsister's cosmetics,
put on one of their dresses.
She tied her dark hair in a knot and hid it
beneath a silver scarf. But still her nose betrayed her.
She didn't care. She slipped on her glass shoes
and made her way across town to the gala event,
dreaming of finding a prince who would love her
and adore her and take her away to an enchanted life
where it did not matter that she looked like a Jew.

The party was as dazzling as she had always dreamed.
No one stopped her at the door, or paid her any
notice at all, it seemed, though some people stared
at her. No one spoke to her. And then a shriek
made Cinderella the center of attention,
as her two stepsisters ran toward her.
"You are not fit to be seen here!" they cried.
They snatched the spectacles from her face
and, in front of the assembled crowd,
crushed them underfoot with a delicate
twist of the toe, grinding downward.

Cinderella's vision blurred without her glasses.
Tears burned in her eyes, and then suddenly
the smoke that had clouded her sight
for as long as she could recall
lifted. She saw, at last, what she had always
overlooked before: these people had killed
her family, had meant to kill her as well.

She stood there, numb, as the stepsisters
poked and pushed her. They stepped
on her toes and broke her glass slippers
into hundreds of sharp splinters.

Cinderella left the shards of her glass shoes
on the dance floor and walked barefoot
out of the hall, leaving footprints of blood
behind her. She was never seen again.

                       ❧ Lawrence Schimel

Labor

No one tells you—
how could they?

They could say
it was like being
drawn and quartered,
—not once,
with death as respite,
but, as in the Inferno,
reconstituted
only to be rent again,
twenty, then thirty
times an hour,
with increasing violence.
(Dante, had he watched,
would have fainted). Or
the perfect engine
of the Inquisition,
inserted
to be opened
and opened till
you're torn apart. Or
crushed
to a single unbearable
point, microcosmos
at the moment of Big Bang—
and the only way out
is to blow yourself apart.

None of these
comes near it.

How does anyone
do it twice?

They say
you forget.

This is to make sure
I don't.

                                         Barbara Louise Ungar

Last Night in London

from the moment you stepped into the old pub's door
till the time you offered to buy me a pint
I wanted to lunge across the table and claim you as my first
a two-hour talk and countless flirts later
we were splitting the taxi fare to Islington
the pounds weighing a ton in my sweaty metallic hand
you laughed as I tried to figure out the cabby's tip
inside I slid my palm over your round left shoulder
fingering the Polo emblem on your blue oxford shirt
your dialect making me smile
your need creeping closer
our hips connecting like hankering magnets
clasping to find true north
mapping out each other's designed topography
now we wrestled out of breath
you pinning me down
tilting your head to gaze at me
all the ways you gazed at me
we dozed off like two worldly teaspoons
but woke like meshed utensils in an overstuffed kitchen drawer
we shared a morning shower
scrubbing out buoyant bodies smooth
by day the eyes confirm what the nightly hands uncover
but later we dressed in silence
divided by the invisible velvet curtain of yesterday's clothes
you snuck me down the side-winding stairs
mindful of the creaks and groans we ignored the night before
the door yawned open on its old hinges
lengthening our image of the Atlantic's actual width
our feet shuffled and hands dug deep into pockets
I took you once more and you squeezed the back of my neck
one last breath together
I scurried off with a courageous look back and wave
humming something all the way to the Stansted Express
all the while still smelling you on my skin during take off
still tasting the way your lips did that thing on mine that
last night in London

                                  ❧ Jonathan Tilley

The Last World of Fire and Trash

I don't know anything anymore
or if that cricket is still singing
in a country where crickets are banned.

I'm Indian in a strange pastiche of hurt and rain
smells like curry and sweat
from a sunset rock and roll restaurant.
A familiar demon groaning with fear
has stalked me here, ruins poetry, then
his swollen pride commandeers.

Beneath the moon rocking above Los Angeles
or outside the stomp dance fire of memory,
I told him, you can choose to hate me
for going too far, or for being a nothing
next to a pretty nothing like you.

So long, goodbye, oh fearful one.
My desires had turned into a small mountain.
Of dirty clothes, sax gig bag, guitar
books, shoes and grief
that I packed and carried
from one raw wound to another.

I can't get betrayal out of my heart,
out of my mind,
in this hotel room where I'm packing for home.
I've seen that same face whirring
in the blur of a glass of wine
after the crashed dance,
the goodbye song
in the last world of fire and trash.

The most dangerous demons spring from fire
and a broken heart, smell of bittersweet aftershave
and the musk of a thousand angels.
And then I let that thought go running away
because I refuse to stay in bondage
to an enemy who thinks he wants what I have.

I turned my cheek as my head parted through a curtain of truth
and erupted from the spirit world to this gambling place—
And I send prayers skyward
on smoke.
Hvsaketvmese, Hvsaketvmese.

Release this suffering.
May the pretty beast and all the world know peace.

I refuse to sum it up anymore; it's not possible.
I give it up
to the battering of songs against the light,
to the singing of the earnest cricket
in the last world of fire and trash.

                         ❧ Joy Harjo

Late in the Day

We continue our grievances at dinner
where the short one is teased,
the thin one maligned,

rivalries rekindled, grown children disowned.
The holiday meal nearly ended, we abandon
turkey bone and gristle, cranberry sauce

sweet and bitter as blood,
and surrender one by one to the children
urging us out to play aerobe.

My son and ex-husband have gone to new families.
Only my brother, sister and children,
and the sturdy man I now love

stand with me in the lengthening light,
to toss the plastic ring
that rises as if to go over the sun,

though it glides up in a slow loop only—
and down, passing from hand to hand.
The brother who has tormented me

tosses carefully now, so that I will catch
and throw to the child between us,
or to my sister who, with her great bulk,

contains all that she has lost,
yet lumbers to catch the ring

as the circle widens like a ripple or shrinks

to hold something we've never known—
how to be together without rancor—
as if life could be just this easy,

and the family we are given by birth (or by choice)
is the right one for us—the only one—
and this life, this one life, is enough.

                        ઠ Patricia Gray

Laughter

There used to be a time when humans gathered in squares,
parks, and stadiums to laugh together
and all would explode in loud giggles looking at one another.

There were those who laughed to keep warm
and those who laughed to fight off the heat.

Yet others, from faraway places,
laughed because of the spontaneous pleasure of the body
and fell to the floor laughing themselves silly.

Others laughed at each other rather than at themselves.
Their laughter bordered on black humor.

Others laughed with word games.
There were those who exorcised pain through laughter,
making fun of themselves.

Where laughter did not exist,
humans lived more prone to metaphysics.

They would stand in front of a mirror,
and they would neither stick their tongues out nor make funny faces.

                     ઠ Isaac Goldemberg
                     ઠ Translation by Stanley H. Barkan with Wanda
                           Rivera and Roy Cravzow

The Law

When the Law was delivered to the humans,
its words echoed from one end
to the other of the universe.
The inhabitants of the galaxy
were panic stricken.
Their rulers gathered together
and asked:
"What is this loud rumbling
we hear? Can it be that a new explosion
in the universe is nearing?"
The Supreme Being had promised
not to cause another explosion of the world.
But they again asked:
"Can it be that another rain of fire will fall?"
The Supreme Being had promised
never again to destroy the human race.
But once more they questioned:
"Then, what does that loud rumbling we hear mean?"
The Supreme Being had promised
to render His word because the humans
had lost the balance between
heaven and earth,
and the physical impulse had
overtaken the spiritual.
Then the Law ordered
human life to be shortened.

       ઢ Isaac Goldemberg
       ઢ Translation by Stanley H. Barkan with Wanda
          Rivera and Roy Cravzow

Legacy

I belong here
where the waves
rock the fisherman's boat
from dream to dream.
Successive arms
have betrayed the source of my river,

now it is only a trickle.

I have put away my clarinet
with its clever keys,
and my taut skin
becomes once more
the membrane of drums.

Now the music I make
echo songs from the wombs
of my grandmothers' mothers.
For me each night
the rhythms weave a world.

                     ❧ Sydney March

Les Places Numérotées
(Paris, 1939
Doc' Dan Mahoney speaking)

Like the unsociable odor
which I discovered had been sleeping in my coat,
I know to recognize my time,
with its shabby
battles in the gutter, I must face a face
in the second class window, under the stenciled words

       LES PLACES NUMÉROTÉES SONT RESERVÉES
           PAR PRIORITÉ AUX MUTILÉS DE GUERRE.

Henri, I do not know one citizen
by birth, but I have seen around me in the metro,
breathing a common flatulence of ill-digested dinners
and excited by the same secretions,
refugees
bringing their dark soils with them,
aliens
with mourning bands still on their nails, heading
from negative landscapes somewhere home.

And yet citizens of the one country
whose borders are an endless ringing out of circles,
agents of intelligence and counter-intelligence,

what are we if not emigrants
in long suspicious coats, where do we stand
if not massed forever in a twilight drizzle
to tear our ministries of propaganda down,
our bureaus of standards and measures,
assassins of all we wait to love
and lovers of our own shadowy assassins.

Light
the only light comes off each man
shuttling under the city: Neuilly to La Villette,
Montparnasse to Ménilmontant, Pigalle to Père-Lachaise.

                     ❧ Peter Klappert

Like the Children of Bororo

It can happen small
as it did to me.

Behind closed office doors
a promise is broken.

No witnesses. No one to stand
by the heart of the one betrayed.

Some sleight of hand is done.
Some tap dance of fear.

Betrayal is an intimate art.
They must know you well

enough to know what you love.
Something matters more

than you do. A great deal more.
You are so much mown hay.

It is not about you. Really.
You were only in the way.

Expendable. Noosed.
Like the children of Bororo.

This is how it happens large.
On the reservation in Brazil,

Kaiwowa Indians—too many
for the land that's left—

hang themselves from trees.
There is no place for me

marks the sand
beneath a young boy's feet.

No witnesses. No one to stand
by the heart of the one betrayed.

This is the world we have made.

                ❧ Kathryn Kirkpatrick

Listen

Because I dwell
between whispers,

like snow,
like swallowed

secrets, I hear you
without words,

verbs of pause,
voice of marble,

the sound of e
in mute, elegant,

invisible in the
miracle of light,

in the sound
of this page

remembering pulp
remembering wood

remembering trunk
and leaves

and breeze
through its branches.

           ❧ Don Cellini

Litany of Waves

Light of dawn
Bread of mourning

Hands of fire
Smoke of memory

Mercury tongue
Music of snow

Wind word
River voice

Ladder of daydream
Garden of thistle

Urn of remembering
Handful of dust

Star song
Sacred silence

           ❧ Don Cellini

La Llorona Considers the State of Tortillas

She knows they come in sanitized packages
Cellophaned and counted

Whole wheat flour, yellow or white corn,
Even red tinted and crisp, ready for tostadas or chalupas

Too easy it seems to her for the truth to be told

She also knows machines can never render
A product true

If flour... one misses
The familiar smell of dough cooking on the comal
The puffing up one must, simply must pat down
And hear the pooof of air escaping like dreams
The taste, hot off the comal with butter, the taste of morning

If corn... one relishes
The smell sweet as homecomings
The touch rougher like a kitten's tongue
The taste *como* of corn on the cob
Or pinole... el que tiene mas saliva traga mas pinole

Weeping woman weeps to see
The chemicals preserve and make these tortillas last

Tortillas are paper yearning for a poem
Fold one up and eat it like a melody.

Tortillas are
At once food and utensil
I scoop up memories with each bite
And watch weeping woman smile.

                       ❧ Norma Elía Cantú

A Long Marriage

Means sex takes a long time
and sometimes pleasure happens in the distance
like watching a symphony play with no sound
and you have to hear it in memory.
When it works there is surprise
new flavors served on the old oak table,
surprise in the flash of the inexplicable
the one fact of the imponderable.

A long marriage means more talk than sex
talk that takes a long time

the details of the day expected and longed for.
It means holding hands as if trying to keep each other
when friends are getting cancer and dying
and life plays like a sax in the distance
and you have to see the performer in memory

and you cling to the one slow fact of the inexplicable
as you float away with all you thought you knew.

A long marriage means living in the smell
of another as much as your own
and when you squeeze his shoulders you think, yes,
these are right, here, now an imponderable
one slow fact, his thin shoulders.

You dig through the long day of a marriage
archaeologists of surprise.
The empty clogs in the much–rained–on grass
become passage graves the mind can enter
graves with bowls or offerings
where light on the solstice comes through
a tiny slit in the chamber where you
hold each other and celebrate
the one slow fact of the inexplicable
in the loss of what you once knew.

There is rawness in the year of a long marriage
awareness of what lies outside the winnowing.
In the night you see not constellations
but stars—listen to one night bird break
sentences into words, hear the voice
of the inexplicable and name one by one
each good the other has done.

                           ❧ Mary Kay Rummel

Lost Voice

No more studying languages.
One is enough. Now I seek
not how to say it

but what must be said.

One blackbird, one rose.
One note at a time.

The poets have drawn their
swords, sworn to protect
the earliest phrases,

those before Babel, not yet
out of Africa. Vocabularies
might then have been thin,

but what have our new words
added? Men still struggle
to say I love you. Women

overflow, but retreat
to touch. New icons now catch
fire: a global campaign

to make up for lost voice.

                 ❧ Mark Saba

Love Affairs

I like it when my side of the world is sleeping. One might pretend the countries are peaceful, that our own country believes in reading more than pummeling people we don't know. I like the little round pillow filled with buckwheat shells or kernels that fits right under the neck attached to the throbbing head. It makes a soft scurrying sound when you adjust it. Mice in a corncrib. Something soft and normal.

The Algerian movie fell on us like hammers. *She just wanted to sing. They put her in an asylum because she wanted to sing.* The brilliant but deeply depressing New Yorker story about Iraq and how our country betrays people who help us—such a nightcap. Iraq: a country where my country had no business being for even one tenth of a second. Except to do business. It's a wonder any Americans have an ounce of libido or can sleep at all. We're wrecked, George. I do think it's all your fault.

I'm not sure where my Arab-American-ness leaves me these days. Shall I lean over so belatedly to the German-Swiss minor tones of my heritage? No, those people were too stern. They scared me at close range. *Put that down!* I can't deal with them at a distance.

When my beautiful friend asked me to help her commit suicide, I used ethnicity as a joke—*don't you think I have enough problems already? You KNOW they'd put Arab in the headline!*

My friend's problems were far greater than mine. She needed to die with dignity right that minute, deeply weary of her disintegrating body, dry of tongue, dry of eye, rich of spirit, begging me. She said, *I will save the pills, then you…*

No!

She grinned. *Okay then. I'll suffer like a true American.* She recited Shakespeare at top volume in the halls of that terrible nursing home—what were her favorite sonnets? Seems I'd remember a few choice phrases, at least, being so hungry for lines all the time—but I was soaking up her bright red lips—*honey, old women & barns do better with a little paint*—opening and closing and opening—and the way, at nearly 100, she talked about love affairs she never had.

                     ☙ Naomi Shihab Nye

Lucky

After the calamity,
you find a way to live—

wreckage everywhere, and still
you have to scrape through it
for food, for water.

Whose well was this?
Whose bridge over the drainage ditch?

Stones. Planks. Bricks. Iron.
These ruins are nothing.

Once you're able
to recognize the dead,
you have to claim and bury them—

but first you have to eat.
What good is your body now,
all its senses humming?

What is there to witness?
Home gone—neighborhood—
the children's voices rising in the yard.

If you're lucky you get to live,
though nothing you've ever loved
is left to live for.

                         ❧ Jody Bolz

[magnetic karma]

magnetic karma
when the paintings around you
start to melt
when the ground you stand on
forms a river you can't swim in
when your inner soul
starts to speak
words you have never known
before
please welcome
my magnetic karma
magnetic karma
you can't escape it
can't control it
got to throw your world
right into it
my magnetic karma
pretty baby
has come to get you
my magnetic karma
is after you
when you take a breath
or light a cigarette
when you look at the sun
or the moon for that matter
you think it's all there
you think it's all happening
don't you
take one look behind you
there will be no one there

look at your shadow
it belongs to me
my magnetic karma
is after you

                   ❧ Arnold Melleby

Man High*

The Air Force needed to know whether crew members could parachute safely from disabled aircraft flying in the stratosphere.... A young test pilot, Capt. Joseph W. Kittinger, Jr., was one of those selected to train for experiments under USAF's Project Man High.... August 16, 1960 was set for the ultimate test. Kittinger rode a four-and-a-half foot open gondola to 102,800 feet....
                         —Air Force Magazine

   "The big drop is the only way home."
                         —Captain Joseph W. Kittinger,
     USAF
            National Geographic

When you see our earth from an hour and a half on high
where it is a soul-chilling 94 degrees below zero Farenheit
you know it in your hummingbird-heart
that there are angels
gods
Because when you
now bathed in this rawest of sunlight
and the trumpet-blast of
silence
You who have mastered yourself
by neatly garroting every mingy cringing fear
You who (as you will tell the press) have confidence in your team
confidence in your equipment
confidence in yourself
confidence in God
step off the balloon's gondola
weightless

arms splayed as if they were wings
You are one
gazing down upon the swirled froth
that is cloud-cover
your back to the velvet canopy of blackness
and the stars
though strangely you cannot see them
they are indeed watching in their eternal sparkling silence
that knows every breath
and every intention that must form the future
You fall like a
knife
You have not one inch of bare skin
you are swaddled in insulation and zipped into a pressurized
suit
You must free-fall for twelve of these fourteen miles or
you will freeze
to death
Suddenly you flip and face the heavens
like a babe on his back in a crib
you are in the light but what you see is blackest night
no stars
your balloon a moth-speck of white disappearing
Now you gasp for the air that is not there
no pressure
confusion
feet-first now you plunge
650 to 700 miles per hour and
beyond
soundlessly
supersonic
the clouds loom up solid as a floor
but
like a spirit you pass into it
this breath inside of time
and here
like the finger of Apollo
your barometric device clicks
and your parachute blooms
open
the cage tight around your chest hauls you back up
where you are not welcome to stay
however staring your courage
however steeled your indifference
however much we all dream of it

And you float down now
strange petal
where the wind
shoves you
a kind of tailless helmeted primate
wearing waffle-weave underwear
strapped into a fifty-seven pound contraption
feeling the awful aliveness of your body
that roaring pain in your blood-swollen right hand
that strap tugging over your crotch
in your belly pushing like a brick into your lungs is
your breakfast
orange juice and strawberry shortcake
a clearness now: the world's spectacles wiped clean:
our gray-blue world
the sweet warmth of earth pulls you
to its scarred hide
bleached with the mottle of the ancient sea's sand
white as salt
white as the clouds far above
white as all the stars melted together
thirteen minutes and forty-five seconds have elapsed since bail-out
when you hear
the thud
of yourself
and you fall to your knees into white sand
and your chute
like the last silken exhalation of the heavens
falls on you

                             ❧ C. M. Mayo

* Despite its title, the poem describes a later jump in the "Excelsior Project."

The Manifestation of Sisíism
(May 10, 2006)

By the dawns of the early light
by the smell of burnt oil
in the midst of selfish greed
run amuck under the cloak
of evangelical hypocrisy,

I sigh and decry the
hostility vented towards
poor Latino immigrants
trying to find a place
in the sun like those
who have come before—
legal and illegal—
I ask: Where is this
country headed?
Blame the weak; the poor;
hate the Spanish-speaker;
the Muslim; the gay;
the agnostic; the liberal,
all but those who have
set it all in motion—
who will be next?
Delusion: the drink
of money and power
blinds and deafens the
senseless stupidity
and bigotry *foxed* across
the land of repeat and repeat
till lies become truth.
When will this country
awaken from the stupor
of veiled infestation?
Let us say sisí,
let us create,
think, make the
positive.
Let art, literature,
music, drama, morality,
and value for humanity
drown out cries of Iraq,
senseless bombings
in Israel and palestine
Let us destroy the
meaningless of present life—
a revolt of Dada's revolt
to Sisí
like twins sprung
from the same
vile seed—to manifest
a new age
of art and life.

                       ❧ Robert L. Giron

March 20, 2003

That's a child missing limbs. I can't determine the sex. The body is small and burned as it floats down like a dark leaf, lazily, rocking, a black snowflake falling though a green forest. There's a war and it's snowing. Bulldozers level trees, the machine roar deafening. Jets fly past barely above the treetops. Hundreds of jets trailing flame. It's hard to believe they're piloted by humans but they are and not monsters but young men and women, most still near childhood just doing what they're told, screaming jets over treetops. It's snowing children. The woods are filling up with black snow.

                 ❧ Edward Falco

The Marvelous Child

On the threshold of adulthood I began to dream of a little girl who followed me everywhere and who was myself and my child at the same time. She was light and joyful, wise, yet sensitive, close, yet far away. As soon as she came into my life, I banned from my soul all desire to ever love a man again, all desire to love, all desire ("All" is a way of speaking, of course). I gave her all my blood and the marrow of my bones, and I saw my reflection in her eyes as if into a bottomless well, and the marvelous child grew, and the more real she was, the more unreal I became.

                 ❧ Alta Ifland

Memories of the Future

My sister awoke me very early
that morning and said to me
"Get up, you must come and see this—
the sea has filled itself with stars"
Marveled by this revelation
I dressed myself hastily and thought
"If the sea has filled itself with stars
I must take the first plane
and gather all the fishes of the sky"

         ❧ Mario Meléndez
         ❧ Translation by Ron Hudson

[Metaphor has died.]

Metaphor has died.
Nothing resembles anything else.
The smallest fraction of each atom engrossed in the task of accomplishing its minimum commandment. To endure, every morning, the effort of being, no matter what. The exhausted anatomy of an elm.... The contorted stubbornness of pines.... The innocuous whiteness of the ice over the lintel.
The urine of the neighbor's dog traces a groove in the snow. Insignificant.
    No more
        than all of the rest. No more
than this rash will, the unavoidable inanity
of this attempt.

         ❧ Mercedes Roffé
         ❧ Translation by Janet Greenberg

Michelangelo's Last Pietà
(after Pietà Rondanini, Michelangelo Buonarroti, 1475-1564)

I wonder
what took Michelangelo so long
to bring Mary to age.
Here, the other women wrinkle like dates.
Parchment tongues writing
in flames. Gladiators and that sort
of thing.
I thought it was a
miracle. A bald faced
lie. She had other
children, but eyes only for
Him,
with the body of a pagan
god's. I want to touch
His legs, still beautiful,
I want to touch
him as Michelangelo did,
behind the favored ear, under
riddled testicles, make him
laugh again,
my rolled tongue to Gorgon's
invisible navel—
o, closed pigeon-eye,
cool dove, come as I listen
as she did, and kiss him
wherever
there is no blood.

                ಶ Paula Goldman

Miles and the Shofar
"Awake, ye sleepers from your sleep! Arise slumberers . . ." –Maimonides

Miles Davis on the trumpet
and I'm wondering how he'd be
with the shofar on ROSH HASHANAH:
I can hear the rabbi introducing him.

This year we've got *The Man*, he says,
pointing to the musician-wunderkind,
who's maybe had ballads
and blues enough, puckers
his lips, and suddenly,
Te-keee-ahh, the cantor chants;
and the ram's horn explodes in a long
(imploring what distant angels or God?) wail.
And yes, there were RIOTS
in Crown Heights, and Yankel Rosenbaum,
the Yeshiva student, had been stabbed
and killed. Only here, on this high holy
day in the fall, a sound that is no
sound, rises upward, tremulous, exhortatory,
as congregants in skullcaps
and prayer shawls, listen, amazed.
Shev-a'rim, the cantor intones,
and the three short
calls follow; then the alarum,
Te-ruuu-ahh, with a staccato-like
series of terse notes, leading
to . . . (somewhere between horripilation
and thrill . . .) that single
unbroken blast, the *Tekiah Gedolah*!
From such a sound
that is no sound,

Yankel is walking again.

                              ❧ Mel Belin

The Milky Way

I am in empathy
with the Kansas sky.
Ghost clusters of clouds
bring back my childhood
when I'd stretch out
on the welcoming grass
and see, deep into space,
my absent mother.

Here she is again
moving tenderly across
my aching heart.
Her florid cotton skirt
turning from white to
deep purple as she hides
then reappears
as if pulled back and
forth by a sacred hand.

Mami, I cry out
into this ghost-loved world
but there is no echo
to my call from afar.
Like a glow swathed
in dust set to keep us
apart, my mother's ghost
fades away to make
way for a star.

                     ❧ Anita Vélez-Mitchell

Morning Star Children

Morning Star radiates blessings
for Mother Earth and all the worlds
Her brilliance is a gift of the Spirit
Maheo sent Morning Star Woman
                with Corn and Squash and Beans and Tobacco
to nourish the People, to feed the Spirit
She delighted the People
                as a shining Star Child
           She inspired the People
                as an Enlightened Elder
She encouraged the People
                as an Everyday Woman
sparkling with hope
Maheo told the Cheyenne People:
           "The Nation will be strong
             So long as the hearts of the Women

                    Are not on the ground"
Dakota and Osage People sing a song, and it is Wakan:
"We are not defeated
                    While the Women are strong"
Messages of Creation
for all Peoples
for all Times
Messages in the hearts of Women from Arawak and Acoma
          as they turned away from hairy faces
          and fixed their eyes on severed hands
          and fixed their eyes, and fixed their eyes
Messages in the hearts of Women from Washita and Palo Duro Canyon
as they were stampeded and invaded
          to the sound of ponies screaming in the sunset
          to the sound of screams, to the sound of screams
Messages in the hearts of Women from Bosque Redondo and the Crazy
          Horse Bar
as they traded themselves for their children
          as they sold themselves for food and drinks
          as they gave nothing away, as they gave nothing away
Messages in the hearts of Women from Warm Springs to Siletz
          as they end a century of missing memory
          as they once again dance in emergence dresses
          as they sing their lost and found song:
"They Never Touched Me"
                    "They Never Touched You"
Messages in the hearts of Native Women
for all who are touched in unkind ways
          for all who pray to end unholy days
          for all who shelter the disheartened in loving ways
                    "They Never Touched You"
"You Are Blessed By The Morning Star Woman and Your Heart Is Not On
          The Ground"
"You Are Blessed By The Morning Star Woman and The People Are Strong"
"You Are Blessed By The Morning Star Woman"
"You Are Blessed By The Morning Star"
"You Are A Blessed Star Child"
"You Are Blessed"
                    ❧ Suzan Shown Harjo

My Language

My language lies buried in the center of the earth. When night comes, dreams open time's gates and the black ravens with rustling wings take off, leaving behind a long, leaden sleep. Language's guardians, mute mummies draped in shrouds, float at the four cardinal points, their faces stiff, lips crimson, eyes painted blue. At dawn, they sink back into memory's cracks.

My language doesn't belong to me. All that belongs to me is a long, flowery absence at whose edges roses are growing alongside my legs, encircling them, climbing and covering my body like a tomb. Deep in the absence, my language unearths its words of fog, dead like me, and holds them for an instant above the tomb, then lets them fall like petals.

                 ❧ Alta Ifland

Naiveté

I thought we'd see the Great Wall,
the Grande Palace,
and study the culture
dating back to the earliest human skull,
a girl named Lucy.
Her voice uncovering thousands of years lost
simply by being found,
shaking the applecart,
changing the perception of time,
nearly the same week we are landing on Mars.

I visit Thailand,
see Buddha's Temple
built over 300 years ago.
Too stunning to grasp
in a twenty-minute tour,
like an assembly line
through an orchid field,
numb to its fragrance and beauty.

So many things to take in,
to wear, taste, digest—
in a spiritual sense, of course.
But soon after the fluster dies down

Starbucks comes up in conversation,
cell phones connect us internationally,
and every woman I see
wants a Prada bag.

      ❧ Anika Paris

Nameless

His body lies on shore in pieces   the flesh alligator eaten   in dark and hungry sleeps   his arm floats in the canal   behind the banyan trees   teeth marks crunch the bent wrist   angled upward   bobbing on rip-pulled waves in the tilted moonlight

before his night-wandering sleep in his bed on the banks   he stumbled shoeless into the canal   cleansed caked mud from his tee shirt   a spot of ketchup his own stink

not crying out   when the beast dragged him   into the undertow of   dodged cars of waved front pages of pocketing the sell   road-weary in the Florida heat of gulping the bottled sun to sear the pain of death of a marriage   his little girl his brother   his parents

not crying out   when the beast dragged him   into the undertow of   blueprints of skyscrapers shimmering love   a home behind the banyan trees   baseball games a little brother   a piggy bank

not crying out   when the beast dragged him   into the undertow of   his mother and father rocking him to sleep   body fed   powdered   bathed   wrist bent baby flesh kissed   fingers counted

      ❧ Lucille Gang Shulklapper

Native Land

I walk with you

I am your ship
your crew

your trade winds
your sail
I am your anchor

Terra firma
I remain
and you take me with you

You take me with you
alter-ego folded
and well-behaved
in your trunk

I am the wheat still green
of your flesh
the ripe wheat
in your hold

I am the wine
which does not turn
the livestock which renews itself

I am the burning
the dull pain of exile
I am your voice
the one I have baptized

I am your sealed references
I am the footbridge
which delivers you
to the new land
and there
I am your firewood
and your spark

Have no fear
I walk with you

                         ❧ Marcelle Kasprowicz

Navigating the Warning
(For Reggie)

October 9, 2004, Honolulu

From eternity to never is a river
Of renegade stars
Home-starved planets
Past the stream of thinking-without-direction:
That's where it comes from—
You'll have no exact address in the mess of humanness
And go down in the punch of red history and earthly cowboys.
The body is a helix
Of the dreams of ancestors
Cultivate the wisdom here, in molecular funk and grease
Navigate swiftly
Beyond the scurry of the mind having a drink
With friends at the café
Beyond the limb of knowledge thick with crows
Perched on a broken overhang
Over crashing fresh waters,
Beyond time.

                       ❧ Joy Harjo

Neologism

The birth of a new word is so secret
you would think it were a sin that needed
to be kept from the public or at least
its synonyms, but only a fool could

not guess its paternity. The lacy
lashes cannot disguise its father's I's,
and that pouty mou is its grandmother's
to a T. Only some Grimm defect keeps

us guessing its roots. Soon enough it will
find its way into the dictionary
its heading topped by Roman caps or dressed
in the frilly tutu of italics—

new wine into old bottlenecks, stalled
on the electronic superhighway,
while down in the small type its archaic
progenitors, thesaurus wrecks, exist

on life supports, the philologists' long
IVs stuck on their vowels like umlauts,
as brain functions remain strictly flatlined.
All night poets have been congregating

to watch heroic effort extended
on an adjective whose skin has the fine
craquelure of an Old Master oil.
It has signed away what portion of its

meaning was assignable, and now it
too is waiting, waiting for the buzzword
that will still its indelible ink and bring
its mighty beating to a glottal stop.

                       ❧ David Bergman

The Night Last Night

Already tonight the night has ended.
And while I empty the ashtray
and collect the glasses, and make the bed
still thinking of your kisses
and of your last smile on the landing,
you launch yourself into the cold of the street
and huddle in your jacket,
and pick up the pace, the metro is closing,
and they want you home for breakfast.

And while I still search the sheets
for some of your heat and your scent
and your constellation shines in the dark,
the train crosses the tunnels of sleep
and you curl up inside a weak memory,
tired, content, and groggy,

smelling on your hands my cologne,
reliving lascivious images,
reciting the lyrics of a bolero.

               ❧ Luis Martínez de Merlo
               ❧ Translation by Lawrence Schimel

Nights at Maya's

As always, I arrive with the Scottish mzungu*
eventually his presence will stop getting us
faster service. He starts by ordering Tusker and we
are armed with conversation on observations.

Once in their eyes I was probably a prostitute.
What black woman hangs with white men?
So I told them, Mimi ni wanafunzi
I am a student, so I don't give me those tsk tsk's.

When I place my order—nyama choma with goat.
I know a saved a chicken's life
because he escapes the pen in the back
and comes out running to thank me.
The servers don't know why I laugh.

Because it is tradition, I wash my hands
in the dirty bowl the little boy carries from table to table,
before cupping the steaming ugali and nyoma choma
to my lips like prayer. This is what I will remember
from Kenya. Not the woman around the corner

with her fresh mangoes, brown eggs with feathers,
fresh food my stomach will not process. Not the planned
monthly riots with crimson tainted rifle butts, the two-handed

gropes in gaudy bars, but the long nights at Maya's when I gave
it all up for roasted goat stewed in onions, tomatoes, maybe
some irio or chips on the side and maize porridge
for capturing all the juices and just talk, under the open studded sky.

               ❧ Teri Ellen Cross

* Swahili for foreigner

No-Man's Land

When dogs run loose and the streets are filled
with the BP noose and the same old drill,
when Saunders sags like an old man's face,
like a plastic bag in a fireplace,
and graffiti's sprayed on a boxcar's hip
by the mayor's maid on last night's trip
'cross the bridge back home to the other side
as she rode the wave of the daily tide,
I know I'm here where the world ends,
where night caves in, where daylight bends
in a big-boned arc, in a flash of steel,
in the flat-ass flap of a punctured wheel.
You can't be home along the Rio Grande,
'cause people say it's no-man's land.
There's nothing strange 'bout a daylight brawl,
or a man gunned down near the Riverdrive Mall,
nothing odd about an amputee
who came apart on the rails, you see.
Nothing sad about the blistered man
with the cardboard sign and the coffee can,
nothing new when the neighbor says
that she's seen the ghost of Hernan Cortés.
All this you'll find where the world ends,
where the sky unfurls and recommends
that we bite our tongues, that we nod our heads,
that we brace ourselves for the flying lead.
Just walk along the Rio Grande,
and you'll know, too, this is no-man's land.
Did you take a look at the sky last night?
Did you see if the stars put up a fight
when the spotlight swung from the dealership,
when the BP searched for a midnight dip,
when the flames leaped up as the warehouse burned
and the cloud of smoke billowed and churned,
when a barefoot kid caught a firefly
but snuffed it out though his sister cried?
The light goes out when the world ends,
when night caves in or just descends
through a sewer line, to a septic tank,
down Chacon Creek, 'cross the river bank.
You can't be home along the Rio Grande,
when the light goes out in no-man's land.
Have you heard the news about the nineteen dead
in a sealed-up truck that stopped instead

of moving on with their human load
away from here on the north-bound road?
Can you read its lips when money talks?
Can you wait all day like a white-tailed hawk?
Would you stand up to a scorpion?
Do you have the strength or would you run
if you think that this is where the world ends,
where night caves in, where daylight bends
in a big-boned arc, in a flash of steel,
in the flat-ass flap of a punctured wheel?
Can you survive along the Rio Grande,
the place some folks call no-man's land?
You can break a sweat sitting in your yard
or find your fate in a tarot card;
you can crush the roach crawling through the trash
or pawn your life for a chunk of cash.
Just don't ignore what's in the brush,
beyond the snakes and the strip-joint rush,
beneath the haze of a jungle fire,
behind the truth from a trusty liar:
you damn well know where the world ends,
though we piss and moan and then contend
that the border's raw and uncivilized.
But it's robbed you now, you been burglarized.
It's sunk your heart in the Rio Grande,
sunk down deep in this no-man's land.
I know that this ain't Mexico;
for the United States, you have to go
a hundred miles north of here.
So where are we? Well, some folks fear
that we're all lost in this borderland,
a place that's tough to understand
with coyotes and the evil eye,
where New Year's rains from a leaden sky,
where La Virgen brings la gente hope,
where smugglers try to cross their dope,
where you burn your hand on the steering wheel,
where faith and curanderas heal,
where you leave your blood on a cactus thorn,
where you bury the cord when your child's born,
where you tie yourself to mesquite and sky,
where the truth is often told in lies.
This might be no-man's land to you,
but if it is, I'm a no-man, too.

                   ❧ Randy Koch

Not This
(Madrid, Spain)

on the tour bus
going back to Madrid
another joke
about Mexicans and how,
when we are drowning
in quick-sand, we are so much
like bean dip.

again

everyone on the bus laughs.

and I want to go home
after this trip and remember
the stone flowers of Segovia
on the inner curve of the cathedral ceiling,

how the light fell from the red stained-glass
dress of the Virgin and spilled out
on the marble floor in soft, pink circles.

not this.

I want to say to my mom,
a Mexican back home in Iowa,
that my journey to El Escorial
filled me with grace. Tell her
of the blue tiles in the Reyes' best rooms
the great carved bed of Isabella, Spain's Queen.

the delicate stars,
curved pieces of wood
matched together with a hundred hands
to give a whole heaven of light
there on her ceiling
for Fernando to point toward
in the night.

not this.

I want to tell of the armory
holding five-hundred-year-old
weapons of war,
burned and pounded at El Alcazar

into flat cutting edges, long rounded points,
the low helmets, gloves of steel, blunt corners
and spurs for wounding. Intricate,

the design of protection and the ability to wound
melded into these suits of armor
a shield in one hand,

a sword in the other.

                          ҙ❧ Emily Lupita Plum

Ö

Shape, the lips to an *o*, say *a*.
That's island.

One word of Swedish has changed the whole neighborhood.
When I look up, the yellow house on the corner
is a galleon stranded in flowers. Around it

the wind. Even the high roar of a leaf-mulcher
could be the horn-blast from a ship
as it skirts the misted shoals.

We don't need much more to keep things going.
Families complete themselves
and refuse to budge from the present,
the present extends its glass forehead to sea
(backyard breezes, scattered cardinals)

and if, one evening, the house on the corner
took off over the marshland,
neither I nor my neighbor
would be amazed. Sometimes

a word is found so right it trembles
at the slightest explanation.
You start out with one thing, end
up with another, and nothing's
like it used to be, not even the future.

                               ҙ❧ Rita Dove

An Obsidian Path

Barely ten, yet she carries
her mother´s womb-load on her back
irasol in rebozo trappings
of what is simply life—
No wings crown her cherub face
yet familiar ashblack pain nudges her
into contained laughter leaving
her secret imagination unruffled—
Her lips are borrowed from the saint her mother
prays to at night when no whispers remain
only light-catching cobwebs strung across the air:
clotheslines for visiting chaneques*—
While her unshod soles unfold each set step
the winds name her from all four corners:
amber-rooted, she moves in her world silently
awhirr with miracles —

                        ช Claire Joysmith

* Mischievous elf-like magical beings who are said to inhabit mountain caves in traditional central Mexican lore.

Okie Monarchs

I never saw so raped a countryside,
this Oklahoma "City," so-called....

the derricks jacking in and out, obscene
beside the swings, the library.... crude rules;

mall posterboard and neon wink their lies
across the Broadway shaft, like mica flickers

across a pit, across the tumbling wrappers...
like condoms, sacks of children's souls... pale

along the median. Never saw a hell
to match this drive-through. When the Monarchs

arrived, they waggled in alternative

rush-hour flow, in cloverleafs mid-air,

among the starving greens of Lowes and Target.
More migrants—lovely, sure, but only Okies—

they spawn, they go, their wings like hot-rod flames,
some Heineken-green, never saw the like

before…. once, in glossy springtime, Cape Cod,
a luna moth, a monster, startled me,
and it was green, and I thought, Dickinson,

gone midnight, strange, her "noon" gone moon; I thought,
Nabokov, sexy lepidopterist,
ripe youth and beauty in his net…. Now,

these Red-Dirt flyers, scribbling on the air,
it's like a note you jot in mid-commute,

no poem. Autumn's on us, Hallowe'en,
the black and orange…décor that's not unlike

these blossom-cruisers: Little People, up
on brooms, their dance to Satan stained the blood
of sunset; male hooks female; howling mute,

invisible yet vivid upward love coils,
a couple climbing spiral steeps, at work
against the vertigo, a pair of pilgrims….

                         ❧ John Domini

An Old Uncle Held Them

In mellow light before time turns crisp
at the edges, skinks scurry over warm rocks
near Rousseau-lush palms. We drowse
while shadows still linger on the sundial.
Time is an umber-tanned man, salt prints
from sea water drying on his chest, as he turns
on his belly toward me. What does it matter
that he's younger? Like Walt, I love muscle-ripple
and maleness. The poet held dying lads in a flux

of lust and endearment. At the moment of death,
it must have seemed to each that an old uncle
held him. So what if Walt mixed brotherly love
and desire? Pushed to the edge, who can sort
its strands? We may break through strongholds
of rules, even deny what we feel, still grasping
for what's true within, even as it hides.

                                      ❧ Patricia Gray

On U.S. 11 (Bear Station, Tennessee, 1968)

Finned cars
line the motel lot,

give comforting sameness
all along the road,

all across the
great wideness.

Summer morning's
dirty fog lifts,

grits and gravy call from
the junction diner.

Even the hills have
a smell that

lifts in the
burn of day.

The road's two-lane,
there's one light.

Forests creep to
town's edge;

it's bowled by
peaks. A new

kind of place,
a new thought; but,

for now, we're just
passing through.

                 ❧ Anthony W. Reevy

The Outskirts

In the slow landscape ceaselessly spreading
from grass and summer's ripening fruit
princess nature in her goodness
launches freedom's lark

In hidden gardens where history's shadows
are rubbed out never to be revealed
water sparkles in its veils
of shimmering mercury and silver

Just in time the sun comes up
to relieve asthma and insomnia
crabs are crawling across the moon
which trembles next to its star

The sea is nothing more than a green opal
far in the distance a sailor sleeps
his aching bones are calm
and he is dreaming of discoveries

                 ❧ Raymond Queneau
                 ❧ New translation by Daniela Hurezanu and
                     Stephen Kessler

The Ox:
(for Andrés Fisher)

"Neither the ploughman's whip nor hardship is pain. What hurts is knowing you draw a single furrow yielded again and again and you plant.

The sharpest pain is the same old pain. From the most intense cold, memory, there is no shelter.

The plough forever snags the root which snags the plough, but the hitch doesn't make the share blunter nor the trace more durable."

      Benito del Pliego
      Translation by Robin Ouzman Hislop

Patrimonial Recipe

I swore never to wear my father's mask.
Yet I meticulously peel and cut tomatoes.
Crush garlic. Pluck basil bent
low in observance. One
by one. Push them off the plank.
Into the fervid blonde of olive oil.
Salt. Pepper. Dash of sugar.
Then I sit down at the table.
Yell at my children for being children.
Ignore my wife——her voice:
the steam of boiling water.
And wait for the perfect consistency.
Al dente. The callous core that weeps
when overcooked.

      Daniele Pantano

The Pavlovian Crux

They've tenured you, professor
and high school teacher
They've tenured you to fear
They've tenured you to keep
your mouth shut
They've tenured you to turn
a blind eye
They've tenured you to dread
with the mocking smirk
of contemptible denial
They've tenured you to cower

even when there is no
threat at all
They've tenured you to seek
comfort in twisted rationalization
They've tenured you to argue
in treacherous blindness
They've tenured you to feel good
about yourself and to actually
believe you're doing good
And they've flooded the nation
with your ilk
for indeed you are
doing good… for them.

                          G. Tod Slone

Persimmons

He taught me about persimmons:
First you have to wait in the rain
For the large orange globes to ripen
On their Texas trees, then
Wait when they squat like tomatoes

On a sheet of tin foil
On your kitchen floor,
Each upturned face as fat
As any Buddha squinting
Through one petalled eye.

Color, of course, means nothing.
Feel is everything. Each day
You have to pulse each scrotum,
Anticipating between your thumb
And tender fingers

That one fruit will relax
Into your touch, giving in
The way soft flesh and fat
Squirm delicately, responding
To the push of bone.

Each baby grows apace,

Its timetable close to its heart.
No two ripen the same day.
Like lovers they come one at a time,
And when you probe that special one,

You stand in the kitchen
And peel back the leather sheath.
Beneath, the mushy strands
Ooze sticky mucous
That you roll across your teeth,

Play on your tongue, and slide
Into your sex-starved throat.
Juice dribbles on your chin.
You let it fall where it will
On your naked chest.

Some rites end in disarray.
Let nature rule a feast.
Never rush the crest of love.
If you rip into a pert round
Before its time, your gift

Is chalk in the mouth,
Regret in your guilty heart,
And days of sad remembrance.

                               George Klawitter

The Philosophy Lesson

Philosophy settled in the gardens of a monastery
where the monks read fairy tales to young children.
Those were moments of true happiness
because the reading was accompanied by slaps
on their tender cheeks.

Then, the first illumination came to pass:
If a lamb were able to speak we would not be able to understand it.
Thus were the games played by language
So it would no longer be possible to reach the essence of words.

Then philosophy sat on an armchair
and devoted itself to watching cowboy movies
while eating popcorn as the Indians fell like flies.

                         ❧ Isaac Goldemberg

The Pilgrimage
(in honor of Walt Whitman)

On a pilgrimage liken to those who knee to Santiago de Compostela,
those who rock before the Wailing Wall, or
those in a dervish daze circling Mecca,
I stand before your bed and touch the wooden railing
smooth as porcelain by countless rubbings by manly hands.
As if wanting to commune with you, I wait
patiently for some sign to revive the first time
I read *Leaves of Grass* and felt my spirit leap,
sensing the brotherhood in your words,
knowing that we had a commonality crossing decades.
I look around and vaguely feel the calling of America,
the brotherhood of muscle, valor, and independence,
the need to be free and oneself among the masses,
the celebration of the body electric, the common man,
the mechanic, the captain of my life, rooted to the earth,
a silver oak of determination but a faithful willow
of pliability, I sing to myself,
calling the joy you felt among the men.
You are with me and I am refreshed,
flowing with the river ebbed by the
sting of life; I quiver, undulating until
I grasp the gossamer thread of my Soul.

                         ❧ Robert L. Giron

Pirateology
(for Merrie Penck and Joey Leto)

I was checking out a stack of pirate
books for my boy. Our librarian said,
I'm related to Captain Morgan,
one of the most famous pirates.
After I saw "Pirates of the Caribbean,"
I dreamt I was a pirate all night &
woke up happier than I've ever been.

We looked him up in Pirateology:
Sir Henry Morgan, Governor of Jamaica,
King of Buccaneers, a most fortunate
pirate, said the caption—and there
she was: the same square jaw and round
Welsh eyes, pale green rimmed in black.

It might've been just another Johnny Depp
fantasy, but I like to think Captain Morgan's
rum-soaked genes lie coiled within her
quiet cells. Perhaps past-life memories
are ancestral blood that rises like sap,
tapped in dreams and rich, obsessive reading.
Scratch the librarian, you'll find a pirate.

Like my Italian hairdresser, Joey,
who's descended from two presidents
on his mother's side, going back to a Leiden
hooker who came over on the Mayflower
as an indentured servant. He's tracked his line
back to Charlemagne, which I think explains
something of his magic with the scissors.

                               ❧ Barbara Louise Ungar

Plastic Hen

Between the gum and underwear
displays, the purple plastic hen
twirls on her dimestore weathervane
and squawks electrically for a quarter.

She stoops on her glass nest to warm
transparent eggs. Through tinmail slots
she warms her chicks—bright whistles, rubber
dinosaurs, fossil superheroes.
One day I saw a woman fish
a quarter from a tattered purse;
her three-year-old compressed his face
against the treasured glass. The hen
awoke like Sleeping Beauty, clucked
her purple polymeric song
and spun before the wide-eyed boy
as if this were a wondrous world.

                         ❧ Miles David Moore

Poema como TRANSLENGUAJE
A Trans-L=A=N=G=U=A=G=E Poem

Taking cabs in the middle of the night driving as if to save your soul where the road goes round and round the park and the meter glares like a moral owl.
    —Elizabeth Bishop

¿Vienes?
Are you coming?
Apúrate, llega
Hurry up, come
sube por el Hudson
go up the Hudson
cruza la ciudad por el Central Park
cross to the other side of the city, by Central Park
y llama.
and call me.

¿Vienes?
Are you coming?
En el East River
Up the East River
un barco nos llevará
a ship will take us
alrededor de la isla,

around the island
una y otra vez,
once and again
para que veas
so you can see
asomarse entre las torres gemelas
appear, through the Twin Towers,
el vacío que nos engendra.
the emptiness that begets us

¿Vienes?
Are you coming?
Brooklyn aún espera
Brooklyn still awaits
ser descubierta
to be discovered
desea ser Manhattan y su puente cuelga
it wishes to be Manhattan and its bridge hangs
como una pérdida.
hopeless.
De envidia no quiere ver
Its envy doesn't let it see
la isla que la niega.
the island that denies it.

¿Vienes?
Are you coming?
Aún te espero
I am still waiting
y veo por la ventana
and I see through the window
la neblina de otra ciudad
the mist of another city
que me marca
that leaves its mark on me
Llega, apura, salgamos
Come, hurry up, let´s go
protegidas por el anonimato.
protected by the anonymity.
La noche nos fuerza
the nigh compels us
a enmascararnos.
to disguise us.

¿Vienes?
Are you coming?

El metro pasa por el Bronx
The subway goes though the Bronx
sus ojos sin pestañas
its eyes without eyelash
te persiguen desde la ventana.
haunts you from the window.

¿Vienes?
Are you coming?
¿O prefieres llegar por la mañana
Or you'd rather come in the morning
cuando la ciudad muera
when the city dies
sin haber cumplido su promesa?
before meeting its promise?

                       ❧ Marta López-Luaces

Poetry Offender

The fourth night, she said that she never liked the one poem he'd ever published in his life in a literary magazine in Utah. That was all right with him, because he wasn't a poet, had never considered himself a poet, and had no aspirations to poet-tude.

He was, in fact, a rocket scientist and had published in a literary magazine in Utah due to a computer glitch, generated when he'd tried to e-mail the formula for liquid booster fuel to a firing range on the salt flats. Through some server quirk, his e-mail had ended up in an English department office, and a teaching assistant had intercepted it and liked it so much that it had appeared under the title "Maximum Thrust" in the college magazine, The Salt Lick.

"But you knew all that, anyway," he said to her, "so why are you bringing this up now?"

"Because tonight is a special occasion," she said, "and even though you've never written more than one bad poem, you should write a second poem, for me, and you should make it a good one."

"Yikes!" he said, slapping his forehead with his open palm. "I'd forgotten all about the occasion and how special it is! I'll get my quill and start scribbling."

                       ❧ Thaddeus Rutkowski

[Poets are bad for the economy.]

Poets are bad for the economy.

They don't get a job immediately after graduating
from college. Ten years later they still
have never owned an automobile.

Their spouses do not pick out new living room furniture
every four years. They spend their own money
fixing up their apartments.

Poets keep things for a very long time.
Like postage scales, typewriters, lovers,
and leather boots. They take vacations

off-season, shun formality, and buy the paperback
versions of classics. Others who are bad for the economy
include housewives, husbands, fathers,

painters, old people, young people, harpsichordists,
and the religious. Those who are good for the economy
do not waste time paying attention to why someone close

may hurt. They would rather go for a run,
order the future from a catalogue,
change the subject. Meanwhile, the economy lives

while those both good and bad for it are just passing by.

&ℯ Mark Saba

The Pond Does Not Ripple

Ophelia, are you mad,
sleeping in the water like that.

You can fall ill;
dry yourself, before fever arrives.

You look peaceful, relieved,
but please go back home
and have a warm bath.

Drink some hot tea
and stay under the covers.

What happens to beauty
when stricken with sickness
and turmoil?

Let us not find out.

                   ❧ Shome Dasgupta

Prove To Me

In a single blizzard more snowflakes fall
    than all the money produced
        in the history of the world.
In a single fall more leaves fall
    than all the money produced
        in the history of the world.
In this Universe alone, not counting
    Universes before and after
        and Universes
            concurrent with this Universe,
More planets with Utopias on them exist
    than all the money produced
        in human history.

Explain to me why
    snow can't be used as money.
Explain to me why each fallen leaf
    can't be pecuniary remuneration.
Prove to me beyond the shadow of a doubt
    why the epiphany zillions of planets
        have Utopias on them
            can't be legal tender.

Why can't I fill my cart with food
    and after the girl rings up my bill
        give her a pinecone?
Why can't I knock on my landlord's door
    and hand him a flower
        for rent?
And when the police take me away

  and demand to see my identification
    what else can I do but
      reach into my pocket
And present them
 a handful of sand
   running through my fingers?

          ॐ Antler

Prozac

Divine and blue,
you're an aspirin fit for the gods,
the powdery ghost of Gandhi
conjured into a bottle,
glorious as the bones of Buddha
ground into white dust.
How truly miraculous
the way you dissolve on my tongue,
like a peppermint, like a host—
the way you bury my grief
like a diamond ring, like a seed.

          ॐ Chris Tusa

Radiolaria

Ernst Haeckel, I can picture you
leaning over your microscope,
left eye closed, the right
open to one-celled worlds
where the quick and the still
yield their secrets.

The miraculous ocean
has entered the scope,
surged through your soul
and is now radiating out

the tips of your fingers,
which grasp a pencil

as you try to capture nature's
art, your Kunstformen.
The marine protozoa
called radiolaria convinced you
Darwin was right,
and your drawings persuaded

all of Europe.
There you are leaning late
with your amazing radiolaria
shaped like snowflakes and spiked crowns,
chandeliers and lobed planets.
This one branches like a crystal.

This one is a net of round holes
so dense it is as much absence
as physical shape. Note the symmetry
of the outstretched arms.
Miniature sunflower, butterfly,
apron, grid, I cannot

get enough of them. Look
at this elaborate helmet
with its quills and its spire.
Ernst Haeckel,
you turned out to be
a racist, an anti-Semite,

to believe in eugenics;
you created your own religion,
the Monist League,
and proclaimed a "crystal soul."
With all your rigor and your beauty,
your fine precision—I see you,

drawing that surprising jewel box
whose inner sanctum,
held in perfect equipoise
by its myriad winding tendrils,
contains nothing but darkness
and the infinite realms of cruelty.

                         ❧ Kim Roberts

Raptors

I walk down the steps are rolled out to the plane in Lima,
and the smell of garbage hits me. A freighter washed up on the coast,
I am told, was simply forgotten there years ago.
                              Behind the city the Andes
rise where the not-so-simple humans swarm in shacks above the dazzle.

Blocks and blocks of the wealthy own not the most,
but the healthiest of the children,
and the name Maria always comes first—
   Maria Isabella, Maria Helena,
so Jesus too will spot them as immaculate for a time. These namesakes of
Blessed-art-thou-amongst-women will never know their hillside sisters
who sleep under bull icon and crucifix astride the makeshift roof.

Airborne again, I see how distance makes headway through the mountains
look easy.
   Roads like whimsical syrup twist through the gorges and over
plateaus where tin roofs blaze back at the equatorial sun. Each settlement
a surprise slipped into the Andes. Each cleft a solitude where the sun comes
to cast light:
Jungle first to the east, uproar of tapir with the sherbet-colored birds.
Heat mounts the vines, the petals, then dips into a glacial green lake.
It glitters on an avalanche stopped for a while
on the baked rock slopes.
               Ages it took to stack
this land on its way through the clouds, sky full of raptors,
earth full of tremors.

                      ࣻ Katherine Soniat

Reality Show

Nizhoniigo no hey nay
Nizhoniigo no hey wa ney
Nizhoniigo no hey nay
Nizhoniigo no hey wa ney

How do we get out of here?
Smoke hole crowded with too much thinking
Too many seers

And prophets of prosperity
We call it real, we call it real

What are we doing in this mess of forgetfulness?
Ruled by sharp things, baby girls in stiletto heels
Beloved ones doing street time
We call it real

What are we doing napping, through war?
We've lost our place of in the order of kindness
Children are killing children
We call it real, we call it real.

What are we doing forgetting love?
Under mountains of trash, a river on fire
We can't be bought, forced or destroyed.
Just what is real?

Nizhoniigo no hey nay
Nizhoniigo no hey wa ney
Nizhoniigo no hey nay
Nizhoniigo no hey wa ney

             ❧ Joy Harjo

Nizhoniigo: Navajo (or Dineh) which means beautiful within and without

Redemption

The river is being dredged
on a pink cloud night so
thick with lilac, gulls seem
suspended in the air.

No sign of the skuffle,
just the trompe d'oeil pastoral,
of picnic blankets weighted
with ice jugs and food cartons.

What were the last words
he spoke into the cypress trunk?
Bees gather around tree roots,
his muscle shirt clotted

around the mossy hollows.

He shouldn't have been so
limp wristed, a gawker remarks.
That sort of thing simply
doesn't belong around here.

The tug treds slower now,
casts its light into the marsh.
Broomstick or collarbone?
A few diners pause to crane
their necks towards the artifact.

The sharp trill of the cicadas
drape over the portrait.
A whisper of oars banked
on the bayou's edge remain
undusted for fingerprints.

The gurgle of swamp water
seems clarified by goldenrods.
Queen Anne's Lace gently folds
together in the wind, the white
blossoms forming a kind of wreath.

❖ Gerard Wozek

Red, White and Blue

Moving together
We press ourselves
Against each other

Where we meet
The red flow
Of your body rhythms
Begins to streak our skin

Pausing
I get up

To remove the flag
Hanging over the back window

Now used as a screen
And not the symbol
The last tenants
Left behind

Spreading it below us
We arch and moan
Tangled in the bars and stars

Later
After washing and dressing
I look back to the bed
To our embrace
Blood smudged rubbings
Our crimson imprints
Drying on America

                 ☙ Josh Gilman

Reformation of the Arsonist

1
Complications of keys collect.
The solenoid immolates itself, hundreds
of composition papers sprout stigmata
and drift to the carpet. Dreams of fame
replace dreams of love and prove equally vain.
The savings book dwindles beneath
your pillow. Flammabilities are displaced,
age reforms the arsonist.

2
A neighborhood consumed with autumn:
for weeks the maples along Morris Street
practice their pyromania, scattering leonine
options along humping turn-of-the-century brick,
pasting orange the hoods of cars, all the age
yellowed love letters ever ripped to shreds
collecting along curbs, inviting passing
children's scuff.
                 In a rocking chair
by the window of November, creaking with

the radiators, watch arsonists take to
the evening, those sunsets your schedule
barely permits. Try to recall reasons
for ardor, for bursting into flame, ways
to rationalize the random. At nightfall,
scrapings of a rake, a train's distance,
the clock grows too loud. Later, leaves
caught in rain and church-bell knell,
peeling off midnight and drifting
embers through your sleep, gestures
a lover made in your last life.

3
Fire evaporates from the top twigs first,
leaflessness working its way down. Take up
the red pen, open the secondary source.
This last week of leaf-fall, the maples
lose colors you lost years ago, when
the body retired from crime, when
bones became kindling laid away
under damp eaves and forgotten, with
no hope of being consumed by autumn.

                       ❧ Jeff Mann

The Religion Lesson

Upon refusing to correctly interpret the situation,
religion set in motion the final catastrophe.
Such was the tragic continuation of history.

It knew that no one could say more about the human than the human.
There existed many things that one could have said,
but the most profound, the most revealing,
the most extreme were found in his conception of himself.

Then religion decided to do and say something.
It wanted to be recognized by the humans
and that they define themselves by its precepts.
It didn't wish to be the fruit of their imagination.

Then it sat itself upon a high and exalted throne,
and from there it spoke, covering its face.

It warned that the humans' house would be destroyed
and any demonic thing
would have free reign to attack them.

It begged the humans and cried out to them,
but the humans wanted no more of it.

                     ❧ Isaac Goldemberg
                     ❧ Translation by Wanda Rivera and Roy
                         Cravzow with Stanley H. Barkan

A Retired Voodoo Priestess Dreams of Revenge from The Psych Ward in Charity Hospital

Only three days and already I loathe this place,
this milk-white morgue, this smiling slaughterhouse,
where girls in straitjackets grow fat on pills,
floating on pale clouds of Clozapine,
sad white angels with their wings lopped off,
their eyes blind as stones rattling in a gris gris bag.

I've had it with these nurses, with their dull
white smocks and their hypodermic needles,
the smiling orderlies with black holes for eyes,
their veins pumped fat with steroids,
psychiatrists with the same filthy grins,
talking through their pink Pepto-Bismol mouths.

Do they know that with one pinch of cayenne
I could turn their liver into a hornet's nest,
make roaches scurry through their black veins?
That with one single strand of horse's hair
I could squeeze the breath from their fat pink necks,
stop the clock from ticking in their chest?

Do they see me in the cold dull afternoon
sewing bloodroot into dolls, drawing Xs in the air?
Do they know that while I stand in line for meds
I'm working a mean batch of spells in my head?
That at night I keep a crow's foot in my pocket,
hidden like a white pill under my tongue?

                             ❧ Chris Tusa

Rip Tide

When we took the rip cord in our delicate hands and yanked the rough yarn of the rope until the skin under our skin began to peel and crack and our palms to blister and burn with certain, unassailable pain, it was then I understood that no one could ever claim to understand me or the predictable patterns that once comprised my life.

I knew I was only to them an aberration, that the red tides of my mind had moved me forever beyond the realm of the life-guard, the lighthouse, the beached schooner with its hollowed heart.

I knew also that the song of the sea, which is the song of our bodies rising, and the song of the brown pelicans swooping to kelp beds containing their nourishment, and even the song of the clam with its eyes shut so tight against the world was something they had stopped singing, a lullaby they would never learn.

We saw everything as if in the blind rush of falling came a moment of invincible clarity—the wife I would not be, the life I would not have—and your heart opened to me wider than the throat of the ocean, red and wild as the parachute that saved us, both our lives.

                 ❧ Julie Marie Wade

The Road

He sometimes felt that he had missed his life
By being far too busy looking for it.
Searching the distance, he often turned to find
That he had passed some milestone unaware,
And someone else was walking next to him,
First friends, then lovers, now children and a wife.
They were good company—generous, kind,
But equally bewildered to be there.
 He noticed then that no one chose the way—
All seemed to drift by some collective will.
The path grew easier with each passing day,
Since it was worn and mostly sloped downhill.
The road ahead seemed hazy in the gloom.
Where was it he had meant to go, and with whom?

                 ❧ Dana Gioia

Robinson

On the dead sea alongside the sunset
The siren has given to the rootless floating
Trees the shadow of her breasts and waist
To those that drowned the sound of waves
Is like fish slipping thru the nightswells
When the hull the iron spikes reject the salty water
The flowery mast and ashen clouds
Invading the beach where the astrolabes
Drawn by death come to sleep in summer
The wooden planks and rum barrels roll down
To the cliffs near dirty tables and unwashed glasses
The coffee spice across the plain in wonder
Reflects no lion strolling in this haze
Wearing the usual purple and gold silk
The forests have lost their leafy smile
And shepherds bite their elderwood flutes
Assiduous tourists young girls and painters
Have fled the city where nobody sings anymore
Since the assassin lost his suspenders
In the dark cells where no one hanged himself.

                         ❧ Raymond Queneau
                         ❧ New translation by Daniela Hurezanu and
                            Stephen Kessler

[St. Anthony's Church]

St. Anthony's Church

in Questa, New Mexico,
erected a plaque
on a pedestal
outside its doors
to honor all the dead
"unborn children"
of the world.

I looked in vain
for a corresponding plaque
to honor the bone-thin

babies starving or dying from HIV
in South Central, L.A.,
in Albuquerque or Santa Fe,
in barrios below the border,
the Sudan, the streets of
Calcutta or North Korea,
the armless children
in Iraq, the legless soldiers of
all countries, the untold numbers
of grieving parents, brothers, sisters,
& lovers.
I looked & found
lovely yellow & orange wild flowers
growing in a white planter shaped
like a cross.

– Clifton Snider

Saved

She never met a man
who didn't like to do it
in the morning.
But Papo was best.
Away the rustle of cotton,
a slick probing in the ear,
to spring her hands to light.
She woke inside wet mouth and shudder,
a blue lagoon
lapping over hip and flank.
All honey, mont Vénus hailing
the sap of the world.
Drink from this tree and ye shall be saved.
Drink from this hallowed earth
and thy tribes shall come
from light breaking.

– Naomi Ayala

Secrets
(for C. L.)

Black currants and bergamot infuse the deep secrets.
The bar serves fevered water as sangria to steep secrets.
Your phone's in love, you say. It calls you without me.
Has it drunk-dialed and left after the beep secrets?
A light bulb is loosened behind the wrought iron gate;
a square under the stairs where we'd heap secrets?
Scanning the dedications in his rare editions,
the ones missing my name belong with the cheap secrets.
Winter's kimono sleeves whirl, wetting the eyes;
a clever cover in daylight while we seep secrets.
An accomplice of rapture rewinds to the crime:
"The shoebox falls twice…between breaths creep secrets."
He peels back his hood and with it hesitation.
Let want be canine. I'll put to sleep secrets.
For food, for thrill, for fucking, the appetite asks:
Isn't a hunger left hungry free to reap secrets?
Your mouth, Daniel's: they've turned into honeycomb.
Hint: their sweet walls—once?—did more than keep secrets.

                         ❧ Daniel W. K. Lee

Seigneurial Rights

Life was easy
—fur against skin—

She might have been content with it
but each morning
she hung her heart
from the big rusty nail
where the beasts are tethered
closed without noise
the door to the stable

She had promised herself she would catalogue
this space without horizon
which stretched all around her
She surveyed it
carved it into lots

that she fenced
with the ineffective barbed wire of her words

But emotions' wild horses
always escaped
They ignored her cries
cared nothing for her petty calculations
her rickety fences
which they tore away
unaware

Space belonged to them
They exercised
their seigneurial rights

                      ❧ Marcelle Kasprowicz

Sexing the Dancers

Jerry won't touch or watch them on parade
because go-go boys are essentially trade.
Bartender Joe thinks they've got to be gay
to put themselves on display that way.
Ken finds he can discriminate
since only straights appreciate
the frills of drag queen excess:
that's how they want women to dress.
Nick says it's all in what they choose
in the way of their dancing shoes:
only a straight dancer ever shoots
at selling himself in cowboy boots.
Joey thinks groping provides the clue:
straight guys never will let you
touch down there in their pants.
Zaki thinks it's how they dance:
gay ones don't camp so much as straight ones do.
Lloyd says that, if they'll go home with you
and you don't have to pay,
you shouldn't care much either way.

                    ❧ Edmund Miller

Sexual Paradox

If I could choose, I'd woo the fairer sex
And let myself get swept up in the spin.
But damned if I don't have this gender hex
That turns me off the softness of their skin.
And so I'm forced to flirt with men instead,
Preparing for that first exciting night
When we decide it's time to brave the bed.
My muscles taut, my stomach knotted tight.
He speaks in terms I barely comprehend.
That is, if he decides to speak at all.
I lie like stone beside him and pretend
That silence is a friend and not a wall.
With women I'd just know what's right to do.
But then why not? Since I'm a woman too.

                         ❧ Jill Williams

Short Cuts

The winter after your death
I freelanced
for Cliffs Notes, tightening

already tight plot summaries
for famous,
boring novels. College undergrads

wrote those study guide masters
letters
more impassioned than anything

they'd scribble to their own families
or lovers:
"Even with your invaluable help,

Remembrance of Things Past
is a bigger challenge
than tracing all the storylines

from the last two years of *The Young
and the Restless.*

I almost feel I need to read

certain passages more than once."
I swore I'd rescue
students from the torture

of sorting out Hamlet's needless
ambiguities, seeing
the welts from Dimmesdale's

self-flagellation, surveying
the duller points
in Dante's tour of hell. Weeks before

you left this world, you gave away
your Dolly Parton albums,
high school track trophies, lucky

pair of glow-in-the-dark shoelaces,
Menudo and Marky
Mark posters, cock rings, unicycle, "Don't Tell

Anyone I'm Gay" t-shirt, lava lamp,
fake refund receipts
from the Gap, and the plastic pink
wading pool. I saved the answering machine
cassette
with the first message you left, erasing

any other voices with the steady silence
of my grief.
Every night for months I listened

to you say, "Pick up the phone, you jerk!
Your books will always
be there." After a few months

I obliterated everything
except "you jerk"
and transferred it onto a regular tape,

playing it in my car whenever I left
my house to visit the forest
preserve. Where gay men in cars circled

around the watertower, looking
for a pretty young face.
Once someone asked my name.

"Let's skip the foreplay," I said.
I rushed
home and worked for hours. Still horny,

I paged through original Shakespeare plays,
drawing lines through any lines
failing to advance the plot. I remembered

when we squirmed through a college
production of *The Winter's Tale*.
You snored during the King's monologues

of sexual jealousy and grief. When I pinched
your love handles,
you jumped and wanted me to say

you didn't miss the part where the wild
bear chases Antigonus.
Weeks ago I abbreviated that scene

to a mere phrase, a present participle,
nothing larger
than the smallest of footnotes.

When I complained to you about having
to read
Crime and Punishment for the survey course

I taught, you said, "Skim the last hundred
pages. Endings
never surprise." You knew you would die

once your suicide note felt right,
unrevisable:
Sorry about the mess.

                                          ❧ Steve Fellner

A Short History of the Corset

Note the necessity of small hands, keyholes,
a dilation of the eyes, or the haunted cabinet.

Like in dancing:

lift the torso from the hips like an egg
from an egg cup, and let the chest
lead as if being drawn forwards
by an upward pulling string.

Taken from the latin, corps,
but then all nouns are accidental,
all grammar, merely chance.

We understand
no more than a pale lick of skin
beneath bone, the sighs
of cloakrooms or lilacs.

While hardly fit for bird calling, or orchards,
the body requires correction, the borders defined.

See how easily one could slip outside of a story.
Even through a locked door, quietly.

             ❧ Kristy Bowen

The Slave's Critique of Practical Reason

Ain't got a reason
to run away—
leastways, not one
would save my life.
So I scoop speculation
into a hopsack.
I scoop fluff till
the ground rears white
and I'm the only dark
spot in the sky.

All day the children
sit in the weeds
to wait out the heat
with the rattlers.
All day Our Lady
of the Milk-Tooth
attends them
while I, the Owl

of the Broken Spirit
keep dipping and
thinking up tunes
that fly off quick
as they hit
the air. As far
as I can see,
it's hotter in heaven
than in the cool
cool earth. I know
'cause I've been there,
a stony mote
circling the mindless
blue, dropping rows
of little clouds,
no-good reasons
for sale.

                       ❧ Rita Dove

Smokers on Break

Reeking of nicotine, coatless
in the cold, we lounge
in a doorway,

a few scant minutes
of kinship and bitching.
Nooses loosen and halos dissolve—

smoke shaking its hips
from tips of cigarettes
like genies escaping

their bottles. We wish
for tanned, tropical lives,
but get the office

carpet, frayed and stained, tired
Muzak droning down
the halls. Between puffs and sighs,

we scheme excuses

to call in sick, rehearse
scratchy voices

as we choke down hits
of swirling, conspiring joy,
eyes flaring.

Soon we'll go back
to our cubicles, framed faces
of kids, lovers we seldom see,

back to glaring
computer screens and the demanding
ring of telephones

where we'll clamp
down with headsets,
longing

for our discarded loves
lying on the hard pavement,
each bright eye slowly fading.

       ❧ Jeff Walt

Social Intercourse

Revealing unexpected social lives,
All the title holders among the men
Fall in with courtly escort duty when
The body builders bring along their wives:
Because they check male bonding at the door,
Like Old Regime French aristocracy
They swap spouses without hypocrisy.
The guys—who aren't out to score—
Exercise conversational passion
To share their small talk like nobility
And—pumped beyond the familiar fashion
Shaping suburban class mobility—
Surprise with relaxed elasticity,
Not uxorious domesticity.

       ❧ Edmund Miller

Song for Fernand Léger

Léger of Argentan in the parade
of mechanical whirs; motors & gears,
railways & tubes, furnaces & factories,
broke with the past.
Beguiled by the grim industrial towns,
he honored scaffolding & beams,
cylinders & slabs, smokestacks & signs,
stairwells & halls, columns & spheres.
Grids & scrolls, semi-abstract,
robot-like shapes leapt from the brush
of this proletarian who turned his back
on that grand parade of art
extolling the bourgeoisie. Yellow boomed
from his canvases, lines banded with black,
furious blues & reds stroking cool whites
through a fracture of forms, mechanical, semi-abstract,
in the dance of *la vie ordinaire*,

Léger, mon frère, like you I've thumbed my nose
at the past, at my prie-dieu, at the chiaroscura garb
of our nuns, their lips brushing cups
of sacramental wine.
I have painted in imagination the milkman's
coat gray white as the doctor who took my pulse,
advising oranges for a fevered throat.
I have thought to paint a faint purple line
between tan stubble & soot-colored sky.
When an iron beast hooted smoke across a field,
I saw the furious red sun blazing through haze,
& hid my head in the wing of my arm
all before the grand parade of art gave me consent
to march with you to the bugle & fife,
the cymbal & drum of la vie extraordinaire.

                           Colette Inez

The Sound of Grass

Let it arrive at my feet
                like a quick falling leaf
        in the first barely

perceived autumn breeze,
                or a favorite aunt's last kiss
        on the forehead

or a silk sleeve forming
                gently as a tear on a child's flushed
        cheek. Where's her lost

catcher's mitt? And will she find it
                before the game? Let it come
        in deep sleep

like the sound of grass sprouting
                in the front yard or even
        like the S.U.V.

that blew me down, crossing
                the street. Let death come
        unerringly and clean.

                                    Paula Goldman

The Speech of Cretans

On my side of the door, not much was being said. There were some people around, people I knew, and they were talking, but what they were saying was unimportant. Theirs was the speech of Cretans. Yes, all of them were from Crete, where the talk was mainly of sheep and olives. They could have talked of important things, of the Minoan culture: King Minos, the Minotaur, the labyrinth, the palace room with leaping dolphins painted on the walls. But these were modern-day Cretans, and we were on the imbecilic side of the door. So I listened to discussions of rubber boots, shepherd's crooks and olive presses. Even bestial sex was mentioned. Meanwhile, on the other side of the door, the real high-wattage speakers, the people of knowledge, the Platonists and such folk, talked about things that meant a lot. They talked about how we all got here and where we'd go after we left here. They asked whether the world was perfect, and if it wasn't, who could bring it closer to perfection—things I'd always wondered about but could never wrap my mind around. I yearned to be on the other side of the door, the side where momentous truths were being uttered, the side where people weren't Cretans.

                   ❧ Thaddeus Rutkowski

Sperm

God's sperm scorched through the void,
Sparked the innards of the bitch of chaos
Who swelling in gassy rapture
Spat worlds
Sneezed moons
Farted stars.

Instantly
Foam-born goddesses
Danced on the wiggle of the waves
Sprouts twigged, armadilloes ached.

To bees with glittering
Helmets of eyes
Tinted petals
Opened oozing nectaries
And pollens black, yellow, red
While swarms
Of skin teasers, gluttons, tiny dissonants
Hatched from bubbles
Of hot mud wakening
To seed stink
And the creep of snails.

JOY
Frog ponds gulped and twanged

TOGETHER
Gasped lovers, those sweet machinists
Panting in unison.

As mystics hymned the spume
Of the divine erection
Through an ecstasy of muck,
In hospitals the sick,

Seeded with germs,
Choked and fevered into vision,
The dying hugged their death.

I AM
Roars the sun's groin
Pumping spasms
Of perpetual fire

WE ARE
Rant the jumpy
Zigzag particles
Their slapstick dance and helter-skelter
Exploding
Into rock, brain
Blood, brine, pus and excrement
(Frantic dream)
The twitch and rage to be.

             ❧ Clifford Browder

Spires and Tunnels

I was born in the shadow of a mighty church
old as the town itself and as gray.
Two tall spires stretched toward the sky
like the legs of a lovesick woman;
she taught us about longing, about love, about
being human, being poor, wanting what you cannot have.

Now in your modern American city I write
to salute your spirit of surprise, the random core
of poets, the loyal hope of lovers, here
everything leads downward to the heart,
down to the river, down south, down to you
and down to me, too, in the subway tunnel.

I stand here now between two gods, belong to both
even when they quarrel. Here I will read you
not from front to back like a scholar of serious intent
or from back to front like a daughter of Israel,

but like a poet I invite the irradiant irreverence
of inconsistency and coincidence.

                           ❧ Gunilla Theander Kester

Starkweather: Numbered for the Bottom

He sees, at sixteen, how the world works.
His hands bruised, torn, infected half the time
from the garbage he hauls, chucking great
bins filled with rancid cheese, rotten meat,
paint cans, maggoty rats, his body drenched
in the filth of it, the stench that brands him,
that doesn't go away no matter how he washes
and scrubs. Even if he puts on a jacket and tie,
takes a girl to a nice restaurant with proper silver
and cloth napkins, he knows they're laughing
at him, garbage man in fancy pants, dumb-looking
as a little girl in her mother's cocktail dress.
They had me numbered for the bottom he'd say
later, even then wondering who did the numbering
in this world, wondering if he could rip away
someone's other, better number, re-number
the entire earth, before his own number was up.

                           ❧ Christopher Conlon

Staying Home on Mother's Day

My mother died when I was three.
My uterus never formed.
Today is a bulky set of hours
sitting on my shoulder blades
and digging like shovels
I can't put away.
I skip the party my sister planned,
stacking excuses like bricks

for an utterly crucial wall.
They will be steeping in booze.
I must avoid their cold glass lips,
reeking of scotch, martinis,
and olives and Chardonnay.

I send along expensive gifts
mushy cards, a special cake—
something to cover
the tracks of my grief,
to prove I'm not glancing
at rims of a grave.
If I sat through the dance
I'd don false courage
like a spear in my chest
or maybe a fading corsage.
I would be a giant lie
scrubbing the dishes to hurry home.

                         Janet I. Buck

Suburban Blues

You live on this planet,
you live among people
you know by sight
(and that is quite all right).
You live in this funny town
that always sleeps,
close to a gas station
and a mini mall.

You have a porch,
a park, a pool (fixed rate)
and stunning sunsets,
(though nobody cares).
You have a girlfriend
with two noisy kids,
a fishing rod, a golf set,
and a few gray hairs.

You toil, you rest,

play tennis once a week
or paint a watercolor,
but that doesn't matter.
At every game
you always keep the score,
as though to make
defeat sweeter.

A pollster once
inquired on the phone
what makes you happy.
Your answers were all wrong.
If anything,
this garbage dump of heaven
is just as good a place
to slit your wrists.

Such thoughts, however,
make you rather sick.
You eat your cornflakes,
waiting for a riot,
and wonder why it is
life gets so quiet
when one turns forty.
So much still ahead.

                       ❧ Piotr Gwiazda

[The suicide bomber is tightening the Laces of his boots.]

The suicide bomber is tightening the laces of his boots.

He doesn't want to trip and call attention to himself
as he strides down the aisle of this crowded morning bus.

Invisible now—but soon he'll be blinding:
a human form exploding, fire-split and shining,

boots tied tight on two scorched feet that fall to earth
within the wreckage and the screaming.

So much to hope for as he finds a seat.

                     ❧ Jody Bolz

Taking Our Measure
(for Jefadam)

Time turns stealthy. My younger
son catches the curve of cycles,
measures his reach, tests the steadiness
of his hands, practices humming.
Only last night he crawled
innocently to every unsafe edge
or clutched my hand like the last
limb in a torrent to the sea.
I held him hard to me, made
a cradle of myself, brimming
with humming and thin gray milk.
We filled ourselves and drifted off.
You can hold this time
in a hand-stitched pocket
with a grandfather's watch
on the end of its golden chain.
One day now, my son will lean
the cradle of himself around his own infant.
They murmur, stretch on the morning bed,
roll easy in their solitary rituals.
In a warm mist like the summer bayou
they tap each other's damp fingers,
a counting that skin remembers.
I wonder how to count the time in between.
I trace the circle and what it makes of my heart.

                          ઽ Patricia Garfinkel

Telling Time

In 1965, somewhere between a saddle shoe and a penny loafer,
a classroom of third graders computes how old they will be
in the year 2000.

Last night, I dreamed I was 43 and I woke up screaming—

Who will do the bridgework on the mouth of a thousand years?
How many pieces of piecework make a sweatshop hour?

We open our eyes to find ourselves out the back door
of one millennium, at the oven door of another wondering
when our turn will come.

Sometimes I dream that my credit cards are digging holes
in the earth to bury me.

Flirtatious first year interest rates beckon, broad oak leaves enticing
with illusions of safe shelter and after a season of spending
the shoveling begins.

I awake to find my IRA's become leg irons; my bank accounts, anchors;
and managed health insurance, an inescapable choke chain.

Do you insist there is no price for following?
I tell you there's always somebody counting.

I dream an old saxophone stooped with osteoporosis stops me
on the road and whispers: If you want to save your shoes
you have to walk through life on your knees.

Before long, I come upon a wealthy woman drowning in a chateau brimming
with overpriced art. Spattered 20th century canvases stretched as far
as cerebral will go. She tells me: the candle is lost to its own wick.

How many pins will prickle the heads of angels before the coming
of a more effective insurrection?

Last night, I dreamed that wisdom gnarled me into bonsai:
my limbs, once reaching their full spread now twist
into branches condensed and autistic.

At six a.m., I wake to the clatter of dumpsters four stories below,
the rhythm of workers clearing away our earthly waste; daily news
like a soiled baby on the Welcome mat screaming for a change.

                        ❧ Nina Corwin

Testament

My dream is to leave them
a forest that does not tremble
that immense stream of their childhood play.

The birds
dawn with all its hues

doves, mocking birds and cardinals
and a family of eagles
on top of the mountain

of firmament and stars.
I want to leave them one clear night
to revel in the galaxies

without the fog that dims the light of the moon,

the Southern Cross, the Milky Way
and the hours of fishing by the lake.

My dream is to leave them a world of peace
no garbage
and the bread of justice and necessity

leave them time to love the Earth
in the small stretch of a walk
the memory of our love
in the eternal brevity of a kiss

leave them the gold of tigers
the libraries
our house and the trees

always prepared
to survive hurricanes

that they do not find in my complaints
the annoyance of flies.

May they take note, yes, of some advice:
above all, to love each other,

not quit piercing through the heavens

to visit Iguazú
the falls, while they are not dry,
the Alhambra, the Taj Majal,
the virgin beaches,
Jerusalem, city of wounds,
Machu Pichu, Teotihuacán.

To make it to the Amazon

while there is life and air enough.

Of my body and my soul
the love that does not burn out

perhaps the joy of some of my verses.

               ❧ Luis Alberto Ambroggio
               ❧ Translation by Xavier Ambroggio and Naomi Ayala

[They saw Christ ...]

They saw Christ suckling the dogs. They saw a void in the heart's place. They saw a heap of hay, a Dumbo's ear, an ox's tail, a grain of cooking salt, a hangar, a telescope. They saw a battle between angels and demons in the depths of a tank. And then the rains came, the rains. Obstinate. Sharp. Intermittent. Impatience's nails tapping on the glass. The hours' teeth sputtering the rosary of tedium.

               ❧ Mercedes Roffé
               ❧ Translation by Janet Greenberg

This Precise Morning, February

opened before me like a submissive woman
enjoying her submission, thankful
for her Christian upbringing,
the wonderful illustrations of curved backs
bending to crooked kings, the thin,
crackling pages of man lying
with woman and woman lying
to man.

Now is the time for a declaration. As men
we are only given two:
No and
Yes, but
this is love's reduction
by heat and the constant pressure of steam.

This is existence concentrated
to separate from question; this
is the only true tendon, bone, tooth and root,
you, not you, this
is what I am crawling between
when the light finally falls my way.

                       ❧ Sean Ross

[Tighter and tighter...]

Tighter and tighter, the horizon. Broader and broader. Diffusion. Difference. As it is said of a transmission—deferred. An assumption of power, an event, a game.... An hour that is not. Which was and which is now verified, feigned and accepted, like a rite. A therapeutic repetition. Monuments. Memories. Constructs. History or creation myth. Mise en scène of a past which explains, suggests, founds, gives a raison d'être to a present somehow failed, imperturbable.

                       ❧ Mercedes Roffé
                       ❧ Translation by Janet Greenberg

To Your Shadow Beast: In Memoriam
(for Gloria E. Anzaldúa, 1942-2004)

You loved water
as only a cactus or a campesina
bred on the thirsty earth
of South Texas
can love water.

Everyone knows about your kinship
with the Goddess,
the One of many names
and the nameless one you called
the Shadow Beast.

You traded dirty secrets with Tlatzolteotl,
swapped nopalito recipes with Tonantzín,

re-membered body parts with Coyolxauqui
and borrowed shadows from Cihuacoatl.
La Llorona gave you voice lessons.

You were Yemayá's child.
In a photograph you flow blue and white
like the waves foaming around your knees.
Laughing hard in long shirtsleeves and jeans
you walk into the holy cross of the Pacific
gathering conch shells and sea horses
for the secret lover that dwells inside.

Once, the tepid tide of the Gulf of Mexico
drew you down into its green depths
and you were reborn in the corpus of the Goddess.

Oshún, too, claimed you.
Mother of the sacred cave where desire
flames into words, where words become flesh
and flesh becomes the dark Goddess of Love,
it was her crescent moon that throbbed in your cunt,
turning pain into amber, blood into gold
in the fiery gush of your tres lenguas.

Some say you had thunderbolts in your eyes
but it was just Changó sparking your warrior spirit
the same way Coatlicue tested
your facultad and forked your tongue.

Straddler of rivers, you bridged
the dark brown currents of the Rio Grande,
the two-fold consciousness of eagle and serpent,
the split in the psyche between English and Spanish,
between Texas and California.

When I met you for the first time in Iowa City
your tejana accent and nahuatl vision
your Virgen de Guadalupe earrings
brought me home to that frontera
I had abandoned like an old lover.

You moved the margins to the middle
the border to the cordillera of my own spine
and taught me what it means to be a fronteriza.

Lover of trees, you spoke
to rattlesnakes and watermelons,

the red and black of Elegua
guiding you at every cruzada.

Nepantlera de aquellas,
you have joined Sor Juana, la Malinche, and Isis
on the black lacquered boat of the dead,
your last passage on the water
where the toll to el otro mundo
is paid with the left hand.

                        ❧ Alicia Gaspar de Alba

Translation as Memory
La traducción como recuerdo

Ample make this Bed	Maple make this bed
Make this Bed with Awe,	Make this bed, so I can rest,
In it wait till Judgment break,	And there I'll Wait for you until
	Dawn Breaks,
Excellent and Fair Excellent and Fair	
Be its Mattress straight—,	Be like a Mattress Firm
Be its Pillow round—,	Be my Pillow
Let not Sunrise's yellow noise,	Let no Sunrise's yellow noise awake me,
Interrupts this Ground—	or interrupts my Peace
La traducción	El recuerdo
Haz esta Cama Amplia	Arce haz esta cama
Haz esta Cama con Reverencia,	Hazla para que descanse
En ella espera hasta el día del Juicio,	Y allí te Esperaré hasta el Alba
Excelente y Justo	Excelente y Justa
Que sea colchón firme—,	Se como un Colchón Firme
Que sea almohada cómoda—,	Se mi almohada
No dejes que el ruido amarillo de la Aurora,	No dejes que el ruido Amarillo de la Aurora me despierte
Interrumpa este Suelo—	ni Interrumpa mi Paz

                        ❧ Marta López-Luaces

Traveling Southeast Asia

America, you haunt me

I hear you like the Ghost Dance in my ears
I see you like the Twin Towers falling in my eyes
I love you like Yosemite National Park in my heart
I fear you like the broken walled Pentagon in my mind
I feel you like the Underground Railroad in my bones

Passing between borders
I keep your passport in my pocket

                        ❧ Josh Gilman

Truce

For the girl abused by her father,
The terrible is the beautiful

In between, he showed range
Embracing a new word from the family dictionary:
Fun

A pumpkin nearly half her size that he let her pick
They came home from the patch and clawed out its guts

He put the face in the window
Without a recipe, they baked happiness on that stunted, grey
afternoon

A can of condensed milk and molasses
The outside, cold as reality

Inside, warm, warm as television
They laughed when the pie turned out to be a horrid tasting neon orange

mess

Because that day, they were not tragic figures:
They were horrible cooks.

                        ❧ Allison Whittenberg

Trying to Sleep, Chicago-Paris, Economy

Now this was unexpected, even here
among the worms, the boneless host, with all
their dim, sore adjustments.

You want a drink, you wrestle for it, you
buck up whole-body, half-obscene, to birth
a bit of change. As if

mere booze could ever drown that toddler, that
mosquito din of iPods (Junior Year
Abroad to either side),

that Elderhostel massacre, next row,
of night-school French: juh sweez eyy-tran-shayy. Then
they started draping heads.

They slumped and covered up. Lopped that blue scruff,
blankets so-called, some wool alternative
(non-flammable, by law),

they lopped it over Cheap-Tix-surfing heads.
You saw whole rows like that,

like ghosts, or those about to turn to ghosts,
in hoods before the axe...

an image you could do without, a jet's
a coffin anyway, and yet beneath
these folds, these glooms—the show

in there was sweet. Was happy. Under wraps,
they had a private screening, dreamy blips.
So here's a honeymoon,

both generous and lewd, and there's a beef
which melts away to clouds whose gray is wine...
delirious the sun itself....

Was unexpected, this, the party in
a shroud, a cattle car. Perhaps I need
to get out more to know.

                             ❧ John Domini

Turning 60

A Lionel train set sufficed
when I was a boy, could carry me off
into joy, like Hopkin's Falcon,
or a slap-shot from a hockey stick

or a roller coaster ride. Birthdays
stretched out ahead, an endless road
across a continent, the pure hellbent dash
for everything. This is no easy candle
to extinguish. You blindfold me

on the way to the porch,
to the rest of my life, where
your gift of a Moon-fire maple waits.
Everything said
in its rusting leaves, the roots
that will fold into autumn's bed.

                         ❧ Arthur Ginsberg

The Twinkle

If there can be a twinkle in the eye
    why not a twinkle in the anus?
Why not a twinkle in the orgasm?
If a mother says to her young son
    once he was the twinkle
        in his father's eyes,
If a father says to his young son
    once he was the twinkle
        in his mother's eyes
And if the spark of their eyes
    and fused thighs
        kindled his life,
Was there not a twinkle
    in their balls and ovaries?
Was there not a twinkle
    in their cock and pussy?
Was there no twinkle
    in their orgasm?

No twinkle
   in their toddler's tinkler
      as it tinkles?
No twinkle
   in tow-headed son's
      boyish wetdream?
If Rip van Winkle laughs
   he's got so many wrinkles
      his wrinkles have wrinkles
Can't a poet have so many twinkles
   his twinkles have twinkles?
Can't there be a twinkle
   in a girl's budding breasts?
Can't there be a twinkle
   in the lubricant drop at the tip
      of a boy's erect dick?
So you don't believe in God,
So you don't believe in Christ,
So you don't believe in the Soul.
Well, what do you believe in?
   The twinkle.

                ஐ Antler

Valentines for a Friend Who Caught Fire
(for Martha: February 3, 1930–
New Year's Day, 1997–February 18, 1997)

                I
While I made resolutions for the year—
ironically, to right myself with friends—
you must have tossed for hours as you had for decades,
depressed, and tangled in your nylon gown.

Midnight you rose to make hot tea. You could
have dozed off, finally, standing up, waiting
for the pot to boil, leaned forward to inhale
the calming herbs—the gown, flammable

as hairspray, feminine aerosols, sheer
as the skin on your face, melted you alive.
Before you're found, unconscious, burned

from the lace neck down, the second hand

vibrated like a gong another day,
while I made resolutions for the year.

II
The cure destroyed what the fire did not;
antibiotics like lye in your veins,
a brew that could shine your oven seared
your organs, kidneys collapsed; it's dialysis

until the death you wished for many times.
But your children overrode your living will,
as children will, while I, a could-be daughter,
send these two valentines, not as a curse

on your children, who forgive you nothing;
nor ointment for a soul you denied, nor
assistance for the doctor to keep his
Hippocratic oath. But a death wish

that burns my mouth. May it kiss your unburned ear
while I keep this resolution for the year.
                                   Kay Murphy

Virginia Woolf's Pockets, Full of Stones

It was just

a simple step from the garden

like any other, the shadow,

that inarticulate specter

whose presence you confirmed again

in the bathroom mirror, abandoned

with the falling bombs, the thunder.

As on other days, there were no

morning mortar-pestle grindings

with your coffee; yet a steady

shower of stones (count the soft thuds,

the comforting clack as they land)

was filling your pockets, and you,

you concluded, life is like this.

                                  ❧ Thomas March

Virtual Freedom

Her last letter, walking papers, burned him
    though not as much as the flashes of
tracer flares, unending shrieks then
    booms of anti-aircraft missile fire imploding
his skull. He'd been promoted again,
    money wasn't an issue, yet he woke up
gasping in night sweats, surrounded by enemies,
    have to drink to sleep. The chest pains
pounding like dropped sand-bags were only
    anxiety attacks from post trauma,
would dwindle to nothing. He dismissed them
    all under slippery dark, tried to submerge
the anguish, report to a fragmented career,
    a commander nothing could piece together.

                                    ❧ Bruce Lader

Voices

Are not forever but travel centuries
strung across stone, skin, paper,
a tablet carved in three languages.

A poet through her long brush strokes
can hear that rain, understand that it fell

all night on the bamboo roof of the boat.

The night a palpable thing, rain insulates
the morning, tears leaves from the trees,
brings down the not-yet-fallen.

After, soft holes in the silence, smell of cinnamon.

                 ?❧ Mary Kay Rummel

Waking In a Borrowed Place, West 85th
(for Hilary Tham)

To wake in the morning is a blessing, you told us,
years before. Traveler from Malaysian seas,
convert, you believed in blessings, made them yours.
Now the river wakes beneath its sleeping towers,
the nightheld barges wallow on their anchorings
as tidal currents slack and turn and fill.
You cannot travel now, except in morphine sleep;
except in drifting, elsewhere, when you wake.
Between the river and its scrim of black-leaved trees
the unseen parkway wakes, grey rush and ebb,
the living carried in recurrent flow.
Gleams, uncertain, catch the river's spine.
Pigeons swoop, wheel down. A black-white cat,
a stray, leaps to its ledge with scrawny grace,
preens beneath the wind-tossed, waking trees.
Take the pathway, traveler, take the turning:
let your soul be ferried, caught, and spilled
as oil in water spills its rainbow sheen,
as silk in water wavers and lets go:
may your soul be carried elsewhere and be blessed:
may you say, to sleep is blessing, and let go.

                 ?❧ Judith McCombs

Wall

Alone, the wall that divides human from human
doesn't know how to break down by itself.
It doesn't know how.
It doesn't know.
It doesn't.

                         ✥ Isaac Goldemberg
                         ✥ Translation by Stanley H. Barkan

The Wall

The wall has pictures on it.
Why? And there are so many books
on the floor and desk.
There is a pen lying next to an elbow
and a pile of paper at a reach
to the right. In one huge way
that's all that needs noting
but in another more confused, more modern way
it's whatever thought
has fallen, like being promised
to be taken somewhere
you've only seen pictures of.
There isn't anything
planned, the whole day just sort of
swings off into the shadow over there,
swings off to the right over there
next to the picture of the farm.

                         ✥ Donald Berger

Weather Warning

Rooftops sag with new snow.
The rotten oak in my tiny yard
Slants further.

The sun, though, is high
Above our heads.

News threatens
Overnight sleet.
Roads will close.

An empty sled
Slips down a hill,
Veers into the trees.

A frozen prayer
Breaks upon a stone.

                 ❧ Jason Tandon

Wedding (after the feast)

The apothecaries of voluptuousness pour enchanted potions into the circumcised glasses left outside, on the table. The guests are gone. At a corner of the table, the bride lies asleep with her mouth open, a string of saliva dribbling into her ravaged cleavage, still feeling the touch of the groom's hands, who several hours before had tried to find what Balzac once called "the two white doves."

Someone is looking for the groom, but he is nowhere to be found. Only the cigarette butts thrown on the ground and the vomit know that he is coiled under the table, with his fly unzipped, his nose bleeding, his eyes full of forgetfulness. He dreams of a big flood, and, inspired, unloads his bladder, floundering soon in a puddle of stinking urine. For her part, the bride moans in her dreams and opens her legs, but not for the groom. For the wind.

                 ❧ Alta Ifland

What Are You Dreaming?

The sheet never covers you. You cover it.
Naked, unashamed, on your back, one knee
bent, breathing short, choked night-breaths.

I never sleep on my back, although the doctor

says I should. I make just enough morning
noise. No competition for the gargantuan
garbage truck grinding dinosaur-large down

Prince Street. Your morning erection points
a little to the left of your stomach. Sometimes
in the morning when I am dressed for work, I
want to climb back into bed, next to you.

I want to whisper in your ear in the language
of sleep, ask you what his name is. I know
he is smooth, blonde, not coarse and muddy

like me. His muscles are taut, intricate,
curvaceous. He glistens, never sweats.
You smack your lips, roll so as not to
disturb the cat, alternately purring and

hissing at your feet. There is no room
in this bed for me now. I put my shoes
back on, fall down the stairs, knowing nothing
will wake you and it's foolish to even try.

                         ❧ Gregg Shapiro

When You Ask About Your Native Country

First we'll describe Asuncion: slow-moving
          but luminous. Hot, then hotter, the sun shining
even when it rains. Lapacho trees shading streets
          with yellow blossoms, butterflies the size
of small birds rising and falling among the flowers.
          In the Rio Paraguay schools of fish move
like silver ribbons, hyacinths mass into floating islands.
          We'll talk about the people, how no one's in a hurry
and even men love babies. Taxi drivers scooped you up,
          waiters waltzed you past the tables.
We never locked the door, walked safely after midnight.
          We'll tell how everyone speaks Guaraní
as well as Spanish—yet nothing of how the Guaraní
          are all but gone, how sidewalks are tiled,
but by the river people live in cardboard boxes.
          That your niñeras kept you in so your skin

wouldn't darken. We'll forget young men in uniforms
            guarding banks with Uzis. Wars that killed
half the population. Thirty years of Stroessner,
            who sheltered Mengele, Somoza. We'll just recall
the scented couryards, that jacaranda blooms in alleys,
            and all the men are fools for children.

                              ❧ Beverly Burch

[When you crossed the line]

When you crossed the line
to Mexico, your girlfriend wouldn't get off
the bus. In the back row, Jane crouched
at the feet of Indian women. She cowered
among their babies, their sacks of dried
beans. Years later and oceans away,
she told me—Cherifa, her toothsome
Moroccan love of her life—everything
scared her—the yapping dogs
in the dusty streets, the drunken
bus driver, the rise and fall
of the land.   In Mexico City, she fled
to the Ritz just like her mama insisted.
Then you found her, flat in bed, losing
all her fluids, surrounded by flowers
she bought for herself. Sick as she
was, you made a foolish lunch date
for the next day, but she ran, flew
to Tucson where she met a carnival
freak—a woman half man or a man half
woman. She said Navajos called
this queer nadle, considered this mis-
fit a blessing.
            Paul Bowles, your lover left
you for a nadle, flirted with this fright
over dinner.

                    ❧ Karren LaLonde Alenier

The Whole Man Blooms

A dahlia Atlas
(wisteria sinewed)
with snapdragon eyes,
sweet pea ears,
the whole man blooms.
His sweat suit (bad curtain,
good theatre) outlines
a glans penis bud.

                          ❧ Blake Robinson

Wind Chill Factor
(for Daisy Rhau)

You point to a photo of your family
taken after they fled from North Korea,
your infant mother in her father's arms,
despots pursuing them the way Uncle Sam
pursued my grandparents after confiscating
their power, their land, its yield of sugar
and coffee, iron and ore, giving them
three weeks—always three weeks!—
to relocate. Before the exodus

your mother awoke each morning
in a tepid bath, her sleeping body phased
into a basin of wrist-warm water to lessen
the shock of life, the anticipated march across
the wide divide between privilege and
anonymity—snipers, land mines at every turn.

As a child I awoke to tepid clothes,
my grandmother warming each tiny garment
with her body—my socks running a low
temperature under each arm, my panties
wedged in her cleavage, my shirt sleeves
embracing her neck, her whole body
a conduit of early morning comfort
as she dressed me under the covers,
easing me into the glare of indifference,

then rage, against an alien shade or sound.

She taught me to braid my hair, gathering
the three strands, like warring factions,
between her fingers, plaiting them over and
under and over and under until a perfect braid
emerged, my world in safe and tidy harmony.

Grown up, I wear my hair in a bun, the skill
of my grandmother's hands in mine,
weaving then coiling the long thin braid
into a perfect circle at the nape of my neck,
insulating me, still, against the chill.

                                 ❧ Gloria Vando

The Winding Path

You tell me
there is a border
one should not violate
a winding path
overgrown with brambles
Their arms their hands
join
like convict's hands
through prison bars

You tell me
take possession
of the healthy arable lands
of your reason
Forget the other side
with its swamps its bogs
Resist the invasion
of your heart's creepers

Oh, do you really want me
to be my own executioner
and raise the ax
which will split me in two?

And that path which tears me apart

how could I find it
when I am still searching for the one
which separates me from you?

                           ❧ Marcelle Kasprowicz

Wing by Wing
(Peace Park, Hiroshima, Japan)

There are no old houses in Hiroshima
except this one circled in flowering trees,
the leaves a green I've never seen before,
they look watercolor, dripping with shine

but the building, the dome, its shell, frail metal,
aches from the weight of all those spirits falling
like rain, all the leaves and hair, bits of fruit
left on kitchen tables to burn, wash away.

Life flourishes past the dome near the river.
Past the Coca Cola truck parked in the road,
past the boy in a yellow hat waiting for his mother,
past an old man smoking, past two hippies

smoking grass in Bob Marley shirts, past
the *Yahoo* BB sales women in short red skirts,
past a young man in khakis sleeping on a bench
stands a cement angel, her wings bent back in the wind.

At her feet thousands of origami peace cranes
from Russia, New Zealand, Maui, and Peru,
cranes of gum wrappers colored purple,
of cardboard painted gold with blue trim,

of paper drawn carefully with small pink flowers
stand naked in the approaching storm. Each waits
for the peace bell to ring, to summon Japan's
dust children to pick them up, wing by wing, and play.

This angel stays. Watches. Stands tall
over the thousands of tiny birds, protects them
from the rain. As the bell rings she spreads out
her wings, gathers her children turned to ash.

                           ❧ Emily Lupita Plum

The Women

Into the circle of women
I entered, not knowing at first

the significance of their power
working as a double-pointed needle—

stitches, like deliberate words,
slipped into strong threads

in the small talk, gossip, and
debate, in the speech unfolding

that flung dice against the white walls
until they wore eyes

while winds lashed at the village square
with unruly tongues

and men wore the black
shadows of women unknowingly,

their deeds interwoven, their give-
and-take a bargaining that

surfaced even in the harshest
elements so that ultimately the women

wore this necklace of pride,
an adornment of rough rope,

frayed where it stretched and rubbed
against the corners of walls

they carefully walked around, which became
sinews of gold in the sunlight,

where their husbands escorted them,
beside their children, along the promenade,

their worth now displayed, portrayed
even to the other women who know

them silently, as they push the needle
through the last hours of afternoon,

as they hover

where the day does not move,

as they guide the thread along patterns
so neatly presented.

                          Donna J. Gelagotis Lee

Work

These walls exude furnace heat.
And beyond? A room to inhabit. We don
suits, state-of-the-art super-resistance.

The place furnished, exquisite
down to the green of books, red
walls, yellow sofa, blue serving set.

A plain room until a worker enters
when walls become Roccoco candy,
pulse at his every movement.

Piece work, the green book to keep tally
of gristly balls with black pattern, random,
exact, followed by violet. One. Two.

Three. That will never be enough.
The room is remade for another
task, the next green book's motif.

                          Greg Baysans

[You're back from Provincetown]

You're back from Provincetown

or Mykonos

or the Pines

fresh from the sun

bright orange joy jell

and another man's arms.

I hate every gay bar you've ever entered,

every gay beach you've ever been.

Not that I wouldn't like to believe

sex simple,

men disposable

and the heart nothing but a quick pump.

It's not so.

Open your mouth, beloved,

and let my bitterness dissolve

in that sweet sea.

John Del Peschio

You're Looking at the Love Interest

It's a long story, but basically
I'm stuck in Lincoln, NE and need to get to Omaha
to catch my flight back to Fort Lauderdale
and the person who is supposed to pick me up
has overslept. When he doesn't answer his cell phone,
I call the local cab company who can't let their cars
leave Lincoln because of some law that takes
the person answering too long to explain. The next hotel shuttle
leaves an hour from now and surely I will miss my flight
if I wait for it. The woman behind the desk says,
There's one more option—a car service—but it'll cost you.
I negotiate a price--$200 for an hour's ride—and run
to the nearest ATM to get the cash. I'm expecting a town car,
but a driver pulls up in a pick up truck. I climb in
and the usual chitchat begins except I keep pressing him—
will I make my plane? *You sure will*, he says,

I used to drive this route all the time. Why was I in Omaha?
To give a lecture, I say. For the most part,
I've stopped telling cab drivers I'm a poet for fear that they'll launch
into how they hated their English teachers
and/or they'll tell me they are poets too and begin
to recite rhyming couplets about life behind the wheel.
A lecture about what? This driver asks. *Poetry,* I say,
clearing my throat. *Oh, so you read last night. You're Denise, right?*
and I'm stuck. *My ex-wife was there. She's a poet, too.*
He describes her to me: long gray hair, red sweater.
She had the first question at the Q&A. And I'm relieved—
he gets it. He has a smart ex. For the first time all morning
I relax. I won't have to talk about Rod McKuen, Tupac
Shakur, or Jewel. *What about Ted Kooser?* he says.
Do you like his work? The driver's favorite book of his:
Weather Central. We talk Nebraska poets: Hilda Raz, Weldon Kees.
The benefits of living here: cheap rent, good air.
It's a long shot, I say, *but do you know my friend
Meghan Daum?* Before I tell him she writes prose—fiction
and nonfiction—his grin fills the rearview mirror.
Know her? he beams. *You are looking at the love interest!*
I ask, *You mean from The Quality of Life Report? But aren't you
supposed to be a carpenter? That's what you are in her book.*
He says Meghan has since talked him into taking work
on the side as a driver since he used to bring her back and forth
to the airport so many times. *Besides, that's a novel,* he explains.
He assures me he's only 70% as bad as she made him out to be
and tells me, scene by scene, his version of the story.
I panic when I see we are in Iowa. *Aren't you taking me
to Omaha? I said Omaha, didn't I?* He explains
what I should already know—that Omaha's on Iowa's
border. *No hard feelings*—he says he understands
why Meghan had to make him out to be a little bit of a jerk.
No conflict, no story, right? As long as he came across
as a sexy guy, what the heck. He slides into
the passenger drop off zone and hoists my bags
to the curb. *Run,* he says. *You're going to make it.*
He checks the crumpled bills I put in his hand—I tip big.
And his tip to me: *Just remember—don't believe everything you read.*

                 ❧ Denise Duhamel

[You've become clear]

You've become clear,
you shine like a mirror,
but looking at you I can't find
my reflection: I've become lost,
I've become transparent,
evaporated, I cloud the air,
a puff of smoke clinging to your skin.

And now that I have learned
to live at last without mass
I feel light, I walk,
I find you on the other side
of the image that I confused with you.
And I am not smoke nor you a mirror.

Perhaps you were an uncertain
series of encounters,
good-byes; I, the tenacious
hunter of forms
that don't exist, rules
of unsuspected games.

You've become clear
smiling in an Adidas t-shirt.
And I've become transparent for you,
I have no form, almost can't remember now
the outline of my skin
or if I existed:
out of so much not searching for you
at last I've found you.

                         ꙮ Luis Cremades
                     ꙮ Translation by Lawrence Schimel

Poems in French

Aquarelle

J'aime les mélanges de couleurs
d'une vague brisée en mousse
sur la grève,
la précaire chaleur
d'un feu de bois dans la clairière,
quand les oiseaux habillent
de leurs ailes les branches dévêtues
et qu'une vitre fêlée évoque
le givre de Janvier.

Comme j'aime alors être
ta reine de coeur,
atout, amie, femme, sœur
quand la tendresse flotte dans l'air
comme dans une toile de Turner
aperçue dans la pénombre
du souvenir,
quand la guitare se fait violon
et se plie aux caprices du temps.

                     ❧ Hedy Habra

Le café turc

Du fond de tes petites tasses,
Des femmes d'un certain âge
Dévoilent, nimbées de grâce,
Aux jeunes filles bien sages
Qui dans ce but les harassent,
Un univers de mirages.

Le coeur battant d'un fol espoir,
Attentives aux présages,
Elles attendront soir après soir,
Dans une ronde d'images,
Tâchant de bien fort y croire,
Des beaux galants, les hommages.

                      Hedy Habra

Chute libre

Tu es la paroi dure, inégale
contre laquelle je m'appuie
de tout mon long

je m'accroche à tes aspérités
à ces racines noueuses
que sont tes bras

et par moments l'envie me
prend de tout lâcher, la chute
libre me tente

une anfractuosité me soutient
l'espace d'un sourire,
d'un clin d'oeil

soudain, la racine s'arrache
d'un sol subitement
mou et friable

je glisse, perds pied
inexorablement
au bord du precipice

                      Hedy Habra

Délire

    Je te revois, courant au loin, sauterelle nocturne
        ponctuant de tes pas l'uniformité poudreuse
simulant dans la neige toute fraîche
      les dunes
          de sable brûlant
   étends-toi sur moi comme sur un lit familier
      j'épouserai tes moindres désirs
ôte ton masque, viens à moi nouveau-né
      suspendu
          au sein maternel
tu as laissé se faner le bouquet printanier
    que je t'avais donné
j'étire le temps sans succès effleurant les pétales froissés
     l'utopie n'est-elle pas
         le désir de durer ?
  face à la page nue, stérile peau douce,
     ma bouche s'emplit de sons que j'étouffe,
je griffonne du bout des doigts parcours ton corps,
    les mots s'entassent pêle-mêle,
se frôlent, s'emmêlent
        tatouage invisible
la soie de ta peau se dévide sous mes lèvres
      ma langue-feutre court, glisse, la pointe crisse,
je bute, trébuche, le trait final se fait trait d'union
      dans l'enceinte
        d'une page qui se creuse.

              ॐ Hedy Habra

Droit de Seigneur

La vie était douce
—une fourrure à même la peau—

Elle aurait pu s'en contenter
mais chaque matin
elle pendait son coeur
au grand clou rouillé
où l'on attache les bêtes
fermait sans bruit

la porte de l'écurie

Elle s'était promis de cataloguer
cet espace sans horizon
qui s'étendait autour d'elle
Elle l'arpentait
le découpait en parcelles
qu'elle clôturait
du faible barbelé de ses mots

Mais les chevaux fous des émotions
s'échappaient toujours
Ils ignoraient ses cris
n'avait que faire de ses petits calculs
de ses minables clôtures
qu'ils arrachaient sans même le savoir

L'espace leur appartenait
Ils exerçaient
leur droit de seigneur

                     ❧ Marcelle Kasprowicz

L'enfant merveilleuse

Au seuil de la maturité, j'ai commencé à rêver les yeux ouverts, d'une petite fille qui m'accompagnait partout et qui était moi et mon enfant à la fois. Elle était légère et vivace, sage et cependant sensible, proche et cependant lointaine. Dès le moment où elle eut apparu dans ma vie, je chassai de mon âme tout désir de jamais aimer un homme, tout désir d'aimer, tout désir ("Tout" est une façon de parler, bien sûr.). Je lui offris tout mon sang et la moelle de mes os, et me mirai dans ses yeux comme dans un puits sans fond, et l'enfant merveilleuse grandissait, et plus elle était réelle, plus je devenais irréelle.

                 ❧ Alta Ifland

L'Ettersberg
(L'Ettersberg est une colline près du camp de concentration de Buchenwald)

Ah, l'audace
l'audace des herbes folles

Oserais-je
du bout des doigts
oserais-je
sous leur peau frémissante
Oserais-je
frôler le passé
enfoui
et son odeur de chair brûlée?

Ah, l'audace
l'audace des oiseaux
Ils reviennent
Ils sont là

Oserais-je
comme eux
oserai-je oublier
le gout de cendres
sur la langue du passé?

Oserais-je
chanter?

                   ❧ Marcelle Kasprowicz

Filles du feu

La flamme s'étire, gémit
éclate scintille en crépitant,
s'élève, ondule, serpentine
pourlèche les tisons

se joint aux autres filles
du feu, esclaves d'un même

harem, démembrées, langoureuses
elles épousent l'ardente mélopée

se touchent, se fondent l'une
dans l'autre, tantôt une, tantôt
distinctes, sœurs, sorcières,
druidesses, initiées aux rites
incantatoires

elles se réjouissent du sacrifice
de nouvelles bûches, sautillent
dessinent de nouvelles rondes
à l'offrande d'aiguilles de pin,
d'herbes sauvages

la bûche rougit, se consume, bat la
mesure, les flammes se fondent, la
pénètrent, tournent sur elles-mêmes,
répètent inlassables leur danse folle,
voluptueuses, désarticulées.

                         ❧ Hedy Habra

Ma langue

Ma langue gît ensevelie au centre de la terre. Quand la nuit vient, les rêves ouvrent les portes du temps et les noirs corbeaux aux ailes bruissantes s'envolent faisant place à un long sommeil de plomb. Les gardiennes de la langue, des momies muettes drapées de linceuls, voguent dans les quatre points cardinaux, visages raides, lèvres couleur de pourpre, yeux peints en bleu. À l'aube, elles se retirent dans les recoins de la mémoire.

Ma langue ne m'appartient pas. Tout ce qui m'appartient est une longue absence fleurie aux bords de laquelle poussent des rosiers qui descendent le long de mes jambes, s'entrelacent et couvrent mon corps comme un tombeau. Ma langue puise dans l'absence ses mots de brume, morts comme moi, pour les tenir un instant au-dessus du tombeau, ensuite les laisse tomber comme des pétales de rose.

                 ❧ Alta Ifland

Mort

Un ami arabe m'a dit un jour : "Je trouve si rassurante la pensée qu'un jour je ne serai plus."

C'est là une manière de voir les choses qui est très naturelle ; mais qui parmi nous, les Occidentaux, pourrait dire cela? Nous luttons contre la mort et nous luttons contre la vie. Il y a quelque part une compagnie qui transforme le corps de votre cher défunt en un diamant. Vous pouvez l'emporter partout, même quand il n'est plus là. "Rien ne se perd dans la nature, tout se transforme," nous a-t-on appris il y a longtemps à l'école. Même la mort n'est plus sans reste.

                      Alta Ifland

Niagara

Ton grondement sourd me parvient,
obscurément étouffé par la double paroi de la baie vitrée.
De ce huitième étage, les yeux rivés à la fenêtre,
je m'extasie devant ta majestueuse beauté.
Si seulement je pouvais m'élancer à l'instar de ces mouettes
me fondre dans la blancheur de ton écume.

Rythme monotone, infernal, tes eaux bouillonnent
dans un roulement incessant, ta buée se dégage,
évanescente, épousant les nuages qui s'estompent
face à ce constant apport émanant de ton cratère ardent,
s'élançant en vapeurs glacées, caressant d'une berge
à l'autre, en guise de gouttelettes accueillantes
les visages étranges qui journellement te côtoient.

Attirés par toi sans distinction de race, ils reçoivent
ainsi le baptême égalitaire de tes puissants torrents.
Gronde, écume, exprime ta rage et ta liberté,
symbole de passion déchaînée, effrénée.
Ton grondement sourd me dérange.

                      Hedy Habra

Les Noces (après la fête)

Les apothicaires des voluptés versent des potions enchantées dans les verres circoncis, laissés dehors, sur la table. Les invités sont partis. À un coin de la table, l'épouse gît endormie, la bouche entrouverte, un fil de salive s'apprêtant à tomber dans le décolleté ravagé, portant encore l'empreinte des mains de l'époux qui, quelques heures auparavant avait essayé de trouver ce que Balzac a une fois appelé "les deux colombes blanches."

Quelqu'un cherche l'époux, mais il est introuvable. Seuls les mégots jetés par terre et les restes de vomissure savent qu'il est lové sous la table, braguette ouverte, nez saignant, oeil oublieux. Il rêve d'une grande étendue d'eau, et, inspiré, décharge sa vessie, pataugeant bientôt en une flaque d'urine puante. De son côté, l'épouse gémit en rêve et ouvre ses jambes, mais non pour l'époux. Pour le vent.

                 ☙ Alta Ifland

Le Sentier Sinueux

Tu me dis
Il y a une frontière
qu'il ne faut pas violer
un sentier sinueux
couvert de ronces
dont les bras les mains
se joignent
mains de forçats
à travers les barreaux

Tu me dis
Prends possession
des terres saines arables
de ta raison
Oublie l'autre côté
ses fondrières
Résiste l'invasion
des lianes de ton coeur

Ah, veux-tu vraiment
que je sois mon propre bourreau
que je lève la hache
qui va me fendre en deux?

Et ce sentier qui me déchire
comment le trouverais-je
alors que je cherche encore
celui qui me sépare de toi?

                     ❧ Marcelle Kasprowicz

Terre Natale

Je t'accompagne

Je suis ton vaisseau
ton équipage
ton alizé
ta voile
Je suis ton ancre

Terra firma
Je demeure
et tu m'emportes

Tu m'emportes
alter-ego replié
et sage
dans ta malle

Je suis le blé en herbe
de ton corps
le blé mûr
dans ta cale

Je suis le vin
qui n'aigrit pas
le cheptel qui se renouvelle

Je suis la brûlure sourde
de l'exil
Je suis ta voix
que j'ai baptisée

Je suis ta lettre de marque
Je suis la passerelle
qui te livre

à la terre nouvelle
et là
je suis ton bois mort
et ton étincelle

N'aie pas peur
Je t'accompagne

❧ Marcelle Kasprowicz

La vieille femme

Car Femme, elle a vécu sans flamme,
Fidèle à son devoir d'état
Noyant jour après jour son âme

Dans une barque sans rames,
Elle a vogué par ci, par là
Car Femme, elle a vécu sans flamme

Ravalant son amertume
Goutte à goutte et sans éclats,
Noyant jour après jour son âme

Et de trop veiller ses mômes,
Parcheminée se retrouva
Car Femme, elle a vécu sans flamme

Privée de fruits et d'arômes,
Ses rêves aussi elle refoula
Noyant jour après jour son âme

Au gré des flots et de son homme
Se dessécha se consuma
Car Femme, elle a vécu sans flamme,
Noyant jour après jour son âme

❧ Hedy Habra

Vouloir qu'on veuille

Une conversation obstinément
semée de moi-je.

Insistez sur l'isolement,
alors, ils seront débiles, vos idiotismes.

Rien au monde qui nous réconforte
comme un on ronde et solidaire.
Nous? Toi et moi, qui acceptons les mains
qu'on veut se tendre.
Bien, et celles de vous tous, du moins
si l'on veut s'entendre.

                     ❧ Alfred Corn

Poems in Spanish

Adagio por una viola d'amore olvidada
(..el hiperespacio proveería un medio
para navegar a través del tiempo y del espacio...
—Michio Kaku)

En el ángulo oscuro
de un desván que recorrí en sueños
        encontré una viola d'amore
reclinada contra una mecedora

único respaldo del penoso peso
        del embarazo
compañera muda
cómplice de largas horas de espera

La compré en la galería Regency,
        la que se quemó durante la guerra civil
veíamos entonces arder piras y hogueras

desde lo alto de la montaña
   lenguas de fuego
lamían los pies de las estrellas

y pensar que me serviría algún día
        en mi ahora de huesos dolientes

¿Qué más da el recuerdo de una mecedora,
cuando lo perdimos todo en Beirut?

La silla se encontraba en el ático

			al lado de una viola d'amore
que reclinaba su espalda

contra el dorso de la silla,
un par de cuerdas flojas
			ecos visibles de silencios rotos

y al cabo del alargado cuello,
la cabeza tallada de un cupido
tan polvoriento
que no se le notaban
los ojos vendados

¿Y qué más da si nadie tocara en la familia?

Sólo quisiera saber lo que esta cabeza
			escuchaba cada vez
que la esbelta alejandrina
			la apretaba con firmeza
bajo el mentón

cuando era joven y fuerte
			y no mi nonna que se deslizaba
por los pasillos
			en una silla de ruedas

sus nudosos dedos
			desgranando el rosario de nácar
bajo la mirada profunda
			del ícono virginal

La imagino tocando en el balcón de nuestra casa
en Heliópolis,
¿o estaría entonces en
Alexandría?

La veo apoyar el cuerpo inerte
de la viola d'amore
contra su pecho
y con cada rasgueo,
resoplaba una y otra nota

gotas de agua cristalinas
el doble juego
de cuerdas haciéndose eco

Tenía una manera de andar

que atraía las miradas...
hasta el día que la casaron

a los diez y seis años
   a un joyero ferviente de masonería
que no sabía nada de música

En esos días decidió guardar la viola en el ático
al lado de mi mecedora

      ❧ Hedy Habra

Alfa amor

La alondra de la tarde
se pierde en el poniente,
busca frondas de tiempo
y susurros de aurora.

Todo tiembla en la sombra,
algo late en el bosque
rumoroso de pájaros.
Libélula de luces.
Sospecha de tinieblas.

Alfa Alfa.

    El latido se extingue
y callado revive
en la forma del beso
La luna toca el sol
en la noche vibrante.

   Alfa Omega

Nada existe en la nada.
Todo vibra en el Todo.
Tu suspiro florece
en tactos y caricias,
y en el aire nocturno
arde el ansia invencible
de mis líquidas grutas.

Alfa Anhelo.

                        La tierra,
tibia y lúcida
reverbera entre el césped
de luciérnagas nuevas.
El siempre y el ayer
emergen en mañana.
Inquieto picaflor,
la madrugada
fluye quedo en tu boca
y estalla en mis cascadas.

           Alfa Aurora.

                      Haces polvo el pasado,
incineras los vientos,
desvelas universos
inconclusos y errantes.

Se despierta el lucero
en tu jardín de polen,
se aclimata el instante
en mi orquídea secreta.

Alfa Amor.

                   ಶ Fanny Carrión de Fierro

Blue jay paixao de vôo
(para Estela Porter Seale)

the drop falls immaculate
into the perennials of red
pájaro azul jay of the night
sí más bien diré que sí
la gota cae inmaculada
por el desliz de tu cintura
apasionada transparentada de luz
y allí se deposita
desprovista de sueños
que le recuerden
que es mero sudor

mero trabajo de amor
una epidermis que en ti se enciende
como canto de las llamas florecidas
para recordar la fuerza la fuerza
de tus manos
de tus músculos
la pureza de tus dedos
que martillan con la furia
de un carpintero joven
del carpintero que construye
la cerca que divide los patios
las propiedades las divisiones
y allí pájaro azul jay of the night
se establece en su vuelo de pasión
observando tu labor de hombre
de humano que bien se conoce
las líneas las separaciones
las fronteras de Robert Frost
good fences buenos vecinos
y el pájaro anonadado en su vuelo
salta de cerca en cerca
hasta llegar a ti
hombre que construyes
cercas propiedades
y te mira de frente
bien de frente
esparciendo alas
azules y negras
y le sonríes como cómplice
de una sola palabra
de una sola frase
que tú bien conoces
hombre que construyes
cercas y propiedades

                               ❧ Benito Pastoriza Iyodo

El buey:
(para Andrés Fisher)

—"Ni la pica del yuntero, ni la inclemencia son dolor. Duele saber que se traza un solo surco y que plantas, una y otra vez, lo recogido.

La punzada mayor, la misma punzada; y del más intenso frío, la memoria, no podemos guarecernos.

El arado se traba siempre en la raíz donde se traba el arado, pero el tropiezo no hace más romo el filo ni la línea que trazó más duradera."

☙ Benito del Pliego

Cabalgadura del siglo actual

Escapa de tu mundo cotidiano,
cruza el desconocido umbral,
novato conquistador de otras tierras
en tu cabalgadura multinacional.

Siente la diversidad de los sentidos:
colores, sonidos, sabores, textura
disfruta la suavidad de la perspectiva
del nuevo ángulo multicultural.

Y el pasado apolillado en el desván,
cesa guardado en el baúl del abandono
cavado en el mausoleo del olvido
y crucificado en el madero bilateral.

Escapa de tu mundo cotidiano,
ensilla tu caballo y cruza el umbral,
ensancha los límites de tus fronteras,
en tu cabalgadura del siglo actual.

☙ Efraín E. Garza

El caballo:
(para Augusto Monterroso)

—"Mienten quienes dicen que son libres porque nadie les maneja.
Oigo decir que hubo caballos sin amo, pero pienso en sus jinetes.
También el que clava tu herradura y te ensilla lleva a lomos la bota que le espolea."

☙ Benito del Pliego

Cartografía sin inventariar

Una línea, un trazo, un límite arbitrario
divide a un país de su vecino
desafiando al pasajero, al emigrante
a seguir por la cañada de las leyes
de países colindantes por destino.

Valija de cuentos fronterizos
relatos en dos lenguas diferentes
confusión que separa y debilita
con borrascas glaciales del norte
y cálidos vientos del oriente.

Precipitación de dos lluvias,
frágiles gotas de colores indecisos,
lágrimas de alegría y tristeza,
caprichosos cauces rebeldes
producidos por deshielos subrepticios.

Legendarios desiertos sedientos,
neolíticas sequías austeras,
subversivos lindes, historia ambivalente
de una geografía vulgar,
con fronteras de amalgamas
y cartografía sin inventariar.

Deslinde de frontera entre naciones,
interminable desafío al ambiente,
un reencuentro con el destino,
kaleidoscopio de múltiples matices
plasmados en mapas y tratados
reelaborados y aceptados por los países.

❦ Efraín E. Garza

Castilla I

i.
El trigo ya cubría estas lomas antes de que hubiese quién lo escribiera.

ii.
El trigo y los girasoles formando geometrías bajo el cielo de Castilla:

iii.
los rastrojos de trigo y los fardos dotando al llano de su propia caligrafía.

Castilla II

i.
El tendido eléctrico abriendo otros caminos en los llanos de Castilla.

ii.
Extendiendo su geometría elíptica sobre las lomas cubiertas de trigo.

iii.
Las torres de acero y hormigón hasta la eternidad sobre los campos de Castilla.

Castilla III
(para Antonio Machado)

i.
Un crucifijo de piedra sobre las lomas del trigo.

ii.
Apenas si crecen árboles en el llano.

iii.
Coches en las carreteras comarcales que cruzan los campos de Castilla.

❧ Andrés S. Fisher

Confesión

Trabajando en el jardín,
descubro un azotador
de color verde tan vivo

que lo miré hasta moverse
para averiguar si estaba vivo.

De repente, recuerdo
otro azotador parecido,
dos niños
y una lata de café vacía
llena de pedazos de periódico

preguntándonos que
pasaría si le prendiera fuego –
una imagen inquietante
ya perdida unos
cincuenta años hasta ahora.

Cerca, los lirios
anaranjados miran al sol,
sus flores de ayer
marchitas, olvidadas,
sin necesidad de absolverse.

Termino el trabajo
con una piedra en el zapato.

                           ᓂ Don Cellini

Contrapunto

Dos figuras invertidas,
        acero bruñido,
                cuñas de milagro unidas
en un sólo punto
        movimiento congelado,
instantánea en plena danza

¿Cómo lograra el escultor
        matizar el azul
                grisáceo de ciertas tardes
nubladas, pulirlas
y, encerarlas con la luz
filtrada de un día
                invernal?

Las contemplo: estáticas,
        sugerente escorzo,
                ademán reprimido
en direcciones opuestas,
me veo a tu lado,
        sentados en un banco
                bajo la sombra del arce

las espaldas rozándose,
        mi cabeza reclinada,
                perdida
entre páginas llenas de ecos
                imaginarios,
        la tuya erguida, buscando
                el áspero respaldo de la corteza

Un soplo de aire fluye
        acaricia las dos caras
                ladeadas
un ángulo de luz
        nos separa en pilares
                de la bóveda del templo
que nos uniera

El leve contacto,
        a través del abrigo forrado,
                nos ata al asiento pétreo
más que al cansancio,
        el cuerpo se entrega
                a su peso de acero,
al imperceptible temblor de
        de un sueño bajo
                los párpados entrecerrados

Y pienso en el otro día,
        en nuestro empeño
                en caminar juntos,
bajo el mismo paraguas,
        mis espaldas
                contra tu pecho reclinado

Recorrimos la acera
        resbalosa,
                empapados, debatiéndonos
entre risas y carcajadas,
        entre alzar o bajar

esta protección inútil
que nos enredaba los pasos.

        ಏ Hedy Habra

Cuero fresco
(Nueva York, Marzo, 2006)

Como estar.

Como vagar.

Como actuar.

Como enfilar la noche.

(bueno, a quienes les interese
el esfuerzo)

Parpadear.

Parpadear
(simplemente).

Algo de como sentir la vibración anónima.

Autosugestión.

Muta

Padre.

You look like the devil's only daughter
penciled eyebrows
dark sand spit
overrun by the evening's tide.

Marea, mareando.

En cuanto la marcha de la Tarde Épica

(Toscano, por supuesto que no, no "manda"—¡a nadie!)

Sociedad Estética Cívica.

"Luria, mijo, luria"

Perfil laboral.

Principios
Creepy.

Crisis
Impossible

Tazota
fabricada en Xianxing.

Cerveza
colombiana Águila.

Buenas noticias
de Venezuela.

Como estar

sin ser
enemigo
propio

Como vagar

contigo, nena.

Como actuar

trans-insurreccional.

Como encuerar
la mañana
con mas ganas que

César

o Hugo.

                        ॐ Rodrigo Toscano

[descubrir noches pintadas por poetas]

descubrir noches pintadas por poetas
bardos viejos de la antigua historia
es verse en los amaneceres de la euforia
que desconociendo van el nuevo pentagrama
de los colores matizados
por lo que santos de los santos
han denominado
lo coloro de lo incoloro
el misticismo de la transparencia
el blanco que ve su blancura
el rojo que entiende su carmesí
el verde reverdecido
en el helecho del jardín
    toda la sutileza de un horizonte muerto
    tragándose en la paleta del espectro
    en una noche de lunas llenas
    astrológicas
    y perplejas
    desanimadas en el sentir
    con letras iluminadas esporádicamente
    un tanto a la imitación neohumana
    un tanto conociendo el mito
    de las lluvias en primavera

                                 ❧ Benito Pastoriza Iyodo

[Dicen los del pueblo]

Dicen los del pueblo
sí, dicen todos
que tu caminar
se fue haciendo sordo
y tus pasos por la calle
                menguaron
desde que el frío azulino de sus palabras
dejó de punzarte las costillas
y los cocuyos
se enfilaron para iluminar tu camino

Entonces te perdiste

te malgastaste en discusiones
interminables discusiones
donde intercambiabas basura
y otras tonterías

Nunca supe de ti
desapareciste
en el descuido de un ápice luminoso
       que desvaneció tu imagen
porque desde aquel tiempo no te veo

Dicen los del pueblo,
sí, dicen todos
que tu andar se perdió en el camino
cuando el río dividió la tarde

                 ❧ Rose Mary Salum

Donde nació la luz

No sentiste
el sonido de la vida
atravesar la lava,

ni el grito
de la lluvia
refrescar las estrellas,

pirata,
sonámbulo juguete
del oro de la reina,

soldado,
servidor de los altos señores
que destruyeron Baltra,

burócrata,
rebuscador
del dinero y la muerte.

Nunca
nunca supiste
de este amor de hoy y siempre

que besa ingenuamente
la seda malva
de los lobos marinos
y las suaves iguanas
al crepúsculo.

     Ni escuchaste
la gentil
misteriosa algarabía
que brota de estas islas,
donde canta el silencio.

Ni encontraste
jamás
ese azul y sereno testimonio
que dejan sobre el mar
los traslúcidos cactos
y las negras tortugas
y los dulces pinzones
y las rojas fragatas
y las tiernas espumas
y las blancas arenas
y las secretas algas
y las amantes sombras
y las calladas manos
de estas islas,
donde nació la luz.

     ಝ Fanny Carrión de Fierro

Escucha

Porque habito
entre susurros,

como nieve,
como secretos

sigilosos, te escucho
sin palabras,

verbos de pausas,
voz de mármol,

el sonido de la h,
en hueco, espacio

invisible en el
milagro de luz,

en el sonido
de esta página

recordando pulpa
recordando madera

recordando tronco
y hojas

y una brisa
por entre sus ramas.

           ❧ Don Cellini

Espacio abierto

Extrañas latitudes visionarias
de fragmentados espacios divididos,
se adueñan de mí las horas solitarias,
los despeñados cristales diluidos.

Podría suponer que al fin he dado
cuanto más de mí han exigido.
Quienes pidieron más me han olvidado,
a nadie he reprochado por su olvido.

Con desvelo y empeño, convertido
en un cajón repleto de ilusiones,
me sorprendió el otoño en raudo giro,

oculto tras un sueño y suspendido
en un extraño aire de gorriones,
en el espacio abierto de un suspiro.

           ❧ Leonel Bernal

Geografía del corazón

En el sol de la tarde,
se arrebuja el crepúsculo.

Hay en el aire
cierta oscura calma
y en el cielo
horizontes de pájaros,
recuerdos.

Cómo esbozar
esta invencible
geografía del corazón,
cómo encontrar
la hora oculta
olvidada
en el péndulo del tiempo.

                      Y el reloj
se apresura.

Y la luz dibuja
las manos de la espera,
vuelve intensos
los ojos más serenos,
pone alegres
los labios
que se trizan en el beso.

Barquero,
navegante,
caballero de luchas y conquistas,
de albatros y gaviotas,
no olvides
que te adentras
en mi país de sueños.

Rema quedo,
remero,
colibrí de las secretas alas
y las tibias colinas
de agua errante,
detente
en la bahía del deseo
y aprenderás del surco,
sembrador y candela.

Y me verás
luciérnagas de amor
en las pupilas
y tocarás
el estallido del liquen
en mi axila.

Y te sabrá fecunda
esta fugaz y agreste
geografía del corazón.

                 ❧ Fanny Carrión de Fierro

El grillo:
(para Alejandra Jaramillo)

—"Quien aplasta con su pie al insecto que entró por una grieta y le incomoda con su ruido, escuchará después, más claramente, el misterio de la oscuridad y el vasto vacío del campo.

Lo difícil de escuchar suele ser lo que con más frecuencia y desazón se escucha".

                 ❧ Benito del Pliego

[el impulso sexual vestido de fiera]

el impulso sexual vestido de fiera
echa sobre mí todo el cuerpo en fuego
allá cerca de la pasión estrujada
cuando la marea despierta
al ardiente animal macho
de su sueño sol embriagado
para sacudir
encender la noche
con juegos pierna labio brazo,
hombre rey seducido
en la oscuridad
del nido de mi pez

                 ❧ Benito Pastoriza Iyodo

Lección de filosofía

La filosofía se instaló en los jardines de un monasterio
donde los monjes leían cuentos de hadas a los niños
Eran momentos de verdadera felicidad
porque la lectura iba acompañada de bofetadas
en sus tiernas mejillas

Aconteció entonces la primera iluminación:
si un cordero pudiera hablar no podríamos entenderlo
Así eran los juegos del lenguaje
y ya no sería posible alcanzar la esencia de las palabras

Entonces la filosofía se sentó en una butaca
y se dedicó a ver películas de cowboys
mientras comía popcorn y los indios caían como moscas

                        ❧ Isaac Goldemberg

Lección de religión

Al rehusar interpretar correctamente la situación
la religión puso en movimiento la catástrofe final.
Tal fue la trágica continuación de la historia.

Sabía que nadie podía decir más del humano como el humano.
Existían muchas cosas que se podían decir
pero las más profundas, las más reveladoras,
las más extremas se hallaban en la concepción de sí mismo.

Entonces la religión decidió hacer y decir algo.
Deseó ser reconocida por el humano
Y que éste se definiera por sus preceptos.
No quiso ser fruto de su imaginación.

Luego se sentó sobre un trono alto y sublime
y desde ahí dio voces, cubriéndose el rostro.
Le advirtió al humano que su casa quedaría destruida
y cualquier cosa demoníaca
tendría libre derecho para atacarlo.
Suplicó y lloró sobre el humano
pero el humano ya no quiso.

                        ❧ Isaac Goldemberg

Letanía de las olas

Para abrirse
Para compartir el dolor

Para ayudar
Para dejar libre el secreto

Para oír
Para llenar la mano

Para escuchar
Para entender el ayer

Para esperar
Para adivinar tu nombre

Para no olvidar
Para sembrar el sueño

Para orar
Para entender el misterio.

ò Don Cellini

La ley

Cuando la Ley fue entregada al humano,
su palabra repercutió de un lado
al otro del universo.
Los habitantes de la galaxia
se llenaron de pánico,
se reunieron sus gobernantes
y preguntaron:
—¿Qué es este tremendo ruido
que escuchamos? ¿Puede que se aproxime
una nueva explosión en el universo?
El Ser Supremo había prometido
no traer otra explosión al mundo.
Pero ellos volvieron a preguntar:
—¿Puede que caiga otra lluvia de fuego?
El Ser Supremo había prometido
no intentar destruir nunca más al humano.

Pero ellos preguntaron una vez más:
—Entonces, ¿qué significa
ese tremendo ruido que escuchamos?
El Ser Supremo había prometido
darles Su palabra porque el humano
había perdido el equilibrio entre
los cielos y la tierra
y el impulso físico había
sobrepasado el espíritu.
Entonces la Ley ordenó
que la vida del humano se volviese más corta.

           Isaac Goldemberg

Llévame

Llévame hacia el sur
de tus caderas
donde la humedad
envuelve los árboles
que brotan de tu cuerpo
Llévame a la tierra profunda
que asoma entre tus piernas
a ese pequeño norte de tus senos
Llévame al desierto frío
que amenaza tu boca
al desterrado oasis de tu ombligo
Llévame al oeste de aquellos pies
que fueron míos
de aquellas manos que encerraron
el mar y las montañas
Llévame a otros pueblos
con el primer beso
a la región interminable
de lengua y flores
a ese camino genital
a ese río de ceniza que derramas
Llévame a todas partes, amor
y a todas partes conduce mis dedos
como si tú fueras la patria
y yo, tu único habitante

           Mario Meléndez

Luchar

Me escurrí velozmente entre las pestañas de tus ojos pardos
al filo de la madrugada
mientras huía del caos y atravesaba continentes y mares,
y así, repleta de heridas aún sangrantes
me refugié en tu órbita sin que te dieras cuenta.

Y transcurrieron así los días, las semanas, los meses
y luego también los años,
incluso cambiamos ya de siglo;
pero la dinámica de la vida me exigió seguir huyendo
de mis heridas, de mis razones, de mis preguntas, de mis fantasmas,
de la dialéctica de la historia y también de mi galaxia.

Aquí estoy ahora; impelida por fuerzas centrípetas
arrojándome a tus brazos cada vez que puedo,
aferrándome a utopías políticas inexorables
para canalizar así mi melancolía y sobre todo mis temores.

Pero la lucha continúa y por lo tanto preciso ser intensa, más aún que el sol,
más fría que la luna; más líquida y salada que las olas de mi infancia;
más fuerte que las rocas del campo; sólida como un tronco;
definida como una Medusa postmoderna
sin cabellos y sin interrogantes metafísicos.

ॐ María-Elvira Luna-Escudero-Alie

Mapas

Un mapa vivo,
　　　nunca confió en líneas
　　　　　trazadas en pieles
con aguja y brújula

El viejo rastreador
　　　sentía
el rápido crecer del árbol,
　　　veía las enredaderas invadir
el cauce del río
　　　desaparecerse surcos, senderos

cuando las tormentas

arrasaban,
retorciendo los miembros nudosos
    del caucho, su tronco
sangrando
a su antojo,
    negándose a entregar su leche

Había visto
    la Corrección roer
con sus mandíbulas,
        pedazo a pedazo
      hasta la última hoja olvidada
que aleteaba al caerse
    el último fragmento de corteza

          o hueso,
había visto
    el tiempo sepultar signos

La naturaleza aborrece marcas,
    cicatrices
      límites y fronteras
    se renueva,
      borrando huellas, rastros
el roce de una mano
el eco de un llanto
    un aliento,
      hasta su recuerdo

        Hedy Habra

Mis manos

Más bien son garras que me aguantan la vida,
mañosas, gentiles y fieles compañeras.
Racimos de tendons y voluntades dolidas,
sostén para mi frente, serias, capaces y altaneras,

aves de precisos vuelos y certeros tinos,
en la curva de tu espalda regalada
y en la aureolas de tus senos vespertinos.
! Tan cual para amasar tu figura deseada..!

Son mis manos, apéndices que adaptan el camino
A mi diario bregar, son ellas las más queridas
Y por ende, de mi cuerpo las más sufridas.

Ponen el pan en la mesa y el cariño en tu destino,
y me hacen exaltar como un poseso
en los acertados momentos cuando escriben versos.

                 ❧ Leonel Bernal

La mosca:

—"La insistencia es virtud y condena. 'Insiste en tu ruina y obtendrás la salvación'—dejó dicho un poeta.

Se acepta el hambre y el frío, pero la insatisfacción es cuchillo que se clava uno mismo.

Un mundo pequeño y miserable, el deseo lo transforma en panal: él nos incita y él nos sacia, él nos encierra."

                 ❧ Benito del Pliego

Mujer

Maíz de Andes Incas
Soy
Vasija de aires
Expansión de fuego

Mujer de chonta azul
Columna y sábila
Liana de selva enmarañada
Mujer- Latina-Color Nuez
Siembra
Cosechada en el clímax del ardor
Dada a luz entre arrayanes y huracanes

Mujer tormenta fiebre

Caderas danza de arco iris
Mujer de flechas al sereno
Devoción infinita de domingos
Alga de mar desnuda
Misa de vírgenes inoportunas
Legítima Estrella desconcertada
Curvas de almohadas y desorden
Inventados oráculos de clásicas naciones
Mujer-Latina-Color Nuez

Dónde hallarte
para oír tus astros con melena bondadosa?

Cuándo veré tu alma desnuda y con sudor
para descubrir en la fórmula del tiempo
la mística locura del íntimo lenguaje?

En qué curva del sol estas metido?
En qué esquina te escondes que no llegas?

Cuándo lograré en tu mano
la cerbatana dicha
que es tuya y mía?

Cómo
podré izar la bandera con mi lengua
tu transparencia atravesando mi conciencia?

Dime que no estás
Arrinconado en ti mismo

              ਠ Desirée Marín

Muro

Solo, el muro que separaba al humano del humano
no sabía cómo derrumbarse.
No sabía cómo.
No sabía.
No.

              ਠ Isaac Goldemberg

Necesidad de cuerpo

Ven y toca mi guitarra
y escríbeme una canción
o un poema, o un corrido

Recuérdame de mijo
menciona los tiempos buenos
has la melodía una sonrisa

Quizás un toque de diana
que despierte mis sentidos
de pertenencia

Ven y toca mi guitarra
y escríbeme una canción
o un poema, o un corrido

de mi padre que nunca conocí
o mi abuela que si
y el influjo de los dos

La melodía puede ser Irlanda
pero no Alemana, no Holanda
Española pero no Francés

Cualquiera la entenderé
porque el alma de las dos
esta en el mismo abrazo

Ven y toca mi guitarra
y escríbeme una canción
o un poema, o un corridor

 ❧ JoseMarGuerr

La noche de anoche

Ya esta noche la noche ha terminado.
Y mientras yo vacío el cenicero
y retiro los vasos, y las mantas
pongo en orden pensando aún en tus besos
y en tu última sonrisa en el rellano,

tú te arrojas al frío de la calle,
y te arrebujas en tu cazadora,
y el paso aprietas pues te cierra el metro
y te quieren en casa al desayuno.

Y mientras en las sábanas aún busco
algo de tu calor y tu perfume
y tu constelación brilla en lo oscuro,
cruza el vagón los túneles del sueño
y en un tibio recuerdo te acurrucas,
fatigado, gozoso y aturdido,
oliéndote en las manos mi colonia,
paladeando imágenes lascivias,
repitiendo la letra de un bolero.

                 ❧ Luis Martínez de Merlo

Nonos de la estrella de la aurora

Estrella de la Aurora radia bendiciones

    Para la Madre Tierra
    Y todo el mundo
    Su esplandor es
    Un regalo del Espíritu.

Maheo mando Mujer Estrella de la Aurora
    Con maíz y calabaza
    Y frijoles y tabaco

    Para nutrir al pueblo
    Para alimentar al Espíritu

    Alegro al pueblo
    Como si fuera una nina estrella brillante

    Inspiro al pueblo
    Como si fuera un anciano iluminado

    Ánimo al pueblo
    Como si fuera una mujer de cada dia chispeando esperanza..

Maheo dijo alo pueblo Cheyenne

"La nación será fuerte
Mientras que los corazones de mujeres
No están en el suelo"

Los pueblos Dakota y Osage cantan una canción, y es el Wakan:

"No estamos vencidos
Mientras las mujeres son fuertes"

Mensajes de la creación

Para todos los pueblos
Para siempre

Mensajes en los corazones de mujeres de Arawak y Acoma

Según se separaron de las caras peludas
Y fijaron sus ojos sobre los manos cortados
Y fijaron sus ojos, y han fijado sus ojos

Mensajes en los corazones de mujeres de Washita y Palo Duro Cañón

Yiendo en desbandada y invadida
al sonido de caballitos gritando en el anochecer
al sonido de gritos, al sonido de gritos

Mensajes en los corazones de mujeres de Bosque Redondo y el bar del Caballo Loco

Según se cambiaron por sus hijos
Según se vendieron por alimentos y bebidas
No dieron nada, no dieron nada

Mensajes en los corazones de muijeres de las aguas calientes hacia sílex

Según se acaba un siglo de memorias perdidas
Según solían bailar en vestidos emergidos
Según cantan sus conciones perdidas y encontradas

"Nunca me tocaron
Nunca te tocaron"

Mensajes en los corazones de Mujeres Nativas

Para todas las que han sido tratado de maneras crueles
Para todos que rezan para acabar los dias profanos
Para todos que alojan al descorazonados en maneras amorosas

"Nunca te tocaron"

"Estás bendecida por la Mujer Estrella de la Aurora
    Y tu corazón no está en el suelo"

"Estás bendecida por la Mujer Estrella de la Aurora
    Y El Pueblo es fuerte"

"Estás bendicida por la Mujer Estrella de la Aurora"

"Estas bendicida por la Estrella de la Aurora"

"Eres un nñna-estrella bendicida"

"Eres bendicida"

                    Suzan Shown Harjo

Paisajes de USA

Si cada ladrillo hablara;
si cada puente hablara;
si hablaran los parques, las plantas, las flores;
si cada trozo de pavimento hablara,
hablarían en español.

Si las torres, los techos,
los aires acondicionados hablaran;
si hablaran las iglesias, los aeropuertos, las fábricas,
hablarían en español.

Si los sudores florecieran con un nombre,
no se llamarían Smith, sino Sánchez,
González, García, Rodriguez o Peña.

Pero no pueden hablar.

                    Luis Alberto Ambroggio

Pasajero de la memoria

I

Las noches te pertenecen
con todos los espectros y sus sombras,
como águilas nocturnas en asecho
que buscan anidarse calladamente
en el contorno de tu espalda.

Y en esas oscuridades desencantadas,
abrirán las aves sus alas de risas alocadas
para anunciar sus vuelos
que son la primicia perpetua
de lo que siempre no eres.

Intervalos negros se harán tardes,
repletos de rostros extraños
que no son sino aves en rapiña,
la envergadura de tus sueños
asolapados por la desmemoria.

Y el sueño ha de persistir,
constante en el ladrido de los perros
constante en el aullido de los lobos
constante en el revés de tu perfil
que es el instrumento del recuerdo.

Entonces, y sólo entonces,
la noche seguirá abandonada
dormida en el lecho insistente de lo eterno,
acurrucada en la sapiencia de su furia,
en las garras de la espalda enamorada
que ha visto vuelo en el éxtasis de su fin.

II

La noche se agudiza con cada sensación de tu piel
la oscuridad se revuelca en el estío de tu mirada,
esperando en el silencio de la noche
en el rotundo silencio de la noche
la imaginación de los sentidos abandonados.

Las defensas amparadas férreas
combatirán el verbo que te entrego
que construyo lentamente suavemente
en el esplendor de la noche.

Las intenciones trémulas,
se descifran en tu aliento
para escuchar para creer
el ardid engañador de la vida.

Manso como el ruiseñor
de la mañana en luz,
¿acaso te atreves a confiar
en la poesía de sus ojos?

Solo te dirán la verdad,
la verdad que no verás
en la oscuridad fácil,
desengañada y arribista.

Y el verbo te acariciará
secretamente
en el fondo del mar,
poseído de su presunción.

Sella tus párpados pues
emprende el viaje
de mundos insólitos
ocultos y perplejos.

Entrégate al desaforo
de tu piel
a la rabia
de tu empeño.

III

La lentitud de tu voz
se deposita en el desquicio
del amor,
como eco de una estela
como estallido de una espada
en espera, en larga espera.

Tarde al desencuentro
como buque a la deriva
perdido en la noche,
perdido en el día
tu sílaba se suspende.

Todo desciende todo termina
y todo será pronto

muy pronto,
en la escena final
de tu vocablo silente.

Pero tu voz sin aire
sigue presente, lenta
hallándose coetánea
de sí misma,
envuelta en su belleza.

Concurrentes de emociones,
tus labios serán los sellos
la perfección de la desmemoria,
la lentitud de un desquicio
imperecederamente enamorado.

                   ~ Benito Pastoriza Iyodo

El perro:

——"Arde la fidelidad con fuego mortecino. La felicidad que la fidelidad aporta es prodigiosa (y su capacidad de descomposición, inmensa).

Quien pinta un perro en una lápida sabe que aguardar es pérdida; la espera es un placer que surge de la nada.

El que ama el pan que dio la mano, amenaza a quien a la mano amenace; si son sus fauces la amenaza, la boca puede amenazarse a sí misma."

                   ~ Benito del Pliego

Quince Pangas

Vuelvo a ti Como
Fuego lluvia bata árbol

Como bicicleta
Montaña
Cielo suelo

Como años
Casa plato
Vestido

Como Cruz aire
Parapente

Como amazonas
Hamaca Río
Panga Palos

Regreso a donde nos dejamos
Vuelvo a mi alma y te encuentro

Pero muerto

                 ❧ Desirée Marín

Recuerdos del futuro

Mi hermana me despertó muy temprano
esa mañana y me dijo
"Levántate, tienes que venir a ver esto
el mar se ha llenado de estrellas"
Maravillado por aquella revelación
me vestí apresuradamente y pensé
"Si el mar se ha llenado de estrellas
yo debo tomar el primer avión
y recoger todos los peces del cielo"

                 ❧ Mario Meléndez

[recuerdo que un día en córdoba]

recuerdo que un día en córdoba
a la salida de la mezquita
una gitana me leyó la mano
—veo un viaje en tu vida, una mujer y dos hijos.
yo sabía que mentía

porque en las cartas de mi vida
sólo salen hombres.
aún así pagué
y seguí bajando la calle

me gustaría contarte esta historia
ahora mismo
para verte reír
pero duermes.
y si te despierto?

                         ⁂ Jesús Encinar

Risas

Hubo un tiempo en que los humanos se reunían en plazas,
parques y estadios para reír juntos
y todos estallaban en carcajadas mirándose unos a otros.

Hubo quienes se reían para entrar en calor
y quienes se reían para combatirlo.

Aun otros, de latitudes más lejanas,
reían por el goce espontáneo del cuerpo
y caían al piso muertos de risa.

Otros se reían del otro antes que de sí mismos.
Su risa bordeaba el humor negro.

Otros se reían con el juego de palabras.
Hubo quienes exorcizaban el dolor por medio de la risa
burlándose de sí mismos.

Donde no existía la risa,
los humanos vivían más dados a la metafísica.

Se paraban delante de un espejo
y no se sacaban la lengua ni hacían morisquetas.

                         ⁂ Isaac Goldemberg

[El sol también tiene su lado oscuro]

El sol también tiene su lado oscuro

pero qué importa, a menos de
penetrar este espacio vedado
ir del otro lado, retroceder
en un reloj de arena como
granos ansiosos de recobrar
su posición inicial en contra
del tiempo sucesivo

y cuán se perdería entre una foto
y su negativo en estas ondas ocultas
como el mensaje oscuro
entre las líneas de una carta
que me eluden sin poder captar
el semblante de la cara inclinada
sobre el papel que aliso con el dedo.

Lo perdimos todo al partir
salvo un álbum de fotos de mi niñez en Egipto
y de mis hijos nacidos en Beirut.
"Qué suerte," me solían decir,
nuestra familia a salvo,
ni un sólo dedo de los suyos
valía el mundo entero dejado atrás.

Nos acostumbramos a dormir
en lugares donde el sol nos hacía trampas,
escondiéndose la mayor parte del tiempo
hasta que aprendimos el moto local
        hay que hacerlo brillar adentro...

Me sentía constantemente renovada,
como una cebolla despojándose, hoja tras hoja,
descubriendo un tierno centro,
        une primeur à déguster,
            pero tan vulnerable,

cada nueva identidad que abrazaba,
eran alas que crecían para doblarse
y envolver la desnudez como manos
unidas en una oración en varias lenguas
mientras los hijos se rebelaban
en contra de lo venido de tierras lejanas
y echaban raíces en el Nuevo Mundo

Año tras año, Navidades y fotos se sucedieron
para apresar la felicidad en sonrisas congeladas
hasta que perdí la cuenta al mirarlas de lo
que se escondiera bajo la superficie.

Como pudiera separarme de mis retratos
en blanco y negro, de cuando era niña
y nadie me obligaba a sonreír
pero sabía lo mucho que me querían...fotos
de mis padres sentados en un aeroplano de cartón
a punto de despegar...
            ...mi madre con un tocado
de fieltro, un velo cubriéndole
parte de la cara ladeada
en una mirada enigmática...
...a la Garbo...
...mi padre de chistera
y pañuelo blanco, a su lado.

Te veo posando con nosotros
en tu papel de madre perfecta,
tu edad, la mía, pero nunca parecías feliz...
...nada como nuestras fotos
los cuatro radiantes año tras año...

Me acostumbré a sonreír, sabes,
ayuda a esconder arrugas,
me hace parecer más joven.
Después de capturar el sol por dentro,
ahora la presión, en estas nuevas tierras
por un ideal de belleza inalcanzable.

                       ❧ Hedy Habra

Soneto a la indiferencia

Desafiante tu cuerpo se desliza
en la penumbra convexa de la noche.
Detrás quedan tus pasos y la brisa,
jugando al Escondido entre los coches.

Desde el blanco árbol y en las ramas se estremece
un torbellino de hojas amputadas

que el frío columpia y columpiando mece
como dorada llovizna en la calzada.

Gime desolado un gato hambriento
desde el abismo profundo de las sombras.
! Que no quiere alcanzarte mi pensamiento...!

Ahora que todo en mi has detenido,
la verdad, no me duele ni me asombra,
sentirme solo, saber que al fin te has ido.

&ep; Leonel Bernal

Son las siete

Son las siete y camino
la ciudad, la mañana,
no sé cómo, con paso
confundido, dos frases
de consuelo y bien pocas
ocupaciones salvo
el tiempo, deambulando.

Sueño, con luz incierta
en la bahía, horas
que no encuentran dueño.
Sin recordar camino
la mañana de zanjas,
las obras del convento.

Sonríe una muchacha:
"Allá se pierde —dice—
mi novio sin memoria."
La miro y no me acuerdo,
de tanto no acordarme
me viene un sentimiento:
soy un niño que mira
y olvida, como
si mirase de nuevo.

La ciudad a las siete,
camino y se deshace.

&ep; Luis Cremades

Sodoma

Y descendieron a la tierra.
Pura belleza masculina jamás por mortal contemplada.
Anduvieron perdidos, desconcertados buscaron la señal.

Guiados por mano divina encontraron a "Sodoma",
y en el neón volandera promesa azul.
Y Lot les dijo: "bienvenidos, son 12 euros, tiempo máximo ocho horas".

Depositaron sus pertenencias. Recibieron toalla, sandalias, condones.
Un chasquido eléctrico les abrió la puerta. Se adentraron por las calles de la
        ciudad.
Níveos zulejos narcisos, cataratas verdiazules, incandescencias termales.

Ya en la sombra docenas de hombres
jóvenes paseaban indolentes toallas y cintura,
celebración de cuerpos livianos, hermandad ancestral.
Los adultos huían de la luz reveladora del tiempo,
sus invisibles cansados cuerpos acechaban la ocasión.

Se refrescaron en la terma jugetona de burbujas.
Reposaron en los gemidos del porno. Se sentaron en el vapor.
Febril calor, deshidratante aliento de horno que abrasa la vista,
agobia la respiración, hace imposible la palabra. Era como estar en el infierno,
mientras la luz esparcía acólitos de las tinieblas.
Los ángeles sudaban copiosamente.

La cercanía de otros cuerpos era tangible como una amenaza.
Los ángeles temieron que los golpearan. Podían haberlos golpeado hasta matarlos

No hubo golpes, sólo caricias y besos.
La semioscuridad velaba el anonimato.
Las manos eran ojos obedeciendo su ley.
Una masa ardiente de lava los cubrio.
Una oleada de deseo los atravesó.
Todo se desarrolló en silencio. Todo fue urbano, elegante, cortés.

Después,
pausado caminar de sandalias, suspiro de puertas, silencio de grifos, rumor que se
        aleja.

De vuelta al cielo, redactaron el informe sobre la hospitalidad de los sodomitas.
Y Dios, premiándolos, les envió un día de abril tan largo que nunca tuvo fin.

ಎ Juan M. Godoy

Sueños hechos añicos

Añicos de un jarrón de porcelana
que cae rotundamente en suelo firme.
Arte del legendario oriente milenario
en segmentos esparcidos por los siglos.

Emigrantes que no coronan sus destinos,
balseros que no arriban a otras riberas
son los sueños hechos pedazos
por las atalayas migratorias sempiternas
que interceptan el sueño legionario
del frustrado y estropeado aventurero.

Sueños sin lograr, sueños hechos añicos
por el código impávido de los hombres,
por intemperantes leyes de la naturaleza
que se confabulan contra el emigrante.

Un río traicionero que sumerge,
un golfo transparente que delata,
por mar y tierra perseguidos,
peregrinos soñadores emigrantes,
eternos prisioneros de los sueños,
de los sueños estrellado, hechos añicos.

                         ༄ Efraín E. Garza

"Te beso"

aunque te asuste el arco de mi deseo porque te conocí tarde
en mis noches lunares
cuando la lluvia del trigo fecunda la tierra
un relámpago acuático
corona mi mente de una luz irasol

aunque sea en mis pensamientos
desde ese lugar que te llena el cuerpo de magnolias
y de irasols que se abren con la luna
busco tu imagen entre las olas

la espuma no te contiene,

es el bramar del mar en su eterno movimiento que te llama
porque con cada rizo vuelve tu nombre
para acariciar la orilla de mis labios

ಊ Rose Mary Salum

Te has vuelto claro

Te has vuelto claro,
brillas como un espejo
pero al mirarte no distingo
mi reflejo: me he perdido,
me he hecho transparente,
evaporado, húmedo el aire,
un vaho pegado a tu piel.

Y ahora que he aprendido
a vivir por fin sin materia
me siento ligero, camino,
te encuentro al otro lado
de la imagen que confundí contigo.
Y no soy vaho ni tú un espejo.

Tal vez fueras una serie
aleatoria de encuentros,
despedidas; yo el tenaz
cazador de formas
que no existen, reglas
de juego insospechadas.

Te has vuelto claro
sonriendo en camiseta adidas.
Y yo transparente por ti,
no tengo forma, ya casi no recuerdo
los contornos de mi piel
ni si tuve existencia:
de tanto no buscarte
al fin te he encontrado.

ಊ Luis Cremades

Testamento

Mi ilusión es dejarles
un bosque que no tiemble
aquel inmenso arroyo de sus juegos infantiles

de los pájaros
el amanecer con todos sus matices

palomas, calandrias y cardenales
y una familia de águilas
unida en la montaña

del firmamento y los astros
quiero dejarles una noche transparente
para que gocen las galaxias

sin esa neblina que apaga el brillo de la luna

la cruz del sur, la vía láctea
y las horas de pesca junto al lago

mi ilusión es dejarles un mundo en paz
nada de basura
y el pan justo y necesario

dejarles tiempo para que amen a la tierra
en el pequeño tramo de una caminata
el recuerdo de nuestro amor
en la brevedad eterna de los besos

dejarles el oro de los tigres
las bibliotecas
nuestra casa y los árboles

siempre dispuestos
a sobrevivir los huracanes

que en mis quejas no encuentren
el fastidio de las moscas.

Guarden, sí, algunos de mis consejos:
sobre todo, que se amen

no dejen de atravesar el cielo

visiten Iguazú
las cataratas, mientras no se sequen

el Alhambra, el Taj Majal
las playas vírgenes
Jerusalem, ciudad de heridas
el Machu Pichu, Teotihuacán.

Lleguen hasta el Amazonas
si les alcanza la vida y el aire.

De mi cuerpo y de mi alma
el amor que no se quema

tal vez la felicidad de algunos de mis versos.

☙ Luis Alberto Ambroggio

Author Biographies

Karren LaLonde Alenier is the author of five collections of poetry, including *Looking for Divine Transportation*, winner of the 2002 Towson University Prize for Literature. *Gertrude Stein Invents a Jump Early On*, her opera with composer William Banfield and Encompass New Opera Theatre artistic director Nancy Rhodes premiered in New York City in June 2005. Her latest book is *The Steiny Road to Operadom: The Making of American Operas*. Website: www.steinopera.com.

Luis Alberto Ambroggio, member of the North American Academy of the Spanish Language and PEN, is the author of ten published books of poetry. His poetry is recorded in the Archives of the Hispanic-American Literature of the Library of Congress.

Xavier Ambroggio is a translator of Spanish literature.

John Amen is the author of two collections of poetry: *Christening the Dancer* (Uccelli Press, 2003) and *More of Me Disappears* (Cross-Cultural Communications, 2005). He has also released one CD, *All I'll Never Need* (Cool Midget, 2004). Amen founded and continues to edit the award-winning literary bimonthly, *The Pedestal Magazine*. Website: www.johnamen.com.

Antler, former Milwaukee Poet Laureate, has recently had work appear in the anthologies *Poets Against the War* and *Comeback Wolves: Welcoming the Wolf Home*. His poem "Whitmansexual" from his *Selected Poems* was just set to music by Pulitzer Prize-winning composer David Del Tredici for New York City's Gay Men's Chorus.

Naomi Ayala, recipient of numerous awards and fellowships, is the author of two books of poetry: *Wild Animals on the Moon* and *This Side of Early*. She has been featured on *Poetry Daily*, and her poems and book reviews have appeared in such publications as *Ploughshares*, *MARGIN: Exploring Modern Magical Realism*, *Saheb Ghalam Daily* (Afghanistan), *Feminist Teacher*, and the *Washington Post*.

Stanley H. Barkan is the editor/publisher of the *Cross-Cultural Review Series of World Literature and Art*, which in the past thirty-six years has produced about 350 titles in fifty different languages. His translations and co-translations, besides Spanish, include Bengali, Hebrew, Italian, Macedonian, Polish, Romanian, Russian, Serbian, and Sicilian, while his own poetry has been translated into twenty-two different languages.

Greg Baysans has recently been published in *Plankton*, *Cherry Blossom Review*, *OYEZ*, and *Coe Review*. Co-founder of the *James White Review* and one-time crossword puzzle creator (cruciverbalist) for *Outweek* magazine, he resides in Portland, Oregon. His biographic essay on poet Harold Norse is posted at *www.glbtq.com*.

Gary Beck has spent most of his adult life as a theater director. His original plays and translations of Moliere, Aristophanes, and Sophocles have been produced Off-Broadway. His short stories have recently appeared in numerous literary magazines.

Mel Belin's first book, *Flesh That Was Chrysalis*, was published by The Word Works, Inc. He has been a winner of *Potomac Review*'s third annual poetry competition, a runner-up in an *Antietam Review* competition, and published widely in journals and magazines nationwide. His poetry has been aired on a program distributed by National Public Radio.

Donald Berger's books are *Quality Hill* (Lost Roads Publishers) and *The Cream-Filled Muse* (Fledermaus Press), and his poems have also appeared in many publications including the *New Republic*, *Conjunctions*, *Tri-Quarterly*, and the *Iowa Review*. He has taught for twenty-seven years, currently in the creative writing program at the University of Maryland and at Montgomery College in Maryland. In 2005 he was the Poet Laureate of the city of Takoma Park, Maryland.

David Bergman, professor at Towson University, is the author of two books of poetry, *Cracking the Code*, the winner of the George Elliston Prize, and *Heroic Measures*. He is also the author of two critical studies, *Gaiety Transfigured* and *The Violet Hour: The Violet Quill and the Making of Gay Culture*. He is the editor of many books, including the award-winning series *Men on Men: New Gay Fiction*. In 2009, the collection *Gay American Autobiography* and a translation (with Katia Sainson) of *The Selected Poems of Jean Senac* will be published.

Leonel Bernal, born in Cuba, resides in the USA where he paints, sculpts, and writes. His work has appeared in various periodicals in New Jersey as well as those in Madrid, such as the anthologies *Calma Infinita* and *Poetic Voices Without Borders*. He has written five novels, four collections of poetry and several unpublished short stories, for his love is the arts.

Jody Bolz, the author of *A Lesson in Narrative Time* (Gihon Books, 2004), has published widely in literary journals (the *American Scholar, Indiana Review,* and *Ploughshares*, among them) and in many poetry anthologies. She taught for more than twenty years at George Washington University, serving twice as acting director of the creative writing program there. Bolz edits *Poet Lore*, America's oldest poetry magazine, established in 1889.

Louis E. Bourgeois teaches philosophy and writing at the University of Mississippi. His latest book, *Colleen*, is forthcoming by Vox Press.

Kristy Bowen is the author of several chapbooks, the most recent titled *the unhappiness of objects* and her work has appeared and/or is forthcoming in *Another Chicago Magazine, Slipstream, Rhino, Cranky,* and *Spoon River*. In 2004, she was awarded first place in the Poetry Center of Chicago's 10th Annual Juried Reading. She edits the online journal *Wicked Alice*, and runs *Dancing Girl Press*, dedicated to publishing chapbooks by women poets.

Clifford Browder's poetry has appeared in *Snake Nation Review, Hawaii Review,* the *Chattahoochee Review, Heliotrope, Runes,* and elsewhere. He is also the author of two published biographies and a critical study of the French Surrealist poet André Breton.

Janet I. Buck, a seven-time Pushcart Nominee, has had poetry appear recently in *2River View, Offcourse,* and the *Pedestal Magazine*. The collection of poetry, *Tickets to a Closing Play*, was the winner of the 2002 Gival Press Poetry Award, and her third collection, *Beckoned by the Reckoning*, was released by PoetWorks Press in the spring of 2004. Buck teaches writing courses for Rogue Community College in southern Oregon.

Beverly Burch's recent work appears in *New England Review, Ontario Review, Poetry Northwest,* the *Antioch Review, Southern Poetry Review, North American Review,* and *Southern Humanities Review*. Her first book, *Sweet to Burn*, won the 2003 Gival Press Poetry Award and a Lambda Literary Award. She is a psychotherapist in Berkeley, California.

Norma Elía Cantú has published articles, essays, poetry and fiction about the USA/Mexican border. Her award winning novel, *Canicula: Snapshots of a Girlhood en la Frontera* received the Premio Aztlán; she is currently finishing another novel, *Champú, or Hair Matters*. She currently serves as professor of English and U.S. Latina/o Studies at the University of Texas at San Antonio.

Fanny Carrión de Fierro has published numerous works of poetry, fiction, and literary criticism, and has received several national and international literary prizes, including the Juana de Ibarbourou Poetry Prize, Lions Club Poetry Prize, Montevideo Poetry Prize, and the Gabriela Mistral Poetry Prize, as well as awards from Feminine Culture Club in Quito. She has taught at several universities in the United States as a Fulbright scholar and a visiting professor. Currently, she teaches at the Catholic University in Quito, Ecuador.

Grace Cavalieri is the author of several books of poetry and twenty-one produced plays; she produces/hosts public radio's "The Poet and the Poem" from the Library of Congress. She holds the Bordighera Poetry Award and a Paterson Prize for Poetry.

Don Cellini is a poet, translator, and photographer who teaches at Adrian College. He is the author of two books of poems, *Approximations/Aproximaciones* (2005) and *Inkblots* (2008), published by March Street Press. His electronic chapbook of translations *Like This Blind Dust/Como esta tierra ciega: Poems by Elías Nandino* was published by www.LanguageandCulture.net (2007).

Ye Chun, a native of China, has published one book of poetry: *Travel Over Water* (The Bitter Oleander Press).

Martha Collins is the author of the book-length poem *Blue Front* (Graywolf, 2006), which focuses on a lynching her father witnessed when he was five years old. She has published four earlier collections of poems and a recent chapbook, *Gone So Far* (Barnwood, 2005), and has co-translated two collections of poetry from the Vietnamese, most recently *Green Rice* by Lam Thi My Da (Curbstone, 2005, with Thuy Dinh). She is one of the editors of *Field* magazine and the Oberlin College Press.

Christopher Conlon is the author of three books of poems *Gilbert and Garbo in Love*, *The Weeping Time*, and *Mary Falls: Requiem for Mrs. Surratt* as well as a novel, *Midnight on Mourn Street*. He lives in Silver Spring, Maryland.

Alfred Corn is the author of nine books of poems, the most recent titled *Contradictions*. Fellowships and prizes awarded for his poetry include the Guggenheim, the NEA, an Award in Literature from the Academy and Institute of Arts and Letters, and one from the Academy of American Poets. In 2005-2006, he taught for the Poetry School in London and in 2007 directed a poetry week at Wroxton College in Oxfordshire.

Nina Corwin is a social worker and the author of one collection of poetry, *Conversations with Friendly Demons and Tainted Saints* (Puddin'head Press, 1999). Recent work is published or forthcoming in *ACM*, *Hotel Amerika*, *Mudfish*, *New Ohio Review*, and *Southern Poetry Reviews*.

Roy Cravzow is a professional translator of literature.

Luis Cremades is the author of the poetry collections *El animal favorito* (Pre-Textos, 1991), *Los límites de un cuerpo* (Pre-Textos, 1999) and *El colgado* (Dilema, 2004), as well as *Don Quijote para triunfar* (Martinez Roca, 2005), a manual for business leaders on learning from El Quijote for executive success. He has translated into Spanish the poetry of Rudyard Kipling, as well as non-fiction books by Harold Bloom and Jonathan Culler. Since 1980 he has lived in Madrid, where he divides his time between the independent consulting firm Ergot Consultores and teaching creative writing at the Escuela de Letras.

Teri Ellen Cross holds an MFA in Poetry from American University. A Cave Canem fellow, her poems have been published in many anthologies and online. She resides in Silver Spring, Maryland.

Shome Dasgupta holds an MFA from Antioch University-Los Angeles in Creative Writing. His work has appeared in the *Quiet Feather*, *Magma Poetry*, the *Chickasaw Plum*, the *Fifth Di...*, and *Si Señor*.

Bradley Warren Davis has worked as a translator and interpreter in various roles as a bilingual attorney and educator. His translations have appeared in newspapers, literary publications, and magazines including *Arte en Luz y Literatura*, *Mystralight*, *Visible and Literal*. He wrote the introduction and English translation for the bilingual edition of *A Matter of Men* by Benito Pastoriza Iyodo, which was published in August 2008.

John Del Peschio lives in Brooklyn Heights. His work has appeared in www.lodestarquarterly.com and *modern words: a thoroughly queer literary journal*. He often walks past a wooden building that in the 1840s was a men's hairdressing parlor; he likes to think Whitman went there.

Benito del Pliego has lived between Spain and the USA since 1997. He teaches at Appalachian State University in North Carolina. His publications include: *Fisions* (Madrid, 1997), *Alcance de la mano* (New Orleans, 1998), *Indice* (Valencia, 2004), and a new collection *Fábula* (Madrid, 2008).

John Domini has won awards in all genres, most recently an Iowa Major Artist grant for creative non-fiction. His poetry has appeared in *Meridian* and elsewhere, and his latest novel is *A Tomb on the Periphery* (Gival Press, 2008).

Rita Dove, former Poet Laureate of the United States and of the Commonwealth of Virginia, has won numerous awards, including the 1987 Pulitzer Prize in Poetry and, most recently, the 2003 Emily Couric Leadership Award. She has written seven books of poetry and a play, *The Darker Face of the Earth*, which was produced at the Kennedy Center in Washington, DC and the Royal National Theatre in London.

Denise Duhamel's most recent poetry title, *Two and Two* (University of Pittsburgh Press, 2005), is the winner of Binghamton University's Milt Kessler Book Award. A recipient of an NEA Fellowship, she teaches poetry at Florida International University in Miami.

Jesús Encinar is a Spanish entrepreneur whose companies include www.Idealista.com, www.Floresfrescas.com, and www.11870.com. Translations of his poems have appeared or are forthcoming in *Knockout*, the *Windy City Times*, and the British journal *Chroma*.

J. Glenn Evans has written three books of poetry: *Window In The Sky*, *Seattle Poems*, and *Buffalo Tracks*; two novels, *Broker Jim* and *Zeke's Revenge*, and several community histories. A native of Oklahoma, he has lived in Seattle since 1960. He is a former stockbroker/investment banker, a founder of *PoetsWest, Activists for a Better World*, and a general all-around political activist.

Edward Falco's most recent books are the collection of short fiction/prose poems, *In the Park of Culture*, from the University of Notre Dame Press; the novel, *Wolf Point*, from Unbridled Books; and the short story collection, *Sabbath Night in the Church of the Piranha*, also from Unbridled. He teaches in the MFA program at Virginia Tech.

Steve Fellner's first book of poems, *Blind Date with Cavafy*, was released last year from Marsh Hawk Press. It won the Thom Gunn Award for Gay Poetry. He currently teaches at SUNY Brockport.

Andrés S. Fisher, born in Washington, DC, was raised in Chile and lived for 15 years in Spain where he obtained his PhD. Since 2004 he's been in the USA and teaches at Appalachian State University, Boone, NC. His last two books of poetry are *Hielo* (Spain, 2000) and *Relación* (Chile, 2008), and his bilingual anthology of Haroldo de Campos's poems was published in 2008 in Spain.

Patricia Garfinkel has published three books of poetry, the latest, *Making the Skeleton Dance* (George Braziller Publishers). She has published numerous poems in literary journals and magazines, won two Poetry-in-Public-Places awards, and gave the first poetry reading ever held at the National Air and Space Museum. She is a senior science policy analyst and speech writer for the director and deputy director of the National Science Foundation.

Efraín E. Garza, professor of Spanish at the University of Northern Colorado, is a member of the Colorado Poets Center. Among his publications are: *Acuarela de la Vida* (Editorial Verbum Madrid, 2003), *Las leyendas de Bécquer y su aproximación al simbolismo francés* (Edwin Mellen Press, 2006).

Alicia Gaspar de Alba, an award-winning native of the El Paso/Ciudad Juárez area, is a professor at UCLA who has written extensively about the Chicana/o experience. Her most recent work includes: *Calligraphy of the Witch: A Novel, Desert Blood: The Juárez Murders*, which won a Lambda Literary Award, and numerous other books and academic articles.

Bernadette Geyer is the author of the chapbook *What Remains* (Argonne House Press). Her poems have appeared in the *Midwest Quarterly, Hotel Amerika, South Dakota Review, Beltway Poetry Quarterly* and elsewhere. Geyer lives in Vienna, Virginia, where she works as a freelance writer and editor.

John Gilgun states, "I fall in love too easily. I fall in love too fast. I fall in love too terribly hard for love to ever last."

Josh Gilman is searched by custom agents every time he leaves the United States. When he asks the agents rummaging through his bag why he is always personally searched at the gate before the plane takes off, one officer once replied, "You have just been to too many strange places in too little time."

Aside from traveling, his writing has appeared in *Exquisite Corpse*, *Earth First! Journal*, and *Napalm Health Spa*.

Shannon Gilreath is a professor and the author of books, essays, and poetry. His writing and poetry appears in numerous national and international publications. He lives in Winston-Salem, North Carolina, where he teaches at Wake Forest University.

Arthur Ginsberg is a neurologist and poet based in Seattle. He has studied poetry at the University of Washington and at Squaw Valley with Galway Kinnell, Sharon Olds, and Lucille Clifton. Recent work appears in the anthologies, *Blood and Bone*, and *Primary Care*, from University of Iowa Press. He was awarded the William Stafford prize in 2003.

Dana Gioia, the outgoing NEA Chairman, is a poet and critic. His poetry collection, *Interrogations at Noon*, won the 2002 American Book Award, and his volume *Can Poetry Matter?*, which was a finalist for the National Book Critics Circle award, is credited with helping to revive the role of poetry in American public culture. Under his direction *The Big Read* has become the largest literary program in the history of the federal government.

Robert L. Giron, founder of Gival Press, has written five collections of poetry and is the editor of the *Poetic Voices Without Borders* series and the online journal ArLiJo.com. He teaches English and creative writing at Montgomery College-Takoma Park/Silver Spring, Maryland, where he also serves as a poetry editor for *Potomac Review*.

Juan M. Godoy, a professor of Spanish at San Diego State University, has published a book, *Cuerpo, deseo e idea en la poesía de Luis Antonio de Villena*, numerous articles on Spanish literature, short stories, and poems. His academic research centers upon twentieth-century gay Spanish authors including Vicente Aleixandre, Luis Cernuda, Federico García Lorca, Juan Gil-Albert, and Emilio Prados.

Isaac Goldemberg, born in Perú, has lived in New York since 1964. He is the author of three novels, a collection of short fiction, twelve collections of poetry and two plays. His novel *The Fragmented Life of Don Jacobo Lerner* was selected by a panel of international scholars convened by the National Yiddish Book Center as one of the hundred greatest Jewish books of the last 150 years. He is the recipient of the 1977 Nuestro Award in Fiction, the Premio Estival de Teatro (2003), and of the Orden de Don Quijote (2005), an award received in previous years by such authors as Camilo José Cela, Fernando Arrabal, and Elena Poniatowska.

Paula Goldman's book *The Great Canopy* won the 2004 Gival Press Poetry Award. New poems are forthcoming in *Prairie Schooner* and *North American Review*. Her award winning poem "In the Musée d'Orsay" is included in *Conversation Pieces: Poems that Talk to Other Poems* (Knopf). She is a docent and lecturer at the Milwaukee Art Museum.

Patricia Gray's book *Rupture* was chosen by the Montserrat Review as one of the best books of poetry for 2005. In 2006, she received an Artist's Fellowship from the DC Commission on the Arts and Humanities, and in June 2007 she was a guest poet at the South Carolina Spoleto Festival. Gray coordinates the Poetry and Literature Center at the Library of Congress, where she has directed the Poetry at Noon reading series for fourteen years.

Janet Greenberg has published pioneering works on the autobiographical genre and Argentine women writers from the 1920s to the present. Her co-authored publications in this area include *Women, Culture and Politics in Latin America* (University of California Press, 1990). Mercedes Roffé's *Like the Rains Come: Selected Poems* (1978-2006) is her first book-length poetry translation.

Benjamin S. Grossberg has taught poetry writing and Early Modern English literature. His poems have appeared in many journals including *Paris Review* and *Southwest Review*, and in *The Pushcart Book of Poetry: The Best Poems from the First 30 Years of the Pushcart Prize*. His chapbook, *The Auctioneer Bangs his Gavel*, was published by Kent State in 2006. *Underwater Lengths in a Single Breath*, winner of the 2005 Snyder Prize, will be published by Ashland Poetry Press.

José Marcial Guerrero, **JoseMarGuerr**, is a disabled veteran living in West Tennessee as a transplant from Laredo, Texas. He writes with the cultural duality that permeates his heart and soul. "De las raíces crece el sentimiento" he always says and, thusly, he walks the rich and varied no man's land which in wisdom truly has no borders.

Piotr Gwiazda is the author of *Gagarin Street: Poems* (Washington Writers' Publishing House, 2005). He has been a Writer-in-Residence at the James Merrill House in Stonington, Connecticut.

Hedy Habra, born in Egypt of Lebanese origin, received her MFA and a PhD in Spanish from Western Michigan University. Her poetry and fiction in English, Spanish, and French appear in anthologies and many journals including *Puerto del Sol*, *Nimrod*, and *Poet Lore*.

Joy Harjo has published six books of poetry. Her latest is *How We Became Human, New and Selected Poems* (W.W. Norton). She has received several awards, including the 2002 Eagle Spirit Award from the American Indian Film Festival for Outstanding Achievement, the 2002 Lifetime Achievement Award from the Oklahoma Center for the Arts, and an Oklahoma Book Arts Award for *How We Became Human*. Harjo's music CD *Native Joy for Real* was released from Mekko Productions. She teaches at the University of New Mexico, but when not teaching and performing she lives in Honolulu, Hawaii.

Suzan Shown Harjo is a writer, curator, and policy advocate who has helped Native Peoples recover over one million acres of land. President of The Morning Star Institute in Washington, DC, and an award-winning columnist for *Indian Country Today*, she was a School of Advanced Research 2004 Poetry Fellow and Summer Scholar in Santa Fe; she was also Executive Director of the National Congress of American Indians, and a Founding Trustee of the National Museum of the American Indian, where she hosts the Native Writers Series.

Robin Ouzman Hislop, poet and translator, born in the UK, has lived in Scotland, Scandinavia, the Far East, and Spain, but now lives in Morocco. His collected works have appeared in *Poetry Life and Times* at www.poetrylifeandtimes.com.

Walter R. Holland is the author of *A Journal of the Plague Years: Poems 1979-1992* and *Transatlantic*, as well as one novel, *The March*. His work most recently has appeared in the *Antioch Review*, *HazMat*, *Redivider*, and *Rhino*. He teaches literature at the New School and is also a physical therapist.

Ron Hudson is a poet and activist who lives in North Carolina.

Daniela Hurezanu's essays and reviews appear regularly in *Rain Taxi*, the *Chattahoochee Review*, and the *Redwood Coast Review*. She has two recent translations: from the Romanian, with Adam J. Sorkin, of Mariana Marin's *The Factory of the Past* (Toad Press); and from the French, with Stephen Kessler, of Raymond Queneau's *Eyeseas* (Black Widow Press).

Alta Ifland grew up in Eastern Europe and emigrated to the United States in her early twenties. She studied literature and philosophy in France and the United States, and currently lives in California. The poems here are from *Voix de Glace/ Voice of Ice* (Les Figues Press, 2007), a bilingual (French-English) collection of prose poems. She has recently finished a collection of short stories.

Colette Inez, the author of nine books of poetry, is the recipient of numerous poetry awards including a Guggenheim Foundation fellowship, two NEA grants and two Pushcart Prizes. She teaches poetry at the Undergraduate School for the Arts at Columbia University. Her memoir *The Secret of M. Dulong* was published in 2005.

Kim Jensen is a writer who has lived and taught in France, California, and the Middle East. Her first novel about a turbulent affair between a Palestinian exile and an American student, *The Woman I Left Behind*, published in 2006 by Curbstone Press, was a finalist in Foreword Magazine's Book of the Year contest. In 2001, Jensen won the Raymond Carver Prize for Short Fiction, and her writings have appeared in *Rain Taxi Review*, *Left Curve*, *Boston Book Review*, *Poetry Flash*, *al-Ahram Weekly*, *So to Speak*, among others. She is on the editorial board of the *Baltimore Review*, and teaches at Community College of Baltimore County. Website: www.kimjensen.org.

Claire Joysmith, professor-researcher at UNAM, Mexico and poet, has published poetry in *Café Bellas Artes, A Quien Corresponda, CLON: Cyberzine, Poetic Voices Without Borders, Tameme, Sofia Poems* (by J. Logghe), *Cantar de espejos/Singing Mirrors*. She is editor of several volumes, the most recent *Speaking desde las heridas. Cibertestimonios Transfronterizos/Transborder* (September 11, 2001-March 11, 2007).

Marcelle Kasprowicz was born in France. She writes in English and French and also translates her French poems into English. She has won several prizes for her poetry, and her work has appeared in *Borderlands, Farfelu Magazine*, among other publications. She is the author of *Organza Skies*, a book of poems about the Davis Mountains of West Texas, published in 2005.

Stephen Kessler's most recent books include *Burning Daylight* (Littoral Press, 2007), a translation entitled *Written in Water: The Prose Poems of Luis Cernuda* (City Lights, 2004; Lambda Literary Award), and a collection of essays entitled *Moving Targets: On Poets, Poetry & Translation* (El León Literary Arts, 2008). He is the editor of the *Redwood Coast Review*.

Gunilla Theander Kester, a Gival Press poetry winner, is the author of one chapbook, *Eyes*, published by Finishing Line Press; her poem "Shiri's Piano" won an International Publishers Prize which was published in the *Atlanta Review*'s International Issue. A Fulbright scholar and an accomplished guitarist she performs regularly and teaches classical guitar at The Amherst School of Music. Visit: *www.thekesters.net/Gunilla*.

Kathryn Kirkpatrick, professor of English at Appalachian State University, is the author of three collections of poetry, *The Body's Horizon* (1996), *Beyond Reason* (2004), and *Out of the Garden* (2007).

Peter Klappert is the author of six collections of poems, including *Lugging Vegetables to Nantucket* (Yale Series of Younger Poets, 1971), *The Idiot Princess of the Last Dynasty* (Knopf, 1984), and *Chokecherries: New and Selected Poems 1966-1999.*

George Klawitter teaches literature at St. Edward's University in Austin, Texas. His book *Let Orpheus Take Your Hand* won the 2002 Gival Press Poetry Award, and his latest book of poetry, *The Agony of Words*, appeared in 2004.

Randy Koch is pursuing an MFA at the University of Wyoming and writes a monthly column called "Serving Sentences" for *LareDOS: A Journal of the Borderlands*. His first collection of poems, *Composing Ourselves*, was published by Fithian Press in 2002 while *The Deaths of the Conquistadores*, a collection of dramatic monologues, was a finalist for the 2001 Gival Press Poetry Award. He also has work published in *Passages North*, the *Raven Chronicles, Concho River Review, English Journal, Mankato Poetry Review, Sparrow*, and many others.

Carolyn Kreiter-Foronda, Virginia's former Poet Laureate, is the author of five poetry books and co-editor of two poetry anthologies. Her award-winning poems have appeared throughout the United States and abroad in numerous publications, including *Nimrod, Prairie Schooner, Poet Lore,* and *Mid-American Review*. In 1992, she was named a Virginia Cultural Laureate for her contributions to American literature.

Bruce Lader, author of the book *Discovering Mortality*, a finalist for the Brockman-Campbell Award, has had poems published in *Poetry, New York Quarterly, International Poetry Review,* and *Poetic Voices Without Borders*. He is the founding director of Bridges Tutoring, an organization educating students from diverse cultures.

Marie Lecrivain is the executive editor of *poeticdiversity: the litzine of Los Angeles*. She works as a grant writer for a non-profit organization. Her prose and poetry have appeared in a variety of publications, and her short story, "The Word Thief," was nominated for a 2007 Pushcart Prize by Ex Machina Press.

Daniel W. K. Lee is a New York City-based writer and artist. He dreams of becoming an expatriate and is taking nominations. Please email suggestions (for exile), accolades, or criticism (of his work) to *strongplum@yahoo.com*.

Donna J. Gelagotis Lee's book, *On the Altar of Greece* (Gival Press, 2006), winner of the Gival Press Poetry Award, received a 2007 Eric Hoffer Book Award: Notable for Art Category and was nominated for a *Los Angeles Times* Book Prize. She lives in New Jersey but lived in Greece for many years. Website: *www.donnajgelagotislee.com*.

Gary Lehmann, twice nominated for the Pushcart Prize, has published essays, poetry and short stories widely—over 100 pieces per year. Books include *The Span I will Cross* (Process Press, 2004) and *Public Lives and Private Secrets* (Foothills Publishing, 2005). His most recent book is *American Sponsored Torture* (FootHills Publishing, 2007). Visit: *www.garylehmann.blogspot.com*.

Vladimir Levchev, a poet and writer who is currently teaching in Sofia, Bulgaria, has written more than ten books of poetry, a book of essays and two novels. He founded the first Bulgarian independent magazine, *Glas*, which was banned by the Communist authorities before November 1989. Levchev's first American book of poetry, *Leaves from the Dry Tree*, was translated into English by the author with the Pulitzer Prize-winning poet Henry Taylor; his poetry has appeared in many anthologies and literary magazines, including *Poetry, Chicago,* and *Child of Europe: Penguin's Anthology of Eastern European Poetry*.

Philip Levine is the author of sixteen books of poetry; *Breath* (Alfred A. Knopf, 2004) is his most recent. His other poetry collections include *The Mercy* (1999); *The Simple Truth* (1994), which won the Pulitzer Prize; *What Work Is* (1991), which won the National Book Award; *New Selected Poems* (1991);

Ashes: Poems New and Old (1979), which received the National Book Critics Circle Award and the first American Book Award for Poetry; *7 Years From Somewhere* (1979), which won the National Book Critics Circle Award; and *The Names of the Lost* (1975), which won the Lenore Marshall Poetry Prize.

Marta López-Luaces has published two books of poetry, *Distancias y destierros* (Red Internacional del Libro, 1998) and *Las lenguas del viajero* (Huerga y Fierro, 2005) and a plaquette entitled *Memorias de un vacío* (Pen Press, 2000). A selection of her work appeared in English in the *Revel Road*'s chapbook series (2004) and in the literary journal, *Literary Review* (New Jersey, 2003). She is the co-director of *Galerna*, a Spanish-language literary journal published in the USA. She was awarded speaker for the New York Council for the Arts and the Humanities (2003-05).

Raymond Luczak has had eight books published, most notably *Men with Their Hands* (Suspect Thoughts Press, 2007), the first-place winner of the *Project: QueerLit* 2006 Contest, and *Eyes of Desire 2: A Deaf GLBT Reader* (Handtype Press, 2007). His books of poetry include *St. Michael's Fall* (Deaf Life Press, 1996) and *This Way to the Acorns* (Tactile Mind Press, 2002). A deaf playwright and filmmaker in Minneapolis, Luczak blogs on his website *www.raymondluczak.com*.

María-Elvira Luna-Escudero-Alie is currently studying at Georgetown University; her dissertation is on the theatre of Mario-Vargas Llosa. She teaches Spanish and French at Montgomery College-Takoma Park/Silver Spring, Maryland.

Jeff Mann's poetry, fiction, and essays have appeared in many literary journals and anthologies. He's published three poetry chapbooks, two full-length collections of poetry, a volume of personal essays, a book of memoir and poetry, a novella, and a collection of short fiction. Mann, a Lambda Literary Award winner, is an associate professor of creative writing at Virginia Tech in Blacksburg, Virginia.

Sydney March, a Jamaican poet, essayist, musician, and journalist, resides in Washington, DC. A former member of the WritersCorps 1996-1998, he is a recipient of grants from The DC Commission on the Arts and Humanities and Poets and Writers (2007), as well as Jenny Moore and Lannan Fellowships. He has recently served as a panelist for the DC Commission's Artist Fellowship Grants in Literature. Publications include *Dark Warriors of the Spanish Main* (Smithsonian New World, Smithsonian Institution, 1992), *The Maroons of Jamaica* (Encounters, University of New Mexico Press, 1994) and a collection of poetry, *Stealing Mangoes* (Mica Press, 1997).

Thomas March, born and raised in the Midwest, is a poet and essayist who lives in New York, where he teaches at an independent school for girls. He was named the 2006 Norma Millay Ellis Fellow by The Millay Colony for the

Arts. Recent work appears in the *Believer, Painted Bride Quarterly, Spoon River Poetry Review,* and *Vallum.*

Desirée Marín is an Ecuadorian poet who lives in the Washington, DC area.

Pablo Miguel Martínez's work has appeared in various literary journals and newspapers. In 2005 he received the Chicano/Latino Literary Prize. His work has also been supported by the Alfredo Cisneros Del Moral Foundation.

Luis Martínez de Merlo has published two collections for young readers, *Oro parece* and *Ahora digo Diego,* as well as numerous volumes for adults, including: *Orphenica lyra* (Poesia Alcalá Prize), *Silva de Sirenas, Alma del tiempo* (a finalist for El Bardo Prize), and *De alguna otras veces* (Puente Cultural Prize). He has translated into Spanish works by Dante, Leopardi, Baudelaire (Stendhal Prize for *Flores del mal*), Verlaine, Laforgue, and Cros, among others, as well as an anthology of French Baroque poets and another of Italian poets from the 16th century. He is also a photographer, whose work is frequently exhibited in Madrid.

C. M. Mayo is the author of *Miraculous Air: Journey of a Thousand Miles through Baja California, the Other Mexico* (Milkweed Editions), and *Sky Over El Nido* (University of Georgia Press), which won the Flannery O'Connor Award for Short Fiction. Her poetry has been widely published in literary journals, among them, *BorderSenses, Lyric, Natural Bridge, Rio Grande Review,* and *West Branch,* and several anthologies, most recently in the first volume of *Poetic Voices Without Borders.* Visit: www.cmmayo.com.

Judith McCombs has published poetry and short-short fiction in *Calyx, Feminist Studies, Kansas Quarterly, Nimrod* (a Neruda Award), *Poet Lore, Poetry, Poetry Northwest, Potomac Review* (Poetry Prize), *Prairie Schooner,* among other publications. Her poetry books include *Against Nature: Wilderness Poems* and *The Habit of Fire: Poems Selected & New,* which was a finalist for the 2006 Milt Kessler Poetry Book Award. She teaches at the Writer's Center in Bethesda, Maryland, and arranges the Kensington Row Bookshop Poetry Readings.

Mario Meléndez's books include: *Autocultura y juicio* (with prologue from the National Prize for Literature, Roque Esteban Scarpa), *Apuntes para una leyenda,* and *Vuelo subterráneo.* In 1993 he received the Municipal Prize for Literature in the Bicentennial of Linares. His poems have appeared in different revues of Hispano-American literature as well as in national and foreign anthologies. Parts of his work have been translated into Italian, English, French, Portuguese, Dutch, Romanian, Farsi, and Catalan.

Arnold Melleby, a native of Norway, is a poet, author, and lyricist. The illustrated book of poetry, *if mountains could swim* (Inner Circle Publishing) published in 2008. He travels the world in search of the right inspiration.

Dante Micheaux is an emerging poet who resides in New York City. His poem "Bread Boy" won the 2006 Gival Press Oscar Wilde Award.

Edmund Miller, chairman of the English Department at the C. W. Post Campus of Long Island University, is the author of scholarly books such as *Drudgerie Divine: The Rhetoric of God and Man in George Herbert*. Miller is also the author of a book of short stories and several books of poetry, including the legendary *Fucking Animals* and, most recently, *The Go-Go Boy Sonnets: Men of the New York Club Scene*.

E. Ethelbert Miller, a literary activist, is board chair of the Institute for Policy Studies and a board member of the Writer's Center and editor of *Poet Lore* magazine. The author of several collections of poems, his last book *How We Sleep on the Nights We Don't Make Love* (Curbstone Press, 2004) was an Independent Publisher Award Finalist. He received the 1995 O.B. Hardison Jr. Poetry Prize. In 2003 his memoir *Fathering Words: The Making of An African American Writer* (St. Martin's Press, 2000) was selected by DC WE READ for its one book, one city program sponsored by the D.C. Public Libraries. Poets & Writers presented him with the 2007 Barnes & Noble/ Writers for Writers Award. Two books will be released in 2009: *On Saturdays I Santana with You* (Curbstone Press) and *The 5th Inning* (Busboys and Poets/PM Press), a second memoir.

Stephen S. Mills recently completed his MFA in poetry at Florida State University. His poems have appeared in the *Gay and Lesbian Review*, *Hoboeye Online Arts Journal*, on Juked.com and others will appear in the *New York Quarterly*, the *Broke Bridge Review*, and the *Quirk*. He won the 2008 Gival Press Oscar Wilde Award.

Michael Montlack has two chapbooks: *Cover Charge* (Winner of the 2007 Gertrude Prize) and *Girls, Girls, Girls* (Pudding House, 2008). His work has appeared in journals including *Cimarron Review*, *Court Green*, *New York Quarterly*, *5 AM*, *Bloom*, *Cream City Review*, *Swink*, and *Columbia Poetry Review*. In March 2009, the University of Wisconsin Press will publish his anthology *Diva Complex: Gay Men on the Women Who Shaped Their Lives*.

Miles David Moore is a member of the board of directors of The Word Works. He is founder and host of the Iota poetry reading series in Arlington, Virginia. His books are *The Bears of Paris* (Word Works, 1995); *Buddha Isn't Laughing* (Argonne House Press, 1999); and *Rollercoaster* (Word Works, 2004).

Kay Murphy is the author of two poetry collections: *The Autopsy* and *Belief Blues*. She has published poetry, fiction, and reviews in journals such as *Ascent*, the *American Book Review*, *Fiction International*, *Chelsea*, *North American Review*, and *Poetry*. She is professor of English at the University of New Orleans and is poetry editor of *Bayou*.

Yvette Neisser Moreno is a poet and translator whose work has appeared in numerous magazines and anthologies. Her translation of Luis Alberto Ambroggio's *Difficult Beauty: Selected Poems* is forthcoming from Cross-Cultural Communications in 2009. She teaches poetry in public schools in both Arlington County, Virginia, and Washington, DC, as part of the Folger Poetry Program.

Naomi Shihab Nye has written several books of poems, including *You and Yours* (BOA Editions, 2005), which received the Isabella Gardner Poetry Award, as well as *19 Varieties of Gazelle: Poems of the Middle East* (2002), a collection of new and selected poems about the Middle East, *Fuel* (1998), *Red Suitcase* (1994), and *Hugging the Jukebox* (1982). Her recent books are *I'll Ask You Three Times, Are You OK?*, *Tales of Driving and Being Driven*, and *Honeybee*, both from Greenwillow, HarperCollins. Nye's work echoes her experience as an Arab-American. She has received awards, including a Lannan Fellow and the Academy of American Poets' Lavan Award, selected by W. S. Merwin.

Alicia Suskin Ostriker is a professional translator of literature.

Daniele Pantano, a Swiss poet, translator, critic, and editor, has had work appear in numerous journals and anthologies worldwide, including *Absinthe: New European Writing*, the *Adirondack Review*, *ARCH*, the *Baltimore Review*, *Gradiva: International Journal of Italian Poetry*, *Italian Americana*, the *Mailer Review*, *Poetry International*, *32 Poems Magazine*, and *Style*. His next books, *The Oldest Hands in the World* (a collection of poems), *The Possible is Monstrous: Selected Poems by Friedrich Dürrenmatt*, and *The Collected Works of Georg Trakl* are forthcoming from Black Lawrence Press, New York. Pantano has taught at the University of South Florida and, as the Visiting Poet-in-Residence, at Florida Southern College. He's senior lecturer in creative writing at Edge Hill University, England.

Anika Paris, an ASCAP award-winning singer/songwriter, teaches Artist Development at the Musicians' Institute in Los Angeles. Her songs have been featured in major motion pictures and on national television. Her poetry has been published in various periodicals and anthologies, most recently in *Chance of a Ghost* (Helicon Nine Editions) and she has just finished her first book of poems, *Life in Check*.

Benito Pastoriza Iyodo, an award-winning author from Puerto Rico, has received various prizes for his poetry and short stories, among them have been the Chicano Latino Literary Prize for his book of poetry entitled *Lo coloro de lo incoloro* (University of California) and others from Australia and Mexico. His works have been published in Australia, Mexico, Chile, Spain, Puerto Rico and the USA.

Richard Peabody is the founding editor of *Gargoyle Magazine*, and co-editor of the Mondo series (*Mondo Barbie*, *Mondo Elvis*, et al.). Between juggling kids, teaching, trying to write, and worrying about the state of the world, he has edited twenty-two anthologies and has five books of poetry and three books of fiction of his own. In addition, he runs Paycock Press in Arlington, Virginia. Visit: *www.gargoylemagazine.com*.

Emily Lupita Plum is the author of *Water and Stone: A Story in Poetry from Japan*, and winner of the Faulkner Gold Medal for the Poem. She received an MFA in Creative Writing and Environment from Iowa State University. Plum is a writer and watercolor artist and works out of her Strong Plum Studio in Atlanta, Georgia.

Raymond Queneau (1903-1976) was one of the most prominent French writers of the 20th century. He was associated with the Surrealist movement and challenged traditional writing forms, both in prose and in poetry. In the 1960s he was part of a group of writers who founded Oulipo, an experimental "Workshop of Potential Literature." The poems included in *Poetic Voices Without Borders 2* are from *Les Ziaux / Eyeseas* (Black Widow Press, 2008).

Anthony W. Reevy's previous publications include poetry in *Asheville Poetry Review*, *Bath Avenue Newsletter*, *Charlotte Poetry Review*, *Now & Then*, *Pembroke Magazine*, the *Poet's Page*, *Writer's Cramp*, and others, as well as non-fiction and short fiction. His books are *Ghost Train!: American Railroad Ghost Legends*, *A Directory of North Carolina's Railroad Structures* (with Art Peterson and Sonny Dowdy), *Green Cove Stop*, *Magdalena*, and *Lightning in Wartime*.

Arthur Rimbaud (1854-1891) was a founder of French symbolism and his collection *Une Saison en Enfer* (*A Season in Hell*) was one of the first collections of free verse. His romantic and erratic relationship with Paul Verlaine ended when Verlaine shot Rimbaud in the hand. Verlaine published Rimbaud's works in 1895 which guaranteed Rimbaud's immortality.

Wanda Rivera is a professional translator of literature.

Kim Roberts is the author of two books of poems, *The Kimnama* (Vrzhu Press, 2007), and *The Wishbone Galaxy* (WWPH, 1994). She edits *Beltway Poetry Quarterly*, an on-line journal of authors from the greater Washington, DC area.

Blake Robinson's poetry has appeared in *Pairs* and the one-volume *Effing the Ineff* and *Distich Farm*. He has translated works by Sandro Penna (*Remember Me, God of Love*), Eugène Fromentin (*Between Sea and Sahara*), Alberto Savinio (*Paris Then*) and, most recently, C. H. Ramuz (*The Young Man from Savoy*).

J. E. Robinson is a widely published essayist, novelist, and poet, who has received an Illinois Arts Countil Literary Award, the Plainsong Poetry Award, and a Pushcart Prize nomination. His poem "Whitmanesque" appeared in

Poetic Voices Without Borders. He lives in Southern Illinois, near St. Louis, Missouri.

Mercedes Roffé, an Argentine poet, has been widely published in Latin America and Spain. Her work has also been translated into Italian, French, and Romanian. An anthology of her work in English translation, *Like the Rains Come: Selected Poems 1987-2006*, has recently appeared in England (Shearsman, 2008). Since 1998 she has edited the New York-based poetry series, Ediciones Pen Press. Among other distinctions, she was awarded in 2001 a John Simon Guggenheim Fellowship in poetry.

Joseph Ross is a poet in the Washington, DC area. His poetry has appeared in many literary journals and anthologies including *Poetic Voices Without Borders, Sojourners, Solo Cafe, DC Poets Against the War*, and *Beltway Poetry Quarterly*. He co-edited a collection of poetry responding to Fernando Botero's Abu Ghraib paintings, published by American University.

Sean Ross's work has appeared in (among other journals) *Mad Poet's Review, GSU Review, GW Review, National Forum*, and *Loop*. He currently teaches English at a funky little private school in Arizona. He can be reached at *seanross42@cox.net*.

Mary Kay Rummel's fifth book of poetry, *Love in the End*, was published by Bright Hill Press in 2008. She divides her time between Minneapolis and Ventura, California, where she teaches part time at California State University, Channel Islands.

Thaddeus Rutkowski is the author of the novels *Tetched* (Behler Publications) and Roughhouse (Kaya Press). Both books were finalists for an Asian American Literary Award. He teaches fiction writing at the Writer's Voice of the West Side YMCA in Manhattan, where he lives with his family. Visit: *www.thaddeusrutkowski.com*.

Mark Saba's poems, fiction, and essays have appeared widely in literary magazines, most recently *Palo Alto Review, Connecticut Review, Steam Ticket*, and *Future Cycle Poetry*. He is the author of a novel, *The Landscapes of Pater* (The Vineyard Press, 2004). Visit: *www.marksabawriter.com*.

Rose Mary Salum is the founder and director of the award winning bilingual magazine *Literal: Latin American Voices*. She is the author of two books of short stories. Her work is included in anthologies of the United States, Argentina, Mexico, India, Australia, and Spain. She has received many international awards for her literary and editorial work.

M. A. Schaffner has had poetry published in *Stand* (UK), the *Beloit Poetry Journal, ARC* (Canada), *Poet Lore*, the *Mississippi Review*, and many other journals in the USA and abroad. He is also the author of the collection, *The Good Opinion of Squirrels* (Word Works, 1997) and the novel, *War Boys*

(Welcome Rain, 2002). When not writing, Schaffner works as a civil servant in Washington, DC.

Lawrence Schimel is an author, anthologist, and translator who has published over ninety books, including *Fairy Tales for Writers, Best Gay Poetry 2008, Two Boys in Love, First Person Queer, The Future is Queer, Desayuno en la cama, La aventura de Cecilia y el dragón,* and *¿Lees un libro conmigo?*. He lives in Madrid, Spain.

Gregg Shapiro, pop-culture journalist, has had interviews and reviews appear in a variety of regional LGBT publications and websites. His poetry and fiction have appeared in numerous outlets including literary journals such as *Beltway, modern words, Bloom, White Crane Journal, Blithe House Quarterly, Mipoesias,* and the anthologies *Sex & Chocolate: Tasty Morsels for Mind and Body* (Paycock Press) and *Blood to Remember*. His collection of poems, *Protection*, was published in 2008 (Gival Press).

Lucille Gang Shulklapper's fiction and poetry appear in numerous journals, anthologies, and three chapbooks: *What You Cannot Have, The Substance of Sunlight,* and *Godd, It's Not Hollywood*. She lives in Coral Springs, Florida.

Ron Singer trawls the genres: poetry, fiction, satire, journalism about Africa, and librettos for two operas. His essay-review on the Caine Prize for African Writing appeared in the Summer 2007 *Georgia Review*, and a second printing of his chapbook, *A Voice for My Grandmother* (Ten Penny Players, Inc.), was issued in Fall 2007. Visit: *www.ronsinger.net*.

G. Tod Slone has a doctorate from the Université de Nantes (France), has been teaching as a visiting professor at Grambling State University (Lousiana), and is founding editor of the *American Dissident*, a literary journal of critical poetry and other writing (*www.theamericandissident.org*). His collection *Where a Poet Ought Not / Où c'qui faut pas* was released in 2008 (Gival Press).

J. D. Smith, who was awarded a 2007 Fellowship in Poetry from the National Endowment for the Arts, is working on his third collection of poems. Visit: *www.jdsmithwriter.com*.

Clifton Snider, an internationally known, award-winning poet, has published eight books of poems, including *The Age of the Mother* and *The Alchemy of Opposites*, three novels, and a book of literary criticism, *The Stuff That Dreams Are Made On*. A specialist in Jungian and Queer Criticism, his article on "Brokeback Mountain" appeared in *Psychological Perspectives* in Spring 2008. He teaches in the English Department at California State University, Long Beach.

Christopher Soden has written film critiques for *AfterElton.com*, *Blogcritics.org*, the *Fort Worth Ally*, and *Tribune*, performance pieces and dramaturgy. He is the poetry editor of *Espejo* and is active in the Dallas poets' community.

His work has appeared in *Gertrude*, *Windy City Times*, the *Chiron Review*, *Sentence*, *Borderlands*, *New Texas 2002*, *Off the Rocks*, *Poetry Super Highway*, *Touch of Eros*, *Gents*, *Bad Boys and Barbarians*, *WordWrights!*, the *James White Review*, and *Best of Texas Writing 2*.

Katherine Soniat's *Swing Girl* is forthcoming from LSU Press. *The Fire Setters* is available through the Web Del Sol On-line Chapbook Series. Her fourth collection, *Alluvial*, was published by Bucknell University Press, and *A Shared Life* won the Iowa Poetry Prize. Poems are in recent issues of the *Kenyon Review*, *Iowa Review*, *Southern Review*, and *Prairie Schooner*.

Jason Tandon's first collection *Give Over the Heckler and Everyone Gets Hurt* was awarded the St. Lawrence Book Award and will be published by Black Lawrence Press in 2009. He is also the author of two chapbooks, *Rumble Strip* (sunnyoutside) and *Flight* (Finishing Line Press), both released in 2007. He teaches English at Holyoke Community College.

Jonathan Tilley, between rehearsals and performances, writes from Stuttgart, Germany, where he has worked for the past eight years as a professional dancer and choreographer. His poetry has appeared in *Red River Review* and *Scene 404*. Visit: *www.jonathantilley.de*.

Rodrigo Toscano is the author of *To Leveling Swerve* (Kruspkaya Books, 2005), *Platform* (Atelos, 2004), *The Disparities* (Green Integer, 2002) and *Partisans* (O Books, 1999). His new manuscript, *Collapsible Poetics Theater*, won the National Poetry Series 2007, while his poetry has appeared in *Best American Poetry 2004*, *War and Peace* (2004), *War and Peace* (2007) and *In the Criminal's Cabinet: An Anthology of Poetry and Fiction* (2004), *Junta: An Anthology of Experimental Latino Poetry* (2008), and *The Gertrude Stein Awards Anthology*. Originally from the Borderlands of California, he lives in Brooklyn and works in Manhattan at the Labor Institute.

Chris Tusa's work has appeared in *Connecticut Review*, *Texas Review*, *Prairie Schooner*, the *New Delta Review*, *Southeast Review*, *South Dakota Review*, and others. With the help of a grant from the Louisiana Division of the Arts, he was able to complete his first chapbook of poetry, *Inventing an End*. His debut collection of poems, *Haunted Bones*, was published by Louisiana Literature Press in 2006.

Barbara Louise Ungar is the author of *The Origin of the Milky Way*, winner of the 2007 Gival Press Poetry Award and the 2007 Adirondack Literary Award for the Best Book of Poetry, among other awards, and *Thrift*, which was a finalist for many awards including the May Swenson Poetry Award and the Tupelo Prize, as well as the chapbooks *Sequel* and *Neoclassical Barbra*, and *Haiku In English*. Her poems have appeared in *Salmagundi*, the *Minnesota Review*, the *Cream City Review*, the *Literary Review*, and other publications. She's an associate professor of English at the College of Saint Rose in Albany.

Alexandra Van de Kamp, Alexandria lives in Port Jefferson, New York and teaches at Stony Brook University. She has work forthcoming in *Quarter After Eight*, *Lake Effect*, and *Court Green*. Her first full-length book, *The Park of Upside-Down Chairs*, is forthcoming from WordTech Press in 2010.

Gloria Vando's latest collection, *Shadows & Supposes* (Arte Público Press), won the Poetry Society of America's Alice Fay Di Castagnola Award and the Latino Literary Hall of Fame's Poetry Book Award. Her work is in many magazines, texts, and anthologies, including the 2007 Grammy-nominated "Poetry on Record: 98 Poets Read Their Work 1888-2006". She is publisher/editor of Helicon Nine Editions, for which she received the Governor's Arts Award (Kansas), and cofounder of The Writers Place, Kansas City.

Anita Vélez-Mitchell was awarded Puerto Rico's Julia de Burgos Poetry Prize for her book, *Primavida: Calendar of Love* (Mairena Press). Her poetry, short stories, essays, and interviews have won many prizes and have appeared in Spanish and English language magazines and anthologies, most recently in *New Letters*, *Institute of Puerto Rico Journal*, *In Other Words* (Arte Público Press), *Chance of a Ghost* (Helicon Nine Editions), *Anales* (Sociedad de Autores Puertorriqueños), and others. She has also distinguished herself as a dancer, choreographer, stage director, and playwright, for which she won the La MaMa E.T.C. INKY Award.

Julie Marie Wade received the Chicago Literary Award in Poetry, the Gulf Coast Nonfiction Prize, the 2005 Gival Press Oscar Wilde Poetry Award, and the Literal Latte Nonfiction Prize. She lives with Angie and their two cats in Pittsburgh, Pennsylvania.

Jeff Walt's poems have appeared recently in *Poetry International*, *Runes*, and *Alehouse Review*. Visit: *www.jeffwalt.com*.

Allison Whittenberg is the author of two young adult novels: *Sweet Thang* and *Life Is Fine* (both from Delacorte). She has published poems and short stories in Columbia, Feminist Studies, and Meridian. She is a former winner of the John Steinbeck Award. Visit: *www.allisonwhittenberg.com*.

Jill Williams, originally from Hartford, Connecticut, divides her time between Vancouver, British Columbia, and Sedona, Arizona. Author of a Broadway musical "Rainbow Jones" and three nonfiction books, she has been published in numerous journals and mainstream magazines. Her poetry books include *The Nature Sonnets* (Gival Press, 2001) and *A Weakness For Men* (Woodley & Watts, 2003). Most recently, her work appears in *Poetic Voices Without Borders* (Gival Press, 2005). Visit: *www.jillwilliams.com*.

Ernie Wormwood, a native Washingtonian, lives in Leonardtown, Maryland. She recently appeared on Grace Cavlaieri's "The Poet and the Poem" at the Library of Congress and has new work coming out in a Walt Whitman anthology from Allbooks entitled *Primal Sanities* and in the book *Poem*

Revised from Marion Street Press. Her work has appeared in *Rhino*, the *Antietam Review*, *Innisfree*, and the *Arabesque Review*.

Gerard Wozek is the author of a collection of short stories, *Postcards from Heartthrob Town* (Southern Tier Editions, 2006). His first book of poems, *Dervish*, won the 2000 Gival Press Poetry Award. He teaches creative writing at Robert Morris College in Chicago.

Katharina Yakovina, an artist and poet, lives in Russia. She creates a space for her art and makes choices among her options.

Acknowledgments

"Adagio por una viola d'amore olvidada..." by Hedy Habra first appeared in *Letras Femeninas*, 2007. Reprinted by permission of the poet.

"All Saint's Day" by Carolyn Kreiter-Foronda first appeared in *Death Comes Riding* (SCOP Publications, Catonsville, MD, 1999). Reprinted by permission of the author.

"Anti-Father" by Rita Dove from *Museum*, Carnegie Mellon University Press. Copyright 1983 by Rita Dove. Reprinted by permission of the author.

"At the Pentecostal Baths" by Pablo Miguel Martínez first appeared on www.givalpress.com as the winner of the 2007 Oscar Wilde Award. Reprinted by permission of the author.

"August Eve" by Anika Paris first appeared in *Chance of a Ghost: An Anthology of Contemporary Ghost Poems* (Helicon Nine Editions, 2005). Copyright © 2005 by Anika Paris. Reprinted by permission of the publisher.

"Blue Jay Paixao de Vôo" by Benito Pastoriza Iyodo appeared in *Elegías de septiembre* (Editorial Tierra Firme, México, D.F., 2003). Reprinted by permission of the author.

"The Border" by Martha Collins first appeared in *Some Things Words Can Do* (Sheep Meadow, 1998). Reprinted by permission of the author.

"Bread Boy" by Dante Micheaux first appeared on www.givalpress.com as the winner of the 2006 Oscar Wilde Award. Reprinted by permission of the author.

"Carry Me Away (Llévame)" by Mario Meléndez (Copyright, 2004) / translation by Ron Hudson. Reprinted by permission of the authors.

"Casualties of War" (formerly "On this Day I Think of the Widows") by Gloria Vando from *Shadows & Supposes* (Arte Público Press, U. of Houston, 2002). Copyright © 2002 Gloria Vando. Reprinted by permission of the publisher.

"Cat Scrabble Ode" by Ron Singer first appeared in *Waterways*, 2005. Reprinted by permission of the author.

"The Climb" by Randy Koch first appeared in *Revista Interamerican* (Vol. 31, 2003). Reprinted by permission of the author.

"Contrapunto" by Hedy Habra first appeared in *Letras Femeninas*, 2007. Reprinted by permission of the author.

"The Courtship of the Morticians" by Peter Klappert first appeared in *Chokecherries* (Orchises Press, 2000). Reprinted by permission of the author.

"Deaf is the night..." by Raymond Queneau; English translation by Daniela Hurezanu and Stephen Kessler first appeared in *Eyeseas* (Black Widow Press, 2008). Reprinted by permission by the publisher and the authors.

"Delft" by Rita Dove from *Museum*, Carnegie Mellon University Press. Copyright 1983 by Rita Dove. Reprinted by permission of the author.

"descubrir noches pintadas por poetas" by Benito Pastoriza Iyodo appeared in *Elegías de septiembre* (Editorial Tierra Firme, México, D.F., 2003). Reprinted by permission of the author.

"The Disappeared" by Colette Inez first appeared in *The Saint Anne's Review*, 2003. Reprinted by permission of the author.

"Donde nació la luz" by Fanny Carrión del Fierro was first published in *Donde nació la luz / Where Light Was Born* (Centro de Publicaciones de la Pontificia Universidad Católica del Ecuador, Quito, 2000). Reprinted by permission of the author.

"The Door" by Bernadette Geyer first appeared in *The Marlboro Review*. Reprinted by permission of the author.

"During the War" by Philip Levine first appeared in the *New Yorker* (2006). Reprinted by permission of the author.

"Eastern Village with Factory" by Daniele Pantano first published in *32 Poems Magazine*, 2007. Reprinted by permission of the author.

"El sol también tiene su lado oscuro" by Hedy Habra first appeared in *Explicación de Textos*, 2002-2003. Reprinted by permission of the author.

"Elena Mesa" by Carolyn Kreiter-Foronda first appeared in *Death Comes Riding* (SCOP Publications, Inc., Catonsville, MD, 1999). Reprinted by permission of the author.

"The Explanation of Metaphors" by Raymond Queneau; English translation by Daniela Hurezanu and Stephen Kessler first appeared in *Eyeseas* (Black Widow Press, 2008). Reprinted by permission of the publisher and the authors.

"Fairy Tales for Writers: Little Red Riding Hood" by Lawrence Schimel first appeared in the chapbook *Fairy Tales for Writers* (A Midsummer Night's Press, 2007). Reprinted by permission of the author.

"Faith" by Edward Falco first appeared in *The Mississippi Review* (34.3, 2006; 58-59). Reprinted by permission of the author.

"Farewell Kiss" by Ron Singer first appeared in *Borderlands: The Texas Poetry Review*, Fall/Winter, 2000. Reprinted by permission of the author.

"Fifi, the dangerous fag dog," by John Del Peschio first appeared in 1997 (Cleis Press). Reprinted by permission of the author.

"Filles du feu" by Hedy Habra first appeared in *Entre Nous*, 1991. Reprinted by permission by the author.

"Final Approach" Lucille Gang Shulklapper first appeared in *The Substance of Sunlight* (Ginninderra Press, Australia, 2004). Reprinted by permission of the author.

"First Breath Last Breath" by Antler first appeared in *The Sun*, as well as *Denver Quarterly* and *Poetry Daily Essentials* (2007). Reprinted by permission of the author.

"The Floor Is Sticky" by Kim Roberts first appeared in *Frontiers* (Vol. XVIII, No. 1, 1997). Reprinted by permission of the author.

"Forgive us our sins" by Katharina Yakovina first appeared on *ArLiJo.com*. Reprinted by permission of the author.

"from the desert" by Raymond Queneau; English translation by Daniela Hurezanu and Stephen Kessler first appeared in *Eyeseas* (Black Widow Press, 2008). Reprinted by permission of the publisher and the authors.

"How to Make a Human" by Lawrence Schimel first appeared in the anthology *Half-Humans* edited by Bruce Coville (Scholastic, 2001). Reprinted by permission of the author.

"i recall a day in cordoba ([recuerdo que un día en córdoba)" by Jesús Encinar / translation by Lawrence Schimel first appeared in *Chroma*, UK, 2007. Reprinted by permission of the authors.

"If I Get This Far" by Kay Murphy first appeared in *North American Review* (Volume 285, No. 1, Jan/Feb, 2000: 35). Reprinted by permission of the author.

"Immigrant Story" by Jason Tandon first appeared in *Colere: A Journal of Cultural Exploration* (Issue 7, 2007). Reprinted by permission of the author.

"el impulso sexual vestido de fiera" by Benito Pastoriza Iyodo appeared in *Cartas a la sombra de tu piel* (Editorial Tierra Firme, México, D.F., 2002). Reprinted by permission of the author.

"In the Attic of My Grief" by Grace Cavalieri first appeared in *Potomac Review*. Reprinted by permission of the author.

"Instructions to Be Followed at the Time of My Death: The service is optional" by Ron Singer first appeared in *Waterways*, 2006. Reprinted by permission of the author.

"Iranian Boys Hanged for Sodomy, July 2005" by Stephen S. Mills first appeared on www.givalpress.com as the winner of the 2008 Oscar Wilde Award. Reprinted by permission of the author.

"It's Seven (Son las siete)" by Luis Cremades / translation by Lawrence Schimel first appeared in *Knockout Magazine*, Issue 2, 2008. Reprinted by permission of the authors.

"Jumper" by Jeff Walt first appeared previously in *Poetry International*. Reprinted by permission of the author.

"Kristallnacht" by Lawrence Schimel first appeared in the journal *Mythic 1*, edited by Mike Allen (Mythic Delirium Books, 2006). Reprinted by permission of the author.

"La Cucaracha" by Grace Cavalieri first appeared in *Ocho Magazine #5* (Ocho Cinco). Reprinted by permission of the author.

"Labor" by Barbara Louise Ungar from *The Origin of the Milky Way* (Gival Press, 2007). Reprinted by permission of the publisher.

"Late in the Day" by Patricia Gray first appeared in *Rupture* (Red Hen Press, 2005). Reprinted by permission of the author.

"Legacy" by Sydney March first appeared in *Stealing Mangoes* (Mica Press, 1997). Reprinted by permission of the author.

"Les Places Numérotées" by Peter Klappert first appeared in *The Idiot Princess of the Last Dynasty* (Alfred A. Knopf, 1984). Reprinted by permission of the author.

"Man High" by C.M. Mayo first appeared in *BorderSenses*. Reprinted by permission of the author.

"The Manifestation of Sisíism" by Robert L. Giron first appeared in *Speaking desde las heridas: Cibertestimonios transfronterizos/Transborder* (September 11, 2001-March 11, 2007), co-published by the CISAN, UNAM, Whittier College, California, and ITESM in Mexico, edited by Claire Joysmith, prologues by John Beverley, Cristina Rivera-Garza and Antonia Oliver-Rotger.

"Mapas" by Hedy Habra first appeared in *Hofstra Hispanic Review* (February, 2008). Reprinted by permission of the author.

"March 20, 2003" by Edward Falco first appeared in *The Mississippi Review* (34.3, 2006; 58-59. Reprinted by permission of the author.

"Memories of the Future" by Mario Meléndez (Copyright 2004) / translation by Ron Hudson. Reprinted by permission of the authors.

"Michelangelo's Last Pietà" by Paula Goldman from *The Great Canopy* (Gival Press, 2005). Reprinted by permission of the publisher.

"Miles and the Shofar" by Mel Belin first appeared in *Poetica Magazine* (July, 2006). Reprinted by permission of the author.

"The Milky Way" by Anita Vélez-Mitchell first appeared in *Chance of a Ghost: An Anthology of Contemporary Ghost Poems* (Helicon Nine Editions, 2005). Copyright © 2005 by Anita Vélez-Mitchell. Reprinted by permission of the publisher.

"Nameless" by Lucille Gang Shulklapper first appeared in *Gulf Stream Magazine* (No. 22, 2004, Florida International University) and won First Prize Soul-Making Contest National League of Pen Women: Nob Hill Branch (prose poem category). Reprinted by permission of the author.

"Navigating the Warning," "Reality Show," and "The Last World of Fire and Trash" by Joy Harjo first appeared in *Poetic Voices Without Borders* (Gival Press, 2005). Reprinted by permission of the author.

"Niagara" by Hedy Habra first appeared in *Chimères*, 1986. Reprinted by permission of the author.

"The Night Last Night (La noche de ancho)" by Luis Martínez de Merlo / translation by Lawrence Schimel appeared in *Velvet Mafia*, Fall 2007 online. Reprinted by permission of the authors.

"No-Man's Land" by Randy Koch first appeared in the *Texas Observer* (August 13, 2004, pp. 20-21). Reprinted by permission of the author.

"Not This" by Emily Lupita Plum first appeared in *Sketch* (2005). Reprinted by permission of the author.

"Ö" by Rita Dove from *The Yellow House* on the Corner, Carnegie Mellon University Press. Copyright 1980 by Rita Dove. Reprinted by permission of the author.

"Okie Monarchs" by John Domini won the Editors' Prize from *Meridian* (Issue 17, Spring / Summer 2006, U. of VA). Reprinted by permission of the author.

"On U.S. 11 (Bear Station, Tennessee, 1968)" by Tony Reevy first appeared in *Magdalena* (Pudding House Publications, 2004). Reprinted by permission of the author.

"The Outskirts" by Raymond Queneau; English translation by Daniela Hurezanu and Stephen Kessler first appeared in *Sulphur River Literary Review* and recently in *Eyeseas* (Black Widow Press, 2008). Reprinted by permission of the publisher and the authors.

"Patrimonial Recipe" by Daniele Pantano first published in *The Baltimore Review*, 2005. Reprinted by permission of the author.

"Persimmons" by George Klawitter first appeared in *Country Matters* (2001). Reprinted by permission of the author.

"The Pilgrimage" by Robert L. Giron first appeared on *Beltway Poetry Quarterly* in 2006 for the Walt Whitman Commemorative Edition. Reprinted by permission of the author.

"Plastic Hen" by Miles David Moore first appeared in *Ruby* (Vol. 1, No. 1, 1994) and later in the book *The Bears of Paris* (Word Works Capital Collection, 1995). Reprinted by permission of the author.

"Poetry Offender" by Thaddeus Rutkowski has appeared in *Barbaric Yawp Magazine* and in the chapbook *White and Wong* (Bone World Publishing, Russell, NY, 2007). Reprinted by permission of the author.

"Prove to Me" by Antler has appeared in *Antler: The Selected Poems* (Soft Skull Press, 2000) and in *The Outpost Exchange*. Reprinted by permission of the author.

"Radiolaria" by Kim Roberts first appeared in *Re)Verb*, Issue 4, Winter 2006. Reprinted by permission of the author.

"Raptors" by Katharine Soniat first appeared in *Quarterly West*. Reprinted by permission of the author.

"Rip Tide" by Julie Marie Wade first appeared as Honorable Mention for the Editors' Prize in *Spoon River Poetry Review* (Summer/Fall 2006, Vol. xxxi, No. 2, 121). Reprinted by permission of the author.

"Robinson" by Raymond Queneau; English translation by Daniela Hurezanu and Stephen Kessler first appeared in *Sulphur River Literary Review* and recently in *Eyeseas* (Black Widow Press, 2008). Reprinted by permission of the publisher and authors.

"St. Anthony's Church" by Clifton Snider first appeared in *Chiron Review*. Reprinted by permission of the author.

"The Slave's Critique of Practical Reason" by Rita Dove from *The Yellow House on the Corner* (Carnegie Mellon University Press). Copyright 1980 by Rita Dove. Reprinted by permission of the author.

"Smokers on Break" by Jeff Walt first appeared in *Alehouse Review* / www.alehousepress.com. Reprinted by permission of the author.

"Song for Fernand Léger" by Colette Inez first appeared in *Indiana Review*, 2002. Reprinted by permission of the author.

"The Speech of Cretans" by Thaddeus Rutkowski has appeared in *Barbaric Yawp Magazine* and in the chapbook *White and Wong* (Bone World Publishing, Russell, NY, 2007). Reprinted by permission of the author.

"Telling Time" by Nina Corwin first appeared in *Nimrod International Journal* (Vol. 50, No. 1, Fall/Winter 2006). Reprinted by permission of the author.

"To Your Shadow Beast" by Alicia Gaspar de Alba was previously published under a different title in the July-August 2004 issue of *La Voz de Esperanza*. Reprinted by permission of the author.

"The Twinkle" by Antler has appeared in *Fuck!*, *Big Scream*, and *Woodland Pattern 11th Annual Marathon Anthology*. Reprinted by permission of the author.

"Virtual Freedom" by Bruce Lader first appeared in the winter issue of *Vox*, 2007. Reprinted by permission of the author.

"What Are You Dreaming?" by Gregg Shapiro first appeared in *Protection* (Gival Press, 2008). Reprinted by permission of the publisher.

"Wind Chill Factor" by Gloria Vando from *Shadows & Supposes* (Arte Público Press, University of Houston, 2002). Copyright © 2002 Gloria Vando. Reprinted by permission of the publisher.

"Wing by Wing" by Emily Lupita Plum first appeared in *International Poetry Review* (Fall, 2007). Reprinted by permission of the author.

"The Women" by Donna J. G. Lee is from *On the Altar of Greece* (Gival Press, 2006) and first appeared in *Southern New Hampshire* University Journal (Vol. 20, No. 1, Spring 2003). Reprinted by permission of Gival Press.

"You're back from Provincetown" by John Del Peschio first appeared on www.lodestarquaterly.com. Reprinted by permission of the author.

"You're Looking at the Love Interest" by Denise Duhamel first appeared in *Luna*, Volume 7, Spring 2007. Reprinted by permission of the author.

"You've Become Clear (Te has vuelto claro)" by Luis Cremades / translation by Lawrence Schimel first appeared in *Knockout Magazine*, Issue 2, 2008. Reprinted by permission of the authors.

Index of Authors

Alenier, Karren LaLonde 55, 61, 189, 253
Ambroggio, Luis Alberto 175, 239, 252, 253
Ambroggio, Xavier 175, 253
Amen, John 2, 253
Antler 64, 146, 182, 253
Ayala, Naomi 57, 86, 156, 175, 253
Barkan, Stanley H. 101, 102, 153, 186, 254
Baysans, Greg 42, 194, 254
Beck, Gary 16, 254
Belin, Mel 119, 254
Berger, Donald 15, 186, 254
Bergman, David 126, 254
Bernal, Leonel 226, 234, 247, 254
Bolz, Jody 111, 171, 255
Bourgeois, Louis E. 2, 36, 47, 255
Bowen, Kristy 162, 255
Browder, Clifford 168, 255
Buck, Janet I. 170, 255
Burch, Beverly 189, 255
Cantú, Norma Elía 107, 255
Carrión de Fierro, Fanny 214, 225, 228, 255
Cavalieri, Grace 45, 88, 256
Cellini, Don 42, 106, 219, 226, 230, 256
Chun, Ye 5, 34, 256
Collins, Martha 22, 256
Conlon, Christopher 169, 256
Corn, Alfred 28, 209, 256
Corwin, Nina 33, 173, 256
Cravzow, Roy 101, 102, 153, 256
Cremades, Luis 92, 197, 247, 250, 256

Cross, Teri Ellen 127, 257
Dasgupta, Shome 145, 257
Davis, Bradley Warren 20, 257
Del Peschio, John 62, 195, 257
del Pliego, Benito 45, 50, 65, 78, 136, 216, 228, 234, 242, 257
Domini, John 133, 180, 257
Dove, Rita 8, 49, 131, 163, 257
Duhamel, Denise 196, 257
Encinar, Jesús 80, 244, 257
Evans, J. Glenn 34, 257
Falco, Edward 60, 116, 258
Fellner, Steve 161, 258
Fisher, Andrés S. 29, 218, 258
Garfinkel, Patricia 172, 258
Garza, Efraín E. 216, 217, 249, 258
Gaspar de Alba, Alicia 72, 178, 258
Geyer, Bernadette 52, 258
Gilgun, John 24, 258
Gilman, Josh 151, 179, 258
Gilreath, Shannon 93, 259
Ginsberg, Arthur 3, 181, 259
Gioia, Dana 9, 13, 16, 74, 154, 259
Giron, Robert L. 115, 139, 259
Godoy, Juan M. 248, 259
Goldemberg, Isaac 101, 102, 139, 153, 186, 229, 231, 235, 244, 259
Goldman, Paula 68, 118, 166, 259
Gray, Patricia 101, 134, 260
Greenberg, Janet 117, 175, 176, 260
Grossberg, Benjamin S. 26, 260
Guerrero, José Marcial 260
Gwiazda, Piotr 171, 260
Habra, Hedy 199, 200, 201, 204, 205, 208, 213, 221, 233, 246, 260
Harjo, Joy 100, 125, 149, 260
Harjo, Suzan Shown 121, 239, 260
Hislop, Robin Ouzman 45, 50, 65, 78, 136, 261
Holland, Walter R. 7, 74, 261
Hudson, Ron 27, 117, 261
Hurezanu, Daniela 47, 59, 67, 135, 155, 261
Ifland, Alta 48, 116, 122, 187, 202, 204, 205, 206, 261
Inez, Colette 50, 165, 261
Jensen, Kim 43, 261
JoseMarGuerr 21, 236, 260
Joysmith, Claire 51, 132, 262
Kasprowicz, Marcelle 124, 158, 192, 202, 203, 207, 208, 262

Kessler, Stephen 47, 59, 67, 135, 155, 262
Kester, Gunilla Theander 83, 169, 262
Kirkpatrick, Kathryn 105, 262
Klappert, Peter 44, 104, 262
Klawitter, George 138, 262
Koch, Randy 41, 129, 262
Kreiter-Foronda, Carolyn 5, 56, 263
Lader, Bruce 93, 184, 263
Lecrivain, Marie 75, 263
Lee, Daniel W. K. 157, 263
Lee, Donna J. Gelagotis 19, 194, 263
Lehmann, Gary 9, 263
Levchev, Vladimir 14, 35, 263
Levine, Philip 53, 263
López-Luaces, Marta 10, 143, 178, 264
Luczak, Raymond 87, 264
Luna-Escudero-Alie, María-Elvira 232, 264
Mann, Jeff 32, 77, 152, 264
March, Sydney 17, 103, 264
March, Thomas 184, 264
Marín, Desirée 235, 243, 265
Martínez, Pablo Miguel 11, 265
Martínez de Merlo, Luis 127, 237, 265
Mayo, C. M. 114, 265
McCombs, Judith 185, 265
Meléndez, Mario 27, 117, 231, 243, 265
Melleby, Arnold 112, 265
Micheaux, Dante 24, 266
Miller, E. Ethelbert 56, 266
Miller, Edmund 158, 164, 266
Mills, Stephen S. 91, 266
Montlack, Michael 18, 266
Moore, Miles David 70, 141, 266
Murphy, Kay 81, 183, 266
Neisser Moreno, Yvette 49, 89, 267
Nye, Naomi Shihab 110, 267
Ostriker, Alicia Suskin 14, 35, 267
Pantano, Daniele 53, 136, 267
Paris, Anika 12, 23, 123, 267
Pastoriza Iyodo, Benito 20, 215, 223, 228, 242, 257, 267
Peabody, Richard 38, 67, 268
Plum, Emily Lupita 131, 192, 268
Queneau, Raymond 47, 59, 67, 135, 155, 261, 268
Reevy, Anthony W. 135, 268

Rimbaud, Arthur 2, 36, 47, 268
Rivera, Wanda 101, 102, 153, 268
Roberts, Kim 65, 147, 268
Robinson, Blake 190, 268
Robinson, J. E. 54, 268
Roffé, Mercedes 117, 175, 176, 269
Ross, Joseph 81, 269
Ross, Sean 176, 269
Rummel, Mary Kay 108, 185, 269
Rutkowski, Thaddeus 143, 167, 269
Saba, Mark 109, 144, 269
Salum, Rose Mary 224, 250, 269
Schaffner, M. A. 69, 269
Schimel, Lawrence 60, 79, 80, 92, 96, 127, 197, 270
Shapiro, Gregg 188, 270
Shulklapper, Lucille Gang 63, 123, 270
Singer, Ron 31, 62, 89, 270
Slone, G. Tod 137, 270
Smith, J. D. 74, 90, 270
Snider, Clifton 156, 270
Soden, Christopher 94, 270
Soniat, Katherine 66, 148, 271
Tandon, Jason 69, 82, 187, 271
Tilley, Jonathan 98, 271
Toscano, Rodrigo 85, 222, 271
Tusa, Chris 146, 153, 271
Ungar, Barbara Louise 97, 140, 271
Vando, Gloria 30, 191, 272
Van de Kamp, Alexandra 10, 272
Vélez-Mitchell, Anita 73, 120, 272
Wade, Julie Marie 154, 272
Walt, Jeff 93, 164, 272
Whittenberg, Allison 179, 272
Williams, Jill 46, 159, 272
Wormwood, Ernie 6, 272
Wozek, Gerard 76, 150, 273
Yakovina, Katharina 65, 273

Books Available from Gival Press
Poetry

Adamah by Céline Zins; translation by Peter Schulman
ISBN 13: 978-1-928589-46-4, $15.00
This bilingual (French/English) collection by an eminent French poet/writer is adeptly translated in this premiere edition.

Bones Washed With Wine: Flint Shards from Sussex and Bliss
by Jeff Mann
ISBN 13: 978-1-928589-14-3, $15.00
Includes the 1999 Gival Press Poetry Award winning collection. Jeff Mann is "a poet to treasure both for the wealth of his language and the generosity of his spirit."
— Edward Falco, author of *Acid*

Canciones para sola cuerda / Songs for a Single String
by Jesús Gardea; English translation by Robert L. Giron
ISBN 13: 978-1-928589-09-9, $15.00
Finalist for the 2003 Violet Crown Book Award—Literary Prose & Poetry. Love poems, with echoes of Neruda à la Mexicana, Gardea writes about the primeval quest for the perfect woman.

Dervish by Gerard Wozek
ISBN 13: 978-1-928589-11-2, $15.00
Winner of the 2000 Gival Press Poetry Award / Finalist for the 2002 Violet Crown Book Award—Literary Prose & Poetry.
"By jove, these poems shimmer."
—Gerry Gomez Pearlberg, author of *Mr. Bluebird*

The Great Canopy by Paula Goldman
ISBN 13: 1-928589-31-0, $15.00
Winner of the 2004 Gival Press Poetry Award / 2006 Independent Publisher Book Award—Honorable Mention for Poetry
"Under this canopy we experience the physicality of the body through Goldman's wonderfully muscular verse as well the analytics of a mind that tackles the meaning of Orpheus or the notion of desire."
— Richard Jackson, author of *Half Lives*

Honey by Richard Carr
ISBN 13: 978-1-928589-45-7, $15.00
Winner of the Gival Press Poetry Award
"Honey is a tour de force. Comprised of 100 electrifying microsonnets . . . The whole sequence creates a narrative that becomes, like the Hapax Legomenon, a form that occurs only once in a literature."
—Barbara Louise Ungar, author of *The Origin of the Milky Way*

Let Orpheus Take Your Hand by George Klawitter
ISBN 13: 978-1-928589-16-7, $15.00
Winner of the 2001 Gival Press Poetry Award
A thought provoking work that mixes the spiritual with stealthy desire, with Orpheus leading us out of the pit.

Metamorphosis of the Serpent God by Robert L. Giron
ISBN 13: 978-1-928589-07-5, $12.00
This collection "…embraces the past and the present, ethnic and sexual identity, themes both mythical and personal."
—*The Midwest Book Review*

On the Altar of Greece by Donna J. Gelagotis Lee
ISBN 13: 978-1-92-8589-36-5, $15.00
Winner of the 2005 Gival Press Poetry Award / 2007 Eric Hoffer Book Award: Notable for Art Category
"…*On the Altar of Greece* is like a good travel guide: it transforms reader into visitor and nearly into resident. It takes the visitor to the authentic places that few tourists find, places delightful yet still surprising, safe yet unexpected…."
—by Simmons B. Buntin, editor of *Terrain.org* Blog

On the Tongue by Jeff Mann
ISBN 13: 978-1-928589-35-8, $15.00
"…These poems are …nothing short of extraordinary."
—Trebor Healey, author of *Sweet Son of Pan*

The Nature Sonnets by Jill Williams
ISBN 13: 978-1-928589-10-5, $8.95
An innovative collection of sonnets that speaks to the cycle of nature and life, crafted with wit and clarity. "Refreshing and pleasing."
— Miles David Moore, author of *The Bears of Paris*

The Origin of the Milky Way by Barbara Louise Ungar
ISBN 13: 978-1-928589-39-6, $15.00
Winner of the 2006 Gival Press Poetry Award
"...a fearless, unflinching collection about birth and motherhood, the transformation of bodies. Ungar's poems are honestly brutal, candidly tender. Their primal immediacy and intense intimacy are realized through her dazzling sense of craft. Ungar delivers a wonderful, sensuous, visceral poetry." —Denise Duhamel

Poetic Voices Without Borders edited by Robert L. Giron
ISBN 13: 978-1-928589-30-3, $20.00
2006 Writer's Notes Magazine Book Award—Notable for Art / 2006 Independent Publisher Book Award—Honorable Mention for Anthology
An international anthology of poetry in English, French, and Spanish, including work by Grace Cavalieri, Jewell Gomez, Joy Harjo, Peter Klappert, Jaime Manrique, C.M. Mayo, E. Ethelbert Miller, Richard Peabody, Myra Sklarew and many others.

Poetic Voices Without Borders 2, edited by Robert L. Giron
ISBN 13: 978-1-928589-43-3, $20.00
Featuring poets Grace Cavalieri, Rita Dove, Dana Gioia, Joy Harjo, Peter Klappert, Philip Levine, Gloria Vando, and many other fine poets in English, French, and Spanish.

Prosody in England and Elsewhere:
A Comparative Approach by Leonardo Malcovati
ISBN 13: 978-1-928589-26-6, $20.00
The perfect tool for the poet but written for a non-specialist audience.

Protection by Gregg Shapiro
ISBN 13: 978-1-928589-41-9, $15.00
"Gregg Shapiro's stunning debut marks the arrival of a new master poet on the scene. His work blows me away."
—Greg Herren, author of *Mardi Gras Mambo*

Songs for the Spirit by Robert L. Giron
ISBN 13: 978-1-928589-0802, $16.95
A psalter for the reader who is not religious but who is spiritually inclined. "This is an extraordinary book."
—John Shelby Spong

Sweet to Burn by Beverly Burch
    ISBN 13: 978-1-928589-23-5, $15.00
    Winner of the 2004 Lambda Literary Award for Lesbian Poetry Winner of the 2003 Gival Press Poetry Award — "Novelistic in scope, but packing the emotional intensity of lyric poetry..."
    — Eloise Klein Healy, author of *Passing*

Tickets to a Closing Play by Janet I. Buck
    ISBN 13: 978-1-928589-25-9, $15.00
    Winner of the 2002 Gival Press Poetry Award
    "…this rich and vibrant collection of poetry [is] not only serious and insightful, but a sheer delight to read."—Jane Butkin Roth, editor of *We Used to Be Wives: Divorce Unveiled Through Poetry*

Where a Poet Ought Not / Où c'qui faut pas by G. Tod Slone
    (in English and French)
    ISBN 13: 978-1-928589-42-6, $15.00
    Poems inspired by French poets Léo Ferré and François Villon and the Québec poet Raymond Lévesque in what Slone characterizes as a need to speak up. "In other words, a poet should speak the truth as he sees it and fight his damnedest to overcome all the forces encouraging not to."

For a list of poetry published by Gival Press, please visit: *www.givalpress.com*.

Books available via Ingram, the Internet, and other outlets.

Or Write:
    Gival Press, LLC
    PO Box 3812
    Arlington, VA 22203
    703.351.0079

www.ingramcontent.com/pod-product-compliance
Lightning Source LLC
Chambersburg PA
CBHW031618160426
43196CB00006B/186